AMAZING
DAYS
OF
GRACE

GOD'S BLESSINGS THROUGH
DIFFICULT AFFLICTIONS AND
UNUSUAL DISABILITIES

JOHN BARTON

innovo
PUBLISHING

Published by Innovo Publishing, LLC
www.innovopublishing.com
1-888-546-2111

Publishing quality books, eBooks, audiobooks, music, screenplays & courses for the Christian & wholesome markets since 2008.

AMAZING DAYS OF GRACE
God's Blessings through Difficult Afflictions and Unusual Disabilities

Library of Congress Control Number: 2023912193
ISBN: 978-1-61314-929-4

Cover Design & Interior Layout: Innovo Publishing, LLC

Printed in the United States of America
U.S. Printing History
First Edition: 2023

Has God called you to create a Christ-centered or wholesome book, eBook, audiobook, music album, screenplay, or online course? Visit Innovo's educational center (cpportal.com) to learn how to accomplish your calling with excellence.

This book is dedicated to my Lord and Savior, Jesus Christ. May everything in this book bring glory to His name.

This book is also dedicated to the memories of Dr. Bob Guinter, Jim Siegfried, Steve Alm, Jack Edmands, and Mildred Wofford. These saints have gone home to the Lord but not before showing me how true Christians glorify God with their lives and make a profound difference for good in the lives of others. I am blessed to be one on whom they made a life-changing impact.

Lastly, I dedicate this book to my delightful wife, Candy. This book would not have been possible without her support and encouragement.

CONTENTS

PREFACE

You make known to me the path of life;
in your presence there is fullness of joy;
at your right hand are pleasures forevermore.
—Psalm 16:11

My wife, Candy, and I hosted a special gathering on March 5, 2022, to celebrate my five thousandth day with a feeding tube. We dubbed the occasion "5,000 Amazing Days of Grace" and were blessed to have two dozen men join us in our home. I dare say none there had ever been to such a celebration. It was, after all, a rather odd thing to celebrate. Why happily commemorate my disability? Why celebrate the fact that I had been unable to enjoy good food and drink for these many years? And why on earth would I ask friends to join me for a celebratory meal that I could not eat?

The answer is that we did not celebrate any of these things. Nor did I host a celebration of myself. The purpose of this gathering was to praise our amazing God and acclaim His amazing grace during the previous five thousand days. Only by God's mercy and grace had I survived Stage 4 cancer, remained cancer free, and been generally healthy. My family, friends, and I celebrated that, by God's grace, I had not merely survived with a feeding tube this long, but for most of the five thousand days, I enjoyed an active, purposeful, fruitful, and joyful life for God's glory and the good of others. We gave thanks to the Lord for graciously and abundantly blessing Candy and me in ways as unique as my disabilities. We praised God for the ways He has opened doors for me to use my unusual story to share His love with others. We celebrated how God has used the purifying fires of my affliction and our altered lifestyle to continually strengthen and lift my marriage to Candy to delightful new heights.

By God's grace, only a couple of the men invited could not attend the celebration. Michael and Joseph, my two sons who lived in the Washington, D.C., area, surprised me by showing up that weekend to help us celebrate. And, oh, what a celebration it was! We laughed, we cried, we told stories, we sang, we prayed, and we thoroughly enjoyed genuine Christian fellowship. It was a grand evening in every way. Throughout my life, God has continually put special people along my path to bless me, encourage me, minister to me, help me, teach me, and provide meaningful and fun fellowship. What a blessing it was to celebrate with many of them that evening!

I speak quite poorly because of my soft voice and cancer-caused speech impediment, but by God's grace, I write much more clearly. My friends were all very gracious when it was my turn to speak to the group that evening. To ensure they understood what was on my heart, I put my thoughts on paper as a story. Since our celebration was a collection of new and old friends, many had never read the other short stories I had written about my experiences over the years. Therefore, I bound the new story and several other stories together in a book titled "5,000 Amazing Days of Grace" and presented it to my guests that night. I also shared copies of the book with other special friends and family members over the next several days.

The book was so well received that I decided to write this expanded second edition. One of the many additions is Appendix A, which includes a selected sample of the many posts Candy and I made to my CarePage blog during the summer and fall of 2008. They display some of our real-time thoughts and emotions as I battled cancer. None of my previous writings have been professionally edited or published. I thank the Lord this one has been so I can tell even more people how the Lord has abundantly blessed me through some unusual afflictions and disabilities. Above all, I pray that God will use this book to graciously bless those who read it, encourage many, and bring glory to the name of my Lord, Jesus Christ.

Not to us, O LORD, not to us, but to your name give glory,
for the sake of your steadfast love and your faithfulness!
—Psalm 115:1

Chapter 1

THE GIFT OF A DAY

O LORD, make me know my end
and what is the measure of my days;
let me know how fleeting I am!
—Psalm 39:4

S ummer has always been my favorite time of year. Those months between May and September seemed blissfully long when I was a young boy in Mississippi. The pace of life was slow and relaxed compared to life today, but we always found plenty of ways to have fun before the sun finally went down. For most summers, the most stressful situation I knew was losing a baseball game. As I grew older, responsibilities increased, schedules filled, and all seasons passed more quickly, including those days of summer that I loved so much. As the years went by and my responsibilities continued to multiply and grow, I began to understand the adage, "The days are long, but the years are short." Yet the summer months always remained special.

Summers, however, have not always been trouble free. Some of my most challenging health battles have been in summer, including a few when I struggled to speak and one when I fought to stay alive. It was through these trials that I began to learn the true value of a day.

The years of our life are seventy, or even by reason of strength eighty;
yet their span is but toil and trouble; they are soon gone, and we fly away.
Who considers the power of your anger, and Your wrath according
to the fear of you?
So teach us to number our days that we may get a heart of wisdom.
—Psalm 90:10-12

I find it interesting that this psalm was penned by Moses, who lived to be one hundred twenty years old. God extended this man's life well beyond the average lifespan because of His unique purposes for Moses as the prophet, mediator, and leader of the Hebrew people. Moses recognized that even his extended life seemed to pass quickly; how much more fleeting would a normal person's life feel? He wrote how foolish it was for anyone to assume a long life and not fearfully consider the wrath of God. In these verses, Moses, inspired by the Holy Spirit, implores God's people—then and now—to consider how short life is so that we will value the quality of our limited number of days, not the quantity. David expressed similar thoughts in Psalm 39:

> *Behold, you have made my days a few handbreadths, and my lifetime is as nothing before you.*
> *Surely all mankind stands as a mere breath! Selah.*
> —Psalm 39:5

As I ponder this and similar verses of Scripture, I am mindful of how short the lives of many of my heroes of the faith have been. You will find several quotes in this book by Charles Spurgeon, "the prince of preachers," who preached multiple times a week, wrote prolifically, and helped found several orphanages. He passed away at the relatively young age of 57, having preached over thirty-six hundred sermons and having written at least forty-nine volumes of work. Other heroes in the faith who died younger than I am today include Martin Luther, 62; John Bunyan, 59; J. Gresham Machen, 55; John Calvin, 54; Jonathan Edwards, 54; Matthew Henry, 51; Oswald Chambers, 43; William Tyndale, 42; David Brainerd, 29; and Jim Elliot, 28. It is astonishing what these men accomplished in their relatively short lives. Oh, the fruit they bore as they genuinely counted their days!

The Lord has not equipped or called me to be used as these heroic men were, but I want to be faithful to that which He has called me. To do so, I must pray for a heart of wisdom and esteem the incalculable value of each day of life granted by God. Indeed, our lives are measured by the quality of our days, not the quantity.

I knew of these truths for most of my life, but it was not until I nearly lost my life that I truly embraced them. When the likelihood of seeing my fiftieth birthday, much less the seventy and eighty years described by Moses, seemed unlikely, the value of the current day became far more valuable. While I had not lived a completely foolish life before, I had not lived as if the current day was the only one of which I could be assured. Coming close to death profoundly affected me. I learned to embrace the value of each day as never before. Yet the Lord taught Candy and me that such value is about much more than mere physical survival. God uses each day to glorify Himself by molding our hearts and minds to be more Christ-like for our own good and the benefit of others.

> *And he [Jesus] told them a parable, saying, "The land of a rich man produced plentifully, and he thought to himself, 'What shall I do, for I have nowhere to store my crops?' And he said, 'I will do this: I will tear down my barns and build larger ones, and there I will store all my grain and my goods. And I will say to my soul, "Soul, you have ample goods laid up for many years; relax, eat, drink, be merry."' But God said to him, 'Fool! This night your soul is required of you, and the things you have prepared, whose will they be?' So is the one who lays up treasure for himself and is not rich toward God."*
> —Luke 12:16-21

When a person seems likely to die but does not, the expression "living on borrowed time" is often used. But the hours, days, and perhaps years I have ahead of me are not borrowed. No indeed! They have been purchased, paid in full, by the atoning blood of Jesus Christ. Each day is a gift—an unmerited, invaluable, and gracious gift that is to be used purposefully, meaningfully, and courageously in ways that honor Christ and help others. Each day is a precious blessing, and I pray I will always value each one with genuine gratitude, for I may never see another tomorrow.

> *Satisfy us in the morning with your steadfast love, that we may rejoice and be glad all our days.*
> —Psalm 90:14

This lesson to not take tomorrow for granted has been dramatically underscored in the two years that preceded this writing. Two of my closest friends, Steve Alm and Jack Edmands, passed away. For most years of our friendship, they were the fit and healthy guys who ministered to me while I dealt with one malady or another. I never considered that either would pass away before me. Yet they have, and their losses have been sobering reinforcements of the truth that life is fleeting at a blistering pace. Each day is a special gift to be treasured and used wisely.

Summer is still my favorite time of year. I love the hot weather, how green the trees and grass are, and how beautifully the flowers bloom. I love how the sun rises very early and sets late in the evening, making for wonderfully long hours of sunshine. Candy and I enjoy celebrating our anniversary every June, often with special trips, and we've had many special summer events with friends and family. But I will never forget the summer of 2008—the most remarkable of all.

> *The heart of man plans his way, but the Lord establishes his steps.*
> —Proverbs 16:9

Chapter 2

STRENGTH AND HOPE
FROM GOD'S WORD

It is good for me that I was afflicted, that I might learn your statutes.
—Psalm 119:71

Tongue cancer is by far the most painful thing I have ever endured. Imagine if someone reached inside one side of your mouth and firmly grabbed half your tongue with a pair of pliers, then squeezed. Tightly. Now imagine they used locking pliers so that the pain never eased. That's a fair assessment of the raw pain I felt in the spring and summer of 2008. I was prescribed multiple high-powered pain medications, but none removed the pain, only softened and blunted its jagged sharpness. As my cancer worsened, the pain rapidly increased each day. My tongue became increasingly less functional, and swallowing became unbearable. A feeding tube was inserted into my stomach in late June to give me a way to hydrate, get some nutrition, and take medications. Candy and I diligently prayed for healing, as did hundreds of other people. In His eternal goodness, the Lord answered my prayer, but in a different way than I imagined.

> *On the day I called, you answered me; my strength of soul you increased.*
> —Psalm 138:3

Even though I was physically in a very bad way, the Lord strengthened my soul daily. During many, sometimes most hours of the day, my mind was understandably fuzzy because of the intense pain and pain medication. Yet almost every day, there were windows of time when my mind was unusually sharp and my heart was at rapt attention while communing with the Lord in His word and in prayer. While I had been somewhat of a student of the word before, it was just one of the many things competing for my attention. But now I was a captive audience, for I was unable to do much else. My body was literally wasting away more and more each day, and I rapidly grew weaker and weaker. I tried to be as self-sufficient as possible, but dear Candy had to do increasingly more for me as my strength waned. Yet my soul was being strengthened as never before. My love for the word steadily grew. I prayed each day for the Lord to give me a window of time with a clear mind to spend with Him and to record my experiences, thoughts, and insights on my CarePage blog for those praying for me. God was indeed faithful!

> *So we do not lose heart. Though our outer self is wasting away, our inner self is being renewed day by day. For this light momentary affliction is preparing for us an eternal weight of glory beyond all comparison, as we look not to the things that are seen but to the things that are unseen. For the things that are seen are transient, but the things that are unseen are eternal.*
> —2 Corinthians 4:16-18

> The afflicted believer is under tuition, he is in training for something higher and better, and all that he meets with is working out his highest good, therefore is he a blessed man, however much his outward circumstances may argue the reverse. (Charles Spurgeon)[1]

That summer, I communed with God in a more focused and personal way than I ever had before. Bible study and prayer had long been spiritual disciplines for me, but I confess they were not always my passion. Yet during the hottest months of 2008, I developed a thirst for the word and prayer like never before. As I did, I developed a deeper understanding of who God is and how holy and good He is. I also saw myself more clearly than ever. His holy word acted as a mirror to my soul, revealing some previously unseen ugliness in my heart. By the Lord's grace, His word led me to repentance and assured me of forgiveness.

Perhaps the most convicting revelation was that I had never truly feared God as He commands. I had previously equated fearing God with simply believing in Him, believing His word, and trying my best to obey Him. But His word clearly showed me that fearing God meant much more.

To fear God is to regard Him as the omnipotent consuming fire that He is. He is a pure, holy God who can never abide with my sin. He is a just and wrathful God who punishes sin with eternal death. Yet fearing Him also includes the clear understanding that Almighty God is good, faithful, and loving. The God of terrible wrath is also the God of tender mercy. In fact, He is so loving and merciful that He sent His only Son to take the just punishment that my sins deserve. He is a strict yet loving Father who patiently teaches and effectively disciplines me for my good. Therefore, the only acceptable way for me to approach God is with genuine humility, trembling, gratitude, and praise.

Fearing God in this way brought higher levels of joy and deeper levels of peace to my soul, even though there was neither joy nor peace in my body. I recognized that my cancer and the horrendous pain were harsh but necessary course corrections for my soul by my loving Father for His glory and my good.

> *For great is the LORD, and greatly to be praised; he is to be feared above all gods.*
> *For all the gods of the peoples are worthless idols, but the LORD made the heavens.*
> *Splendor and majesty are before him; strength and beauty are in his sanctuary.*
> *Ascribe to the LORD, O families of the peoples, ascribe to the LORD glory and strength!*
> *Ascribe to the LORD the glory due his name; bring an offering, and come into his courts!*
> *Worship the LORD in the splendor of holiness; tremble before him, all the earth!*
> —Psalm 96:4-9

> *The fear of the LORD is the beginning of wisdom;*
> *all those who practice it have a good understanding. His praise endures forever!*
> —Psalm 111:10

The more time I spent in the word of God, the more I became aware of a persistent theme. The Lord promised me that no matter what happened, He would always, always, always be with me. He had called me, redeemed me, cleansed me, and made me His own, and nothing could ever change that. He did not remove my pain, and it would most certainly get worse, probably much worse, before it got better. It might never get better while on this earth.

The aggressive cancer in me was spreading and could easily lead to bodily death. Yet my Lord promised He would be with me through it all, no matter what may come. My days that summer were spent in the paradox of unending pain and unceasing joy.

It is the LORD who goes before you. He will be with you; he will not leave you or forsake you. Do not fear or be dismayed.
—The words of Moses in Deuteronomy 31:8

"Have I not commanded you? Be strong and courageous. Do not be frightened, and do not be dismayed, for the LORD your God is with you wherever you go."
—The words of Yahweh to Joshua in Joshua 1:9

. . . fear not, for I am with you; be not dismayed, for I am your God; I will strengthen you, I will help you, I will uphold you with my righteous right hand.
—Isaiah 41:10

But now thus says the LORD, he who created you, O Jacob, he who formed you, O Israel:
"Fear not, for I have redeemed you; I have called you by name, you are mine. When you pass through the waters, I will be with you; and through the rivers, they shall not overwhelm you; when you walk through fire you shall not be burned, and the flame shall not consume you. For I am the LORD your God, the Holy One of Israel, your Savior."
—Isaiah 43:1-3a

"And behold, I am with you always, to the end of the age."
—The words of Jesus in Matthew 28:20b

Excerpt from CarePage entry

July 31, 2008

The last few days have continued to be very tough. I cannot seem to get over the nausea and vomiting from chemo and have been very sick. My weight continues to fall as I struggle to keep any nourishment down. Candy and I will be returning to West Clinic today; hopefully they will help get these turned around.

Yet each day has also brought blessings of encouragement. I have indeed felt quite discouraged at times, but a fresh word from the Lord or a note of gracious encouragement from a friend is never far behind. God's word never fails to assure of His great love for us, and that He is with us each step of the way. We also are constantly buoyed by the prayers, the love, the friendship, the encouragement, and the many helping hands and feet from people near and far.*

As Candy and I prepared to head to Houston in early August, my life seemed increasingly paradoxical. I had no idea what lay before me. I knew I could not live much longer in my quickly deteriorating condition. Yet the destiny of my soul had never been clearer. The God I fearfully loved had indeed strengthened my soul and allowed me to know Him better than ever before. Was He preparing me for heaven, or was He preparing me for a different sort of life on this earth? I had no idea, but I was more assured than ever that my wonderful Savior would be with me, and I would be with Him, in bodily life or death, for His glory and my good. I had no option but to rejoice!

Rejoice always, pray without ceasing, give thanks in all circumstances; for this is the will of God in Christ Jesus for you.
—1 Thessalonians 5:16-18

For this reason I bow my knees before the Father, from whom every family in heaven and on earth is named, that according to the riches of his glory he may grant you to be strengthened with power through his Spirit in your inner being, so that Christ may dwell in your hearts through faith—that you, being rooted and grounded in love, may have strength to comprehend with all the saints what is the breadth and length and height and depth, and to know the love of Christ that surpasses knowledge, that you may be filled with all the fullness of God.
—Ephesians 3:14-19

Comfort is desirable at all times; but comfort in affliction is like a lamp in a dark place. Some are unable to find comfort at such

---

* This book contains many CarePage entry excerpts copied verbatim. They were treated as historical text and have therefore not been edited.

times; but it is not so with believers, for their Saviour has said to them, "I will not leave you comfortless." Some have comfort and no affliction, others have affliction and no comfort; but the saints have comfort in their affliction. (Charles Spurgeon)[2]

Chapter 3

GOD'S PROMISES FAITHFULLY KEPT

Where shall I go from your Spirit? Or where shall I flee from your presence?
If I ascend to heaven, you are there! If I make my bed in Sheol, you are there!
If I take the wings of the morning and dwell in the uttermost parts of the sea,
even there your hand shall lead me, and your right hand shall hold me.
If I say, "Surely the darkness shall cover me,
and the light about me be night," even the darkness is not dark to you;
the night is bright as the day, for darkness is as light with you.
—Psalm 139:7-12

The University of Texas MD Anderson Cancer Center in Houston, usually referred to simply as "MD Anderson," is an absolutely terrible place to feel sorry for yourself. No matter how painful, debilitating, and life-threatening your cancer is, it usually takes only a few minutes to see a patient who is worse off. That's because MD Anderson is so good at what they do: fighting cancer. People from across the country and around the world with severe cases of cancer travel to Houston for a chance to survive. Candy and I considered it an extraordinary blessing to be there in the summer of 2008.

After my first diagnosis of tongue cancer in November 2007, I was treated at the University of Arkansas Medical Center in Little Rock. After surgery and a few months of rehab, but no chemotherapy or radiation, we hoped that cancer would be but a fading painful memory for the rest of our lives. But the excruciating pain in my tongue returned in the spring of 2008. In May, my ear, nose, and throat (ENT) physician in Memphis, Dr. Dean

Klug, gave me the bad news that the pain was again due to cancer, and it looked very serious. I knew I needed a higher level of care this time. I asked Dr. Klug if there was any way he could refer me to MD Anderson, one of the premier cancer hospitals in the world. I got a delicious taste of the grace that lay in store for me when Dr. Klug said that his best friend from medical school, Dr. Eduardo Diaz, Jr., was the head of head and neck oncology at MD Anderson. After one phone call from Dr. Klug, I was set for an early June appointment with Dr. Diaz in Houston.

Candy and I spent much of the next few months of 2008 going back and forth between Memphis and Houston. I was primarily treated by Dr. Diaz, who coordinated his efforts with Dr. Matthew Hanasono, an outstanding oncology plastic surgeon, and a host of other doctors, nurses, and technicians at MD Anderson. Dr. Diaz also coordinated the efforts in Houston with multiple doctors in Memphis, including Dr. Klug; Dr. Kurt Tauer, my oncologist at West Clinic; Dr. Holger Gieschen, my oncology radiologist; Dr. Zack Taylor, my gastroenterologist and friend. I will be forever grateful to our gracious God for the incredible team of world-class physicians He put together to care for me.

In my initial appointment with Dr. Diaz, he told me the bad news: my cancer had already advanced to Stage 4, meaning it had spread beyond the large tumor inside my tongue to other parts of my mouth and throat. He also gave me the good news: he thought there was a chance he could save my life because I was relatively young and otherwise healthy compared to most of his Stage 4 tongue cancer patients. I was in so much pain that I did not feel "young and healthy" at all, but I accepted his words as good news and a challenge to stay mentally and spiritually tough for the very trying physical battle ahead. But Dr. Diaz warned me, "To save your life, we will have to beat the crap out of you." The good doctor would prove to be a man of his word.

Over the next six weeks, I had a variety of treatments in Memphis, including the insertion of my feeding tube by Dr. Zack Taylor in June and chemotherapy treatments in July that made me sicker than I had ever been before. In early August Candy and I headed back to MD Anderson in Houston.

Dr. Diaz scheduled the primary surgery for Thursday, August 14th, to remove most of my tongue and all other cancerous tissue found during the surgery. In the last pre-surgery appointment that Tuesday, he warned me of the worst-case scenarios, as he was ethically bound to do. He prepared me for the possibility that surgery might permanently disfigure my face and completely alter my lifestyle should I survive. After Dr. Diaz's surgery, Dr. Hanasono would immediately take as much tissue as necessary from my legs and arms, starting with my right thigh, to fill in the gaps left by Dr. Diaz's surgery. The surgeries would take most of the day; afterward, I would remain fully sedated in ICU until the nursing shift change on Friday morning. That frank discussion only intensified the prayers Candy and I lifted as we prepared for surgery.

Excerpt from CarePage entry

August 12, 2008

Reporting From Houston

Today (Tuesday) we had several appointments, starting with the most important, the appointment with Dr. Eduardo Diaz, the head and neck surgeon. … The latest scans and tests indicate a strong likelihood that the cancer has spread to places we had hoped that it would not. Of course, they will not know for sure until they start cutting Thursday morning. He asked us to not overlook the good news that surgery can be done, which is not always the case, and surgery is a must in defeating this cancer. For that we are grateful, yet Dr. Diaz could not help but notice the disappointment in our faces as he talked about the various procedures that are likely to be done. He said, "I'm sorry. I don't know if you were expecting miracles, but we're not in that business."

Fortunately, we do indeed know Someone in the miracle business. We continue to pray that the Lord will do something that only He can do. Perhaps that will be in providing a healing prior to the surgery. Perhaps He will leave the doctors wondering what went wrong with their scans. Perhaps He will strengthen me to recover faster and better than expected. Perhaps He will provide His wisdom and peace so that we may minister in His name more effectively than ever before, despite my physical condition. Or maybe He will do what He often does, bless us in ways that we never would have imagined. But this we do know with all certainty: There is no love greater than God's love for us. There is no place or circumstance that can separate us from the love of Christ. There is no greater hope than that which we place in Him.

As I was taken to surgery early Thursday morning, I kept Philippians 4:4-7 in mind and prayed every waking second except when listening to and answering questions from the medical staff. I asked the Lord for His protection but primarily focused on praise and thanksgiving. In the past, I had found that praying for others before surgery kept my heart from anxiousness. Therefore I prayed for my family and friends, as well as the doctors, nurses, and attendants who would care for me.

Rejoice in the Lord always; again I will say, rejoice. Let your reasonableness be known to everyone. The Lord is at hand; do not be anxious about anything, but in everything by prayer and supplication with thanksgiving let your requests be made known to God. And the peace of God, which surpasses all understanding, will guard your hearts and your minds in Christ Jesus.
—Philippians 4:4-7

After the surgeries were completed, Dr. Diaz told Candy that all procedures had gone well and were not as extensive as we feared they might be. He found that the cancer was confined to my tongue and soft tissue in the floor of my mouth and throat and had not spread into my jaw, larynx, or facial bones. Candy rejoiced in the continued grace of God that covered us!

In the hours that followed, however, there were complications, and I awoke sometime in the night. I was concerned about waking up earlier than scheduled since Dr. Diaz had been so emphatic about me staying under anesthesia all night. But I also chuckled to myself, for I had a long history of waking up too early: from sleepovers when I was a young boy to waking up on the operating table during a surgery several years before my cancer.

As I awoke, I realized I was lying on my back in a dark room, which I assumed was in the ICU. I'm not sure if I was exactly horizontal, but it was close enough that I felt choked by a large glob of mucus in my throat. Because of my inability to swallow, it had been months since I was able to lie down without choking. I tried to sit up and quickly realized I could not. I also had minimal movement in my neck. I could tilt my head slightly to the right but could not tilt it to the left at all. That surprised me because the tumor had primarily been on the right side of my tongue, or at least that is how it started. Oh, I hoped it had not spread completely through the left side and into my face!

I could only see the ceiling above me. I sensed I was alone in the room, but without the ability to look around, I was not sure. I tried to ask if anyone else was in the room but found I could not speak. That sent a chill to my heart, and I immediately prayed that Dr. Diaz had not found it necessary to remove my larynx. In my pre-operation appointment, he said he would not know the extent of the cancer until he opened me up and explored inside. He planned to remove all cancerous tissue, and the larynx was one of the possibilities.

Dr. Diaz had also warned that he might have to remove part of my right jaw bone if he found cancer there. To get to all the cancerous tissue, he said he might have to split my lower lip and chin. Remembering that warning, I instinctively tried to reach to feel my neck, jaw, and chin but realized my wrists were strapped to the metal bed railings on either side. I then moved to plan B as I remembered that the plastic surgeon, Dr. Hanasono, planned to remove, if necessary, part of my right tibia to use as a graft to the jawbone. Thankfully, I discovered I could move my legs enough to feel my right tibia with my left foot. It was still intact! I also found the left tibia to be untouched. Thank You, Lord!

But I was still struggling with the big blob in my throat. I knew I had a trach in my throat; perhaps it was clogged, for I was struggling to breathe. I needed some help. I didn't know where the nurses were located, so I did the only thing I knew to do: tap lightly on the metal bed rails. There was no response, so I tapped louder. There was still no response, so I tapped even louder. No one came. I did not want to get off on the wrong foot with whoever was assigned to care for me, so I waited in silence, praying and hoping they would come soon.

Meanwhile, my struggle to breathe continued as the blob in my throat seemed to be growing. I also felt extremely nauseous. I hated to do it, but I really needed some help, so I banged the bed rails quite loudly until a nurse arrived. She tried to comfort me and assure me that I was all right, but I knew I was not. She unfastened my wrists, for which I was grateful. But she did not raise me up, which I desperately desired so I could cough or spit out the clog in my throat. I motioned with my hands a request for her to raise me to a sitting position, but she did not understand. She suctioned out my mouth, which helped some, then pleaded with me to relax and go back to sleep. She left the room with me still lying on my back, desperate to sit up.

After the nurse left, I quickly took an inventory of my body parts. My jaws, lips, and chin were all intact! Hallelujah! Maybe the cancer wasn't nearly as bad as they feared. Dr. Hanasono planned to remove a large chunk of my right thigh to construct a *flap*, which was simply a non-functional filler for the empty space in my mouth left after the tongue resection. Perhaps even that hadn't been necessary! I tapped my right thigh to see if it was unscathed. Yowee! That hurt! The whole thigh was bandaged, from my knee to my hip, and was very sensitive. That meant most, perhaps all, of my tongue was gone.

I thanked the Lord for the many parts I still had and again asked Him to get me the help I needed to breathe clearly.

Not long after the nurse left, I vomited, which was quite challenging while lying down. I turned my head as far to the right as possible, which wasn't much, and spit out as much vomit as possible. My nose apparently still worked fine because as soon as I vomited, I got a big whiff of blood. The bloody vomit temporarily cleared the clog of mucus but created a whole new set of issues. I really needed help now. I felt around for a nurse's call button, but there was none.

Unfortunately I had lots of experience with hospitals and nurses, and I had always tried to be every nurse's favorite patient by being as compliant as possible. I certainly did not want to get on this nurse's bad side right off the bat, so I hoped there was a way I could get her attention without tapping on the bed rails again. I had no idea how the ICU was laid out, so I did not know if the nurses were close enough to see me. I raised one hand and politely waved. No one responded. I waved more frantically. Nothing happened. I waved both arms for half a minute. Still no nurse. So I reluctantly conceded that I wasn't getting any "favorite patient" awards that night and resumed tapping on the bed rail. Within half a minute, my tapping became banging as I felt more desperate to get some help.

The same nurse reentered my room, cleaned me off, and suctioned out my mouth again. I may have twitched my head while she did because the suction wand hit an exceptionally sensitive area on my tongue—or rather where my tongue used to be—and a dagger of intense pain shot through me. I again tried to motion that I needed to sit up, and she again begged me to relax and get some sleep. Oh, how I wished I could speak! The lack of a means to communicate frustrated me and possibly her too.

As the large clog in my throat returned, breathing became much more laborious. The nurse and I replayed a similar dance as before with the same results. I was still lying down, looking at a dark ceiling, and struggling to breathe. I am not sure what caused it, but after she left the room that time, I suddenly felt very sleepy—as if I were passing out. Yet at the same time, I felt terribly nauseous and knew I would soon be vomiting up more blood. If I were not awake to spit out the vomit, what would keep it from going back down into my lungs? I told myself to stay calm and think of a solution, even as I fought with all my might to stay awake. I thought and thought, but there seemed to be no solution to this predicament. But how could that be? I desperately prayed for wisdom to figure out what to do next. But I had to come up with something fast because I couldn't keep my eyes open and was getting more nauseous by the second. Several seconds later, I concluded there really was nothing I could do to rescue myself. I had no doubt that my time on this earth was ending that night, for within the next few minutes, I would either drown in my own bloody vomit or asphyxiate from a clogged windpipe.

To this day, the most surprising aspect of that night was the complete lack of fear. God's clear and strong words throughout the summer to not fear because He was with me became a reality. This is the part of the story where many people become very skeptical, but I promise it is the truth. I could feel the bed rails in my hands, and I could see the dark ceiling above me, but the most real thing in that darkened room was the presence of the Lord. He was faithfully keeping His repeated promises, for He was with me, just as He had said, and therefore I was not afraid of the bodily death that seemed imminent. On the contrary, the thought of being face-to-face with Jesus in a few minutes thrilled my soul! Yes, those few minutes would likely be horrible, especially if I drowned in my vomit. What an awful way to die! But then I would be with my glorious Savior, and all would be better than I had ever known anything to be. How could I be afraid?

I confess that this lack of fear caught me off guard. Since I became a Christian, I had never feared my body being dead because I knew my soul would be at home with the Lord. But I was quite sure that I would be terrified while going through the process of dying. Yet, amazingly, I was not afraid in the least. My fear was swallowed up by the God who I had more deeply learned to fear and trust in the three months leading up to this night. There was no doubt whatsoever that He was with me, just as He promised. I prayed, "Lord, this seems to be a problem with two right answers. If I am soon with You in heaven, I will fall at Your feet and praise You, praise You, praise You. Or if You miraculously allow me to keep living here a while longer, I will still be with You because You will always be with me, and I will praise You, praise You, praise You. Either way, You are my Lord, and I trust You. You are my Father, and I am Your boy. I know You will do what is best."

This feel-good moment was interrupted by the sense that the Lord was leading me not to be so quick to stop fighting for my life. He had called me to certain responsibilities—primarily to be the spiritual leader of my wife and children—and I should not willingly abandon those duties. All I could do was say, "Yes, Lord," and pray for His wisdom and strength to help me stay awake, fight, and breathe. He was sovereign over my life and sovereign over my death. He would decide when it was my time to go, not me.

I concentrated completely on staying awake and breathing steadily, yet calmly and very gently, to keep from sucking the clog of mucus and vomit into my windpipe. In my mind, I pictured the air gently flowing around the clog and into my starving lungs. *Slowly in, slowly out. Stay awake and concentrate. Slowly in, slowly out. Don't panic. The Lord is with me. Slowly in, slowly out. Fight hard, but do so gently and steadily. Slowly in, slowly out. Rely on God's strength and wisdom. Slowly in, slowly out.*

Somehow, I got the idea that if I could hold on until the morning shift nurse arrived, all would be okay. So I asked the Lord to help me hang on that long. *Slowly in and slowly out.* I did vomit again but was able to spit enough out not to choke on the residual. Again, that removed the clog temporarily, but it returned soon enough. So I returned to the fight. *Slowly in, slowly out. Slowly in, slowly out. Stay alert by praying constantly. Slowly in, slowly out. Keep praying for Candy and the kids. Slowly in, slowly out. Keep praying for the Lord to bless all those dear friends who have been praying for me. Slowly in, slowly out. Stay calm. Slowly in, slowly out. Keep praying for strength in the fight to stay awake. Slowly in, slowly out. Slowly in, slowly out.*

I have no idea how long that went on, but it certainly seemed like hours. I may have vomited again, but I cannot say for sure. I know the night shift nurse came in a couple more times, but I did not pay much attention to her because I was too busy. I was in the fight of my life, and I had to keep giving the Lord my full attention as He coached me.

Finally, I felt my breathing get much shallower; I was getting less and less air into my lungs. I knew my time was coming to an end. I had fought well, and I prayed that Candy would somehow know that I had. But in the very next moment, I noticed the left side of the ceiling was gradually getting brighter. When the door had opened to my room, the right side of the ceiling brightened from front to back. The left side had remained very dark all night, but now it was slowly yet most certainly growing brighter from back to front. I excitedly reasoned that there must be a window behind me on that side of the room, and the sun was rising. It was morning! Oh, I was so close to the finish line! I begged the Lord to help me hold on for a few more minutes until the morning shift nurse arrived. Our faithful Redeemer strengthened me as I fought hard for each breath.

Suddenly my eyes were filled with a very bright light. I blinked repeatedly, trying to adjust the focus of my eyes. I figured I was either blinded by heaven's glory or the morning shift ICU nurse had turned on the lights. Either way, I was so thankful the long night's fight was ending. I saw a female face smiling as she looked down at me. Was it an angel or the morning shift nurse? Frankly, I didn't care; I was just so glad to see her!

Then I heard the very welcomed words, "G'mornin', Sugar!" I doubt I could smile much with my post-surgery face, but my heart beamed from ear to ear. Unless this was an angel with an East Texas accent, God had allowed me to live through the night! She said, "My name is Trish, and I am here to take great care of you." And she most certainly did.

Nurse Trish immediately raised my bed to a sitting position, and I coughed out huge blobs of mucus mixed with bloody vomit. At last, I could breathe! I gleefully gulped fresh air into my lungs again and again, praising God with every deep inhale and every exhale. Oh, that felt so good! I thanked the Lord over and over, for He had indeed been with me, just as He promised! But it all seemed so surreal. Had all that actually happened, or had I just awakened from the most realistic, most vivid, and wildest dream of my life? I looked down and saw bloody vomit in various stages of drying on my hospital gown, which confirmed that it hadn't been a dream.

As Trish began cleaning me and my bed, my thoughts turned to the night shift nurse. I had been frustrated with her, but I never felt angry at her, just as I never felt afraid. Instead, I felt compassion for her and was moved to pray that she would not get in trouble if she had not followed protocol correctly. Did that seem like an odd emotion after the night I had? Perhaps, but many things seemed different within my mind and heart. My wristband still said that I was John Barton, but it certainly felt like I was a different version of the guy who went into surgery twenty-four hours before.

Candy came in within a few minutes of Trish's arrival. I don't know if I had ever seen a more beautiful sight! I hadn't been this glad to see my beautiful bride since she walked down the aisle on our wedding day. I signaled that I needed my notepad and pen, and she quickly brought them. Oh boy, did I have a story to tell her! But first, she told me what Dr. Diaz said after surgery, and I rejoiced at the news that no cancer was found in my larynx. My inability to speak was apparently because my vocal cords were traumatized during surgery (they recovered within two days). Candy explained that most of my tongue was gone, as was some cancerous tissue in the floor of my mouth and in my throat. I thanked the Lord for that fantastic news, then began to relay to Candy about the events of the night. I wrote and wrote and wrote and wrote and wrote, for I had quite a story to tell.

I thought of Psalm 23, verse 4: "Even though I walk through the valley of the shadow of death, I will fear no evil, for you are with me." Just as our faithful and gracious Lord came to rescue and deliver my soul through the valley of the shadow of death long ago, he did so, at least temporarily, for my physical body in the previous hours. It certainly had not been a sudden rescue. God strengthened me for the fight of my life all through the night and made His presence felt. More importantly, however, He worked intently within my soul all summer in preparation for this night. Had I not been so calmed by the assurance of God's promises kept, I am absolutely certain that I would not have survived that night.

> *If your law had not been my delight, I would have perished in my affliction. . . .*
> *Your word is a lamp to my feet and a light to my path.*
> —Psalm 119:92, 105

The word of God had never been more delightful than it was in the summer of 2008. That delight sank deep into my soul and became a guiding light on the dark path in the ICU to see dear sweet Candy that August morning. Oh, what a Savior!

> *He who dwells in the shelter of the Most High will abide in the shadow of the Almighty.*
> *I will say to the LORD, "My refuge and my fortress, my God, in whom I trust."*
> *For he will deliver you from the snare of the fowler and from the deadly pestilence.*
> *He will cover you with his pinions, and under his wings you will find refuge;*
> *his faithfulness is a shield and buckler.*
> *You will not fear the terror of the night, nor the arrow that flies by day, nor the pestilence that stalks in darkness, nor the destruction that wastes at noonday.*
> —Psalm 91:1-6

MD Anderson's medical records undoubtedly report that I spent the night of August 14th in their Intensive Care Unit. But the report of my soul is that I was safely tucked away under the Lord's sheltering wings. Therefore I did not fear the terror of the night nor the pestilence that stalked in the darkness. My faith in Christ years earlier was a gift from my faithful heavenly Father by the power of the Holy Spirit, as was the strengthening of my faith in the months leading up to that night. His undeniable presence that night affirmed His faithfulness and care. Therefore I never panicked but remained calm, trusting Him fully, even when death lurked so near. Oh, what a Savior!

A couple of years passed before I told this story to anyone besides Candy and a few very close friends. It felt so personal, almost sacred to me. And quite frankly, I wondered if anyone would believe me. Eventually, however, I felt that the Lord wanted me to share what He did for me that night, and I retold the story to many people at our church and other friends and relatives. Putting it in writing like this, even after all these years, feels like another step of transparency with which I am not entirely comfortable. Yet again, I feel the Lord is leading me to do this, and I pray that it will encourage many.

However, it is extremely important that you not misconstrue the primary reason I tell you about the night God rescued me in the ICU room. The moral of this story is *not* that God miraculously saved my life that night. He did that two thousand years ago on a rocky hill called Golgotha outside of Jerusalem. What the Lord did for me on August 14th and the predawn hours of August 15th, 2008, was gloriously confirm that I am His child by His own choosing and that I was, am, and forever will be in His grip. He never let go of me that night, and He never will. His undeniable presence confirmed His repeated promises and left no room for fearful thoughts. And the joyous anticipation of being face-to-face with Jesus eviscerated any remaining vestiges of fear. My soul was safely in the arms of my heavenly Father, no matter what happened. How could I be afraid?

In Psalm 91:16, God says of the psalmist—and of me, "With long life I will satisfy him and show him my salvation." By the time I saw Nurse Trish that Friday morning, I felt the Lord had indeed shown me His salvation and assured me of everlasting life with Him in monumental and unforgettable ways. Yes, He sustained my earthly life that night and has since. But the part of me that will never die—my soul—was never in danger, nor will it ever be, because God never, ever forsakes the sheep of His pasture. And that is what I am!

> *Jesus said to her, "I am the resurrection and the life. Whoever believes in me, though he die, yet shall he live, and everyone who lives and believes in me shall never die. Do you believe this?" She said to him, "Yes, Lord; I believe that you are the Christ, the Son of God, who is coming into the world."*
> —John 11:25-27

I pray that all who read this story will pay close attention to this next part because it is crucial. When I have told people this story in the past, some have said they were sorry I had to go through that terrible experience and blamed the night shift nurse for incompetence. That completely misses the point of the story. I never want to cast MD Anderson or any of their staff in a bad light. It is one of the greatest hospitals in the world, and from a human perspective, Dr. Diaz and his staff saved my life that summer. Every person there who cared for me in any capacity was outstanding in their work. All that happened that night was under the control of our sovereign and almighty God. He allowed those events to happen just precisely as they did for my good and His glory. (Read John 9:1-3.) Those were some of the most important hours of my life, and their effect on me was immediate, profound, and life-changing. Just as my great friend Jim Siegfried taught me to be thankful for my cancer, I was and always will be thankful for that night. Without Jesus, it would have been absolutely terrifying, but with Jesus, it was sensationally glorious. Without Him, there would have been only death; with Him, there was only life. My Savior was glorified, and I was blessed in unimaginable ways. I pray the Lord has also blessed you as you have read this story.

> *I love the LORD, because he has heard my voice and my pleas for mercy. Because he inclined his ear to me, therefore I will call on him as long as I live. The snares of death encompassed me; the pangs of Sheol laid hold on me; I suffered distress and anguish. Then I called on the name of the LORD: "O LORD, I pray, deliver my soul!" Gracious is the LORD, and righteous; our God is merciful. The Lord preserves the simple; when I was brought low, he saved me. Return, O my soul, to your rest; for the LORD has dealt bountifully with you.*
> —Psalm 116:1-7

Chapter 4

PROVIDENTIAL PATHS OF GOD'S STEADFAST LOVE

*Teach me to do your will, for you are my God;
let your good Spirit lead me on level ground.*
—Psalm 143:10

I n the hours after I first saw the angelic Nurse Trish, who did indeed take great care of me, I was still utterly amazed at what I had experienced. I'm sure the Lord and His angels had intervened before to extend my life on earth, but I never experienced anything like this. I felt the Lord's presence in that dark room as much as I felt my own. The total absence of fear and the absolute assurance of my soul's security in Christ, no matter what happened to my body, confirmed my salvation and faith in Jesus. While I wished the night shift nurse and I had been able to communicate with each other, I could not bring myself to wish the experience had played out any differently. It reinforced the truth that our lives are entirely in the sovereign hands of the Lord and Him alone. My life on earth will end when He wills, not a minute before or after. And I know with all certainty that my soul will remain alive on that day and will forevermore be in the presence of the one true God.

On my second day in the ICU, I was still in great pain but much more functional. I was able to read my Bible, and, as usual, I started in Psalms.

I happened to be on Psalm 91 that day, and its power and relevance were striking. My eyes widened as I read the final three verses:

"Because he loves me," says the LORD, *"I will rescue him;*
I will protect him, for he acknowledges my name.
He will call upon me, and I will answer him;
I will be with him in trouble, I will deliver him and honor him.
With long life will I satisfy him and show him my salvation."
—Psalm 91:14-16 NIV

The words jumped off the page and into my heart. That was precisely what God did for me during those perilous hours! I called out to Him, and He answered and rescued me. In my time of trouble, He was truly with me, just as He promised and just as He had been with me so many times before. The Lord God was indeed my blessed Deliverer! By the time I read those verses, I had tried to lie flat a couple of times and got terribly choked within seconds. I could not lie flat on my back even for an entire minute. My utter amazement continued as I pondered what had happened—and not happened. *How did I last for hours that night after surgery without choking? How did the blood from my mouth fall only into my stomach and not my lungs? What kept the vomit out of my lungs? How could my survival be explained by anything else except the protective hand of God being upon me?* I again praised the Lord for His gracious protection.

Excerpt from CarePage entry

August 18, 2008

Recovery Day 4

John is slowly getting various tubes and wires taken out (Yeah!). The foot-long incision on his thigh has been much more sore than the tongue, but it will heal much faster. John started walking a little on Sunday and will be increasing each day. The biggest risk in surgeries like these is pneumonia (in fact the doctors say that it is a given that he will get it), so he is doing tons of breathing treatments and exercises to try to keep his lungs opened up and not infected. Today we talked to a LOT of people, including a physical therapist and a speech therapist who told us John will need both therapies extensively in the months to come. We also had visits today from Dietary Dept.,

Social Services, Housekeeping, Volunteer Services, Accounting, Valet parking, and some guy named Kenny who just wanted to talk to someone. (Just kidding about Kenny!) As you can imagine, getting rest is quite a challenge. Last night, John sent me back to the hotel so that I could get some uninterrupted sleep and it helped tremendously! All in all, John is getting better every day. It is a good, strong start to a long road of recovery. We continue to see evidence of answered prayers with every step. Please pray that John will get some rest tonight and that he will not get pneumonia (a "given").

By the following Tuesday, however, I started having doubts about the events of that first night. I had been out of the ICU for a couple of days and in a regular room. I thought a lot about the events of that night. I was clear on what happened but recognized that I had been under sedation for many hours and probably still felt its effects after waking. Perhaps my perception of life-threatening danger was not entirely accurate. After all, this was one of the finest hospitals in the world. Candy and I had spent many days and hours at MD Anderson, and the care provided was phenomenal. Every nurse, doctor, technician, and therapist was exemplary in their skills, compassion, and kindness.

Throughout my stay in Houston, there were concerns about my below-normal blood pressure, and we later learned that was why I was awake during the night after surgery. My blood pressure dropped to a dangerously low level, and they brought me out from under sedation much sooner than planned. The nurse that night undoubtedly tried to care for me the best she could. I do wish she would have explained my situation to me and been more helpful in providing a means for me to communicate. She probably thought that all the technologically advanced monitoring devices hooked up to me communicated all she needed to know.

With those events now in my rearview mirror, I began to think that the advanced monitoring technology probably would have alerted the nursing staff if I had aspirated, and they would have rushed in to help me and clear my lungs. Could my life have really been in mortal danger in such a place as this, one of the most outstanding hospitals in all the world? (Dr. Diaz refers to it as *the* best cancer hospital in the world.) Although the events of that night were intimately personal, almost sacred, I knew there would probably come a day for me to share what happened with others. When that time came, I wanted to be as accurate as possible, and God certainly didn't need me to exaggerate the level of danger I was in for Him to be praised for His presence with me. Yet if my thinking was clear about my life being in imminent danger, I didn't want to withhold that glory from the Lord. I prayed for the Lord to give me clarity.

Each day Candy and I walked the halls of the hospital as part of my recovery. A large strip of my right thigh, including muscle and nerve tissue, had been used for reconstructive surgery in my mouth during the operation, and I was slowly working to restrengthen that leg. At first, I could only walk a short distance from my room, but Candy and I walked a little farther each day. We always kept to the section of patient rooms near mine. The walls were painted cheerful colors and adorned with many beautiful paintings. The friendliness of the nurses and attendants passing by us made our walks even more pleasant.

On that Tuesday, however, I felt rather adventurous. As Candy and I approached an intersection on our usual route, I felt a desire to turn and walk down a hall we hadn't walked before. Candy questioned my desire, as that hall was not nearly as decorative and bright as the ones we were accustomed to, and there was nothing special to see. I told her I didn't know, but I just had a powerful urge to walk that hall. She reluctantly obliged.

As we neared the end of the hall, I saw that it intersected a very busy hall, one buzzing with the activity of fast-paced doctors, nurses, and technicians. Even though I still had the urge to venture into it, I knew this was not a hall I should be walking at my slow, recuperative pace. Candy asked if I was ready to go back, and I reluctantly said I would, even though I still had an odd urge to go on. Candy detected my reluctance and suggested we pause there, recalling that she needed to call the Rotary House (the hotel connected to the hospital). But alas, her cell phone had no reception. It seemed as if we were in a zone with no cell phone reception, the only one outside of the ICU we experienced in the hospital that summer. Candy suggested we return to the area near my room so she could make her call, but I boldly suggested we continue further into this busy section of the hospital because they would likely have cell phone coverage. Again, my sweet, patient wife reluctantly agreed.

After we walked six feet or so in the busy hallway, Candy checked her phone, but she still didn't have a signal for her phone, which seemed quite odd. I suggested we walk a bit farther, and we did, but there was still no signal for her phone. The foot traffic and noise grew, yet we continued walking.

Finally, Candy got a signal on her cell phone, and we stopped just past a set of elevators. My eyes were immediately drawn to the large windows on either side of the hall and the rain outside. For several days, my view had been restricted to interior walls and a few narrow exterior windows. While Candy made her call, I walked a few yards ahead to one of the windows to watch the rain. It seemed a long time since I had seen the blessing of God watering His earth, especially in Houston, and it was a beautiful sight.

I heard both elevators ding near me, and several talkative people got on them, but strangely, no one exited. The hall suddenly became much, much quieter. Directly behind me, on the other side of the hall, there was a middle-aged lady with a mournful expression and eyes that were bloodshot and puffy. I could hear her softly crying. I glanced back and saw that she sat on a windowsill. She dialed her cell phone while wiping away her tears. She cleared her throat and tried to compose herself as she slowly pushed the final number on her phone. Then she said, "Hey, Mom, it's me. Oh, yes, I'm fine, Mom, but I'm calling about Frank. He's in very critical condition. You know his surgery was today...."

About that time, Candy walked over and told me she was having trouble getting through to the right person at the Rotary House and was put on hold. She told me what she needed to tell the person. While listening to Candy, I missed the next few things Frank's wife said. Candy quit speaking and walked away to try to complete her call. As she did, I heard Frank's wife say, "At some point Frank vomited and hiccupped at the same time. When he did, his lungs sucked in the vomit, and there is no way they can get it out. He's barely hanging on, and, Mom...oh, Mom...they say there's nothing they can do for him." Frank's wife was sobbing too much at that point to continue speaking.

Tears filled my eyes and ran down my cheeks. I heard the pain and grief in this dear lady's voice, and I prayed for the Lord to comfort her. I wished I could tell her of my prayers, but I was in the first stages of trying to learn how to speak with no tongue, and no one could understand my grunts besides Candy and Nurse Trish. I prayed for the Lord to miraculously rescue Frank as He had done for me.

My earlier doubts about God's rescue of me shattered as I wept and prayed. It was quite obvious that the Lord had put in my heart a desire to walk an unknown hallway, confounded Candy's cell phone, brought a gentle rain for me to watch, and quieted the hallway to providentially put me in that exact spot at that precise time to overhear the lady's conversation. He wanted me to know that my perceptions of danger from aspiration had been on the money. It could and did happen, even in this wonderful hospital. The Lord had indeed rescued me, possibly from immediate bodily death, or at least from major oxygen deprivation and massive brain damage. In any case, my life on earth was in grave danger, and He rescued me. The eternal life of my soul was never in danger because it had been saved by the Lord long ago. I was grievingly overwhelmed at the thought that God spared me but apparently not Frank. It was my first experience with survivor's guilt, although certainly not the last. I again prayed for God to come to Frank's rescue. As Frank's wife and I continued to cry separately, I prayed that these people knew Christ personally or would very soon.

Candy soon completed her call, noted my tears, and asked what was wrong. I told her I would explain later, and we turned to return to my room. But because of God's remarkable providence, I was not the same man on the return trip that I had been a few minutes earlier.

Some may say all these things were mere coincidences, but there were too many things with God's fingerprints on them to ignore. This was the sovereign hand of God Almighty providentially guiding me, Candy, Frank's wife, the talkative people who left the hall, the rain, the phone, and all the other circumstances surrounding us, all for His glory and my good. I never again doubted whether my experiences and perceptions during those dark hours in the MD Anderson ICU were real. Those were indeed my Psalm 91 hours, and it is only by God's steadfast love that I am here to proclaim His mercy and His grace upon me.

> *Trust in the LORD with all your heart, and do not lean on your own understanding.*
> *In all your ways acknowledge him, and he will make straight your paths.*
> —Proverbs 3:5-6

> *All the paths of the LORD are steadfast love and faithfulness,*
> *for those who keep his covenant and his testimonies.*
> —Psalm 25:10

> *You have multiplied, O LORD my God, your wondrous deeds and your thoughts toward us;*
> *none can compare with you! I will proclaim and tell of them, yet they are more than can be told.*
> —Psalm 40:5

Chapter 5

UNHARMED

"Fear not, for I have redeemed you;
I have called you by name, you are mine.
When you pass through the waters, I will be with you;
and through the rivers, they shall not overwhelm you;
when you walk through fire you shall not be burned,
and the flame shall not consume you.
For I am the LORD your God,
the Holy One of Israel, your Savior.
—Isaiah 43:1b-3a

B y God's grace and to the surprise of my doctors, I never developed pneumonia after the surgery, a rare occurrence for the type of surgery I had. It was especially shocking, considering how I struggled to breathe throughout the first night in the ICU. So after recuperating for only a couple of weeks from my surgery in Houston, Candy and I returned to our home in Collierville, Tennessee, at the end of August. I looked forward to a chance to rest and heal before starting the next phase of cancer treatments. We were thankful for MD Anderson, Dr. Diaz, Dr. Hanasono, Nurse Trish, and all the other wonderful people in Houston who helped us. Most of all, we were thankful for the ways the Lord made His presence known to us in such incredible ways while we were there.

As they say, there's no place like home, and we were thankful to have recovered enough to make the trip. It was a delight to see our daughter, Laura, and son Joseph, again. We missed seeing our son Michael; he was a member of Mississippi State's Famous Maroon Band's drumline and performed that afternoon and evening at State's first football game of the season. For the next six weeks, I focused on healing for my mouth, physical therapy for my weakened right leg, and overall strength for my body.

I began six weeks of chemotherapy and radiation treatments in mid-October of 2008. The chemo treatments were done weekly at West Clinic in Memphis, and the radiation treatments were done each weekday at Methodist Germantown Radiology Center (MGRC). The radiation treatments were administered while I lay flat on a metal table with my head in a rigid plastic mask, which was bolted to the table. The mask was designed to shield me from radiation except for holes in the mask at precise points where radiation was needed to wage war against any remaining cancer cells. There was also a hole for a rather uncomfortable mouthpiece to be inserted to protect my teeth. The mask was custom designed by a team that included Dr. Holger Gieschen at MGRC, Dr. Eduardo Diaz and radiology oncologist Dr. Anita Sabichi at MD Anderson, and Dr. Kurt Tauer at West Clinic. These were four of the world's finest, most knowledgeable oncologists, and we were so very thankful that the Lord assembled such a stellar team to treat me!

As I mentioned before, I could not lie flat for very long without choking on my saliva, yet I had to do so for these treatments. After arriving at MGRC for each treatment, I exchanged my shirt and undershirt for a hospital scrub top in the men's locker room. I always arrived early enough to spend several minutes praying in the locker room before each session. I asked the Lord to do for me what I could not do myself: lie flat and still long enough to receive the treatment for that day. I asked God to put the remaining cancer cells in the line of fire of the radiation beams. I prayed for the technicians and for the precision equipment they used. With gratitude, I reminded the Lord of what He did for me in the ICU at MD Anderson and asked Him to do the undoable again.

> Good men know how to turn the darkest trials into arguments
> at the throne of grace. (Charles Haddon Spurgeon)[3]

Each session included twenty-two minutes of radiation. It also took a few minutes to bolt me and my mask to the table before the session and unbolt me afterward. Therefore, each session, theoretically, should take twenty-five to thirty minutes. My sessions, however, always took longer. The MGRC technicians knew of my limitations and were incredibly kind and patient. Whenever I began to choke, I raised my hand; the technicians immediately stopped the treatment and rushed in to unbolt my mask so I could sit up and spit and cough out the saliva from my throat. Then they bolted me back down, and the treatment resumed. Normally I could not lie flat for over a minute before choking, but with the Lord's help, I usually made it about halfway through a session before I had to raise my hand. Once again, the Lord was faithful in keeping His promises to be with me, to protect me, and to do what was impossible for me to do myself.

The first couple of weeks of these treatments were not too damaging. Eventually, however, the cumulative effect of absorbing so much radiation began to take its toll, producing painful blisters on my neck and multiple sores in my mouth and throat. With each treatment, the blisters, sores, and pain worsened. My saliva continued to thicken, which complicated the treatments at MGRC and normal functions at home. By mid-November, I had second-degree burns on my neck and tender sores throughout my throat and mouth.

Excerpt from CarePage entry

November 14, 2008

This is not an easy season. Each treatment is more difficult and the side effects get a little worse each day. My digestive system has made lots of music this week, but can't seem to decide between just Sitting on the Dock of the Bay or doing the Flight of the Bumblebee. In addition to the sores in my throat, mouth, and lips, some skin on my neck and face is chafed and painful. All my neck and lower face are red and hairless, as the hair follicles have been destroyed by the radiation. My face has taken on a definite starboard list, as the right side of my face and neck are quite swollen. The thick secretions continue to be difficult to manage. Speaking continues to get more difficult.

My intention is not to whine about my situation. I do want to be honest with you folks on the difficulties of going through radiation. But I also want to share the great message of hope, that even in times like this our days can be full of joy and joyous songs as we read and hear the Lord's melodious words of truth, and our hearts sing praises to Him.

(Several other CarePage posts related to my experiences with the radiation treatments during the six-week period from October 13 through November 26 can be found in Appendix A)

One day while gingerly dabbing burn ointment on my neck, I surveyed the damage in the bathroom mirror. My neck was bright red except for the worst of the burns, which were much darker and oozed with pus. The inside of my mouth and the visible part of my throat looked awful, with too many sores to count, although many were hidden by thick, sticky saliva that clung like cobwebs inside my mouth. The burns and sores were fiercely painful, and it was depressing to think I still had another week of remaining treatments that would only make them worse. I felt like a piece of burnt toast that someone kept putting back in a microwave. My eyes moistened as I looked in the mirror, and I recalled Isaiah 43:2: "When you pass through the waters, I will be with you; and through the rivers, they shall not overwhelm you; when you walk through fire you shall not be burned, and the flame shall not consume you."

I prayed, "O Lord, I know You said these things to Israel, not me. But You miraculously allowed me to pass through the high waters that night in the ICU and not asphyxiate or drown in my own bloody vomit. So I thought You would also protect me from getting severely burned from radiation. But look at me, Lord, I am burned! So terribly, terribly burned! You know how badly it hurts, and it's only going to get worse!" Immediately the Holy Spirit brought to mind a word of truth:

> *For we know that if the tent that is our earthly home is destroyed, we have a building from God, a house not made with hands, eternal in the heavens. For in this tent we groan, longing to put on our heavenly dwelling,… He who has prepared us for this very thing is God, who has given us the Spirit as a guarantee.*
> —2 Corinthians 5:1-2, 5

God the Holy Spirit gently reminded me that these injuries were only to my body and only for a season. My soul, by His grace, was unharmed. It was stronger and healthier than it had ever been. God would continue to be with me, heal me in His perfect timing, and strengthen my soul. I bowed my head, took a deep breath, and said, "Yes, Lord." My spirits lifted, and I dried my eyes. I told myself, *The Lord's got this; He will see me through.* And, in due time, our faithful Savior kept His promises once again.

> *See, I have refined you, though not as silver; I have tested you in the furnace of affliction.*
> —Isaiah 48:10 NIV

> *I am afflicted very much: quicken me, O LORD, according unto thy word.*
> —Psalm 119:107 KJV

Our service of the Lord does not screen us from trial, but rather secures it for us.…This [quickening and renewal] is the best remedy for tribulation; the soul is raised above the thought of present distress, and is filled with that holy joy which attends all vigorous spiritual life, and so the affliction grows light. Jehovah alone can quicken: he has life in himself, and therefore can communicate it readily; he can give us life at any moment, yea, at this present instant; for it is of the nature of quickening to be quick in its operation. The Lord has promised, prepared, and provided this blessing of renewed life for all his waiting servants: it is a covenant blessing, and it is as obtainable as it is needful. (Charles Haddon Spurgeon, commenting on Psalm 119:107)[4]

Trouble and anguish have found me out, but your commandments are my delight.
—Psalm 119:143

On the day I called, you answered me; my strength of soul you increased.
—Psalm 138:3

I completed the thirtieth and final radiation treatment the afternoon before Thanksgiving. The pain was excruciating, but I was exceedingly thankful that I would not again be put into the MGRC "microwave oven" and now could focus solely on healing. Yet it only took a bit of reflection to realize that I had much to be thankful for on this Thanksgiving Eve. I had survived an incredible battering of my body. I could not help but think of my first appointment with Dr. Diaz five months before—five months that felt like every bit of five years. He promised "to beat the crap out of me," and he proved to be a man of his word. Yet I was so very thankful for him, as well as for Drs. Hanasono, Tauer, Sabichi, Gieschen, Klug, and Taylor. I was thankful for the chemotherapy in early summer that made me so sick, for the life-altering yet life-saving surgery in August, for the Lord's miraculous protection of me, and, yes, for these torturous radiation treatments. All of these played crucial roles in Dr. Diaz's brilliant plan to defeat my cancer. I was thankful the chemo and radiation treatments were in Memphis rather than Houston. I was so thankful to be home with my beloved family for Thanksgiving. Above all, I was thankful that by the strength of the word of God and His kept promises, my soul was not only unharmed but stronger than ever.

This is my comfort in my affliction, that your promise gives me life.
—Psalm 119:50

Count it all joy, my brothers, when you meet trials of various kinds, for you know that the testing of your faith produces steadfastness. And let steadfastness have its full effect, that you may be perfect and complete, lacking in nothing.
—James 1:2-4

Keep me as the apple of your eye; hide me in the shadow of your wings.
—Psalm 17:8

As I entered this extended time of healing, I was still the apple of my Father's eye and safely in the shadow of His wings. The enemy may have meant this time for my eternal harm with his taunts of discouragement, but God meant it for my good and clearly showed me His mercy and steadfast love. Yes, indeed, I had much to be thankful for on this exceedingly painful yet victorious and blessed Thanksgiving.

Because you have made the LORD your dwelling place—the Most High, who is my refuge—
no evil shall be allowed to befall you, no plague come near your tent.
—Psalm 91:9-10

It is impossible that any ill should happen to the man who is beloved of the Lord; the most crushing calamities can only shorten his journey and hasten him to his reward. Ill to him is no ill, but only good in a mysterious form. Losses enrich him, sickness is his medicine, reproach is his honour, death is his gain. No evil in the strict sense of the word can happen to him, for everything is overruled for good. Happy is he who is in such a case. He is secure where others are in peril, he lives where others die. (Charles Haddon Spurgeon)[5]

Chapter 6

OLDIES BUT GOODIES

When I am afraid, I put my trust in you.
—Psalm 56:3

As you can imagine, my journey through life-threatening cancer was difficult for our entire family. Candy certainly bore the brunt of the impact, but it was also trying on our three children, especially during the summer and fall of 2008. Michael was nineteen and a sophomore at Mississippi State University; Laura was a junior, and Joseph was a freshman, both at Collierville High School.

That school year started while Candy and I were in Houston. We were very blessed to have some wonderful friends who essentially adopted Laura and Joseph as their own for the month of August. Laura stayed with Shawn and Monica Roberts, while Joseph stayed with Carter and Sandy Tate. It was such a relief for Candy and me to know that our children were in such capable hands of people we implicitly trusted. That did not mean, however, that having a dad whose life was threatened by cancer was emotionally easy for our children. Michael, Laura, and Joseph have different personalities and struggled in their own way.

The following year, Laura wrote a short paper about the experience as part of an assignment for her AP English class. She is our family's best writer, and she aced the class. More importantly, her story touched my heart then and still does to this day. I am not sure I have ever read it without my eyes leaking a bit. I hope that you will enjoy it also.

*My heart is steadfast, O God, my heart is steadfast! I will sing and
make melody!*
—Psalm 57:7

Oldies But Goodies
By Laura Barton

About once a month, my friend Patsy Cline finds her way out of
her CD case and back into my heart. Every time I listen to her
country blues, I always come back to the same question: Why
do I like this? But the simple truth is that I just do. She makes
me smile, she makes me brave, and she reminds me of what is
truly important in life, that in the end, things like family and
tradition are integral parts of my identity. And good ole Patsy
Cline has been doing it for a long time.

Ever since I can remember, my father and I have listened to oldies together. From Sly and the Family Stone to Elton John and
Michael Jackson, we have grooved, rocked, and moon-walked
through the decades of musical history together. Sure, I have fa-
vorites like the B52's "Love Shack" or the Go-Go's "Head Over
Heels," but Patsy Cline, she was the first. My enthusiastic rendi-
tions of her classic tunes were, in fact, the spark for the many
musical adventures that were to come. Even now, whenever I
hear her 1957 hit single "Walkin' After Midnight," I cannot help
but dramatically lip-sync the words into my handy imaginary
microphone.

And as I've grown up, my dad's oldies have stayed with me; in
fact, they have become part of who I am too. When the CD
became popular, the first order of business was to trade out my
worn-out cassette tape of *Patsy Cline's Greatest Hits* for a shiny
new CD version. Now, the album is safely stored away in my
MP3 player for unlimited access. By keeping the music close, I
can keep my dad close by too.

While I always knew this hobby of ours was unusual, I only
recently realized how much I took it for granted. From the moment my father was diagnosed with cancer two years ago, the
music took on new meaning. It ceased to be just instruments
and voices; it became a lifeline, an escape from doubt, worry,

and the terrible "what-ifs." While my parents were in Houston, Texas, for my dad's treatment at MD Anderson Cancer Hospital, "Walkin' After Midnight" became a staple, a must before prayers and bed. The song is a part of our relationship, and even though my parents were away from me, I still had my oldies. I believed that surely if the music remained, my father would pull through, too.

When he finally returned home and the worst stages of the cancer passed, Patsy Cline was joined by other greats like Fleetwood Mac, Stevie Wonder, and the Doobie Brothers as if to celebrate the confirmation that, yes, my father and I would be enjoying old music and tune-filled life together for many more years to come.

Chapter 7

WEAKNESS IN STRENGTH, STRENGTH IN WEAKNESS

His delight is not in the strength of the horse,
Nor his pleasure in the legs of a man,
but the LORD takes pleasure in those who fear him,
in those who hope in his steadfast love.
—Psalm 147:10-11

L ike most healthy young men, I was pretty strong in my teens and twenties. I played sports, worked out, and was in excellent physical condition. However, many of those years were also marked by a frail spiritual condition. I usually had part-time jobs that required me to work most weekends, including Sundays, and my church attendance became increasingly less frequent. I also fell out of the habit of reading my Bible, and predictably I was not walking with the Lord and did some very foolish things.

> *Do not be deceived: God is not mocked, for whatever one sows, that*
> *will he also reap.*
> —Galatians 6:7

By God's grace, He awakened me from my spiritual slumber when I was twenty-four years old. My faith in Christ continued to deepen and grow stronger in the years that followed.

Fast-forward another twenty-four years to 2007. My fifteen-year-old daughter, Laura, was playing in her final softball tournament of the summer, a "world series" tournament in Mesquite, Texas. She capped off a great season with an outstanding tournament, and her team came in third place. (Please don't ask me about the last-inning call in the semifinal game that kept us out of the championship game; I'm almost over being upset about it. Almost.) That evening we celebrated the girls' performance at a local hamburger joint in Mesquite. While eating my hamburger, I noticed my tongue hurt on the right side. A quick look in a bathroom mirror later that night revealed that I had an ulcer on the underside of my tongue on the right side. I occasionally had ulcers like that before, and they always went away quickly. But this ulcer didn't go away. It was still there and a bit more painful a few weeks later.

I eventually saw a couple of doctors about it, including an ENT, and both were puzzled. They agreed that it certainly didn't look like an oral cancer sore but weren't sure what to make of it. A biopsy indicated it was a fungal infection, and I was treated for that for a couple of months. Yet the ulcer became more painful and showed no signs of improvement. A second and deeper biopsy by a different ENT, Dr. Dean Klug, revealed it was indeed cancer. That was the beginning of my cancer journey. At the time, I was not in great physical shape—definitely overweight—yet still quite strong. But not for long. From the previous chapters of this book, you know that over the next year and a half, I had a brutal battle with cancer, and I became severely weak physically yet much stronger spiritually.

> But he said to me, "My grace is sufficient for you, for my power is made perfect in weakness." Therefore I will boast all the more gladly of my weaknesses, so that the power of Christ may rest upon me. For the sake of Christ, then, I am content with weaknesses, insults, hardships, persecutions, and calamities. For when I am weak, then I am strong.
> —2 Corinthians 12:9-10

Indeed, the Lord used my weakness to display His strength. I would never wish anyone to suffer the pain I did in my cancer journey, yet I will be eternally grateful for my affliction. God used it to draw me ever closer to Him. He taught me many things about Himself and revealed many things about myself. He showed me that His blessings are not for me to store away for myself but to share with others. God uses both our hardships and blessings to display His glory.

I had my first appointment at MD Anderson Hospital in Houston, Texas, on June 16, 2008. By God's grace, He worked it out so that my friend and mentor, Jim Siegfried, was also in Houston at that time to receive radiation treatments. To this day, I can't think about Jim and not picture him with a smile on his face, an encouraging word on his lips, and a prayer easily spoken from his heart. Candy and I got to visit with him and his wife, Cyndi, for about an hour that day, and it was a welcomed touch of normality as we stepped into this new and perilous world. But it was also another invaluable lesson from our friends on how genuine believers in Christ handle a health crisis.

Within a few years of Jim's first cancer diagnosis in 2003, he and Cyndi began a ministry they called "f.a.i.t.H: facing an illness through Him." It was a Christian-based support group for people fighting cancer or other long-term illnesses and for their primary caregivers. Candy and I were extremely grateful to be a part of the group. Jim and Cyndi were great friends and constant examples of how Christians are to share the love of Christ in all seasons of life. Jim, a lifelong athlete, had been an outstanding businessman and church leader for decades. But now, in the weakest era of his life, Jim relied on the strength of Christ more than ever. His ministry had an incredible impact on the lives of many hurting people. Little did we know as we visited with the Siegfrieds that afternoon that God would also display His strength through my weakness in the coming days.

The remainder of our first day in Houston was spent in orientation sessions to introduce us to the world of MD Anderson Hospital. We learned how to get around the massive complex, how to check appointment schedules, where to eat, and where to do other necessary activities. At one of the sessions, we were introduced to the hospital's "CarePage" system—a blog kept by the patient or caregiver to inform and update interested friends and family members of the patient's health status. (Many people these days use a similar "CaringBridge" system.) That evening Candy and I sat in one of the lobbies and discussed the CarePage. Candy suggested that I do the updates, and I agreed. She suggested I just stick to medical updates without giving too many time-consuming details. I pondered it for a few minutes and then said, "No, we desperately need prayer. I want to write from my heart to hopefully touch the heart of those who read it so they'll pray for us." And that's what I did. My initial appointment with Dr. Eduardo Diaz was the following day, and I began to use my CarePage that evening.

Soon after my first posts on the CarePage, friends and family members posted kind and supportive messages. That was not unexpected, but the volume of responses within a few days was shocking. As more and more people signed onto the blog, the responses to my entries continued to grow. Many noted how inspirational my updates were. At first, I was touched that friends would be kind enough to say such things. But then I began to get similar messages from people I didn't know. I was utterly baffled. What was going on here? I made A's in English in high school and college and knew how to string together a few cohesive sentences with reasonably good grammar, but I did not have the ability to touch a person's heart in the ways they described.

I realized that the Lord was working through the simple words I wrote to touch people in ways that were way, way beyond my abilities. A lady in Nebraska wrote to say her dad also had Stage 4 tongue cancer but had little chance of survival because of his age. She said he asked her every day if I had posted an update so she could read it to him, as it was the highlight of his day. Another lady in North Carolina had a similar story. A group of young men in Louisiana used my updates for their Bible study. These responses bewildered me. I knew this was extending far beyond my use of words and syntax in my postings; the Lord was using me for His kingdom purposes. It was His strength working through my weakness, for His glory and for the good of many. It may have been my CarePage, but God's fingerprints were all over it. That spring, summer, and fall, while fighting for my life, I shared the love of Christ with more people than I had in total for the first forty-nine years of my life!

Occasionally I get out my book of printed messages from my old CarePage and look through them. I have yet to do so with dry eyes. Yes, memories of the excruciating things I endured in 2008 are painful, but my tears flow from a heart that is still overwhelmed by the ways God poured out His grace. Oh, what a Savior!

> *And my speech and my message were not in plausible words of wisdom, but in demonstration of the Spirit and of power, so that your faith might not rest in the wisdom of men but in the power of God.*
> —1 Corinthians 2:4-5

As I recently re-read my CarePage entries, I was reminded that our usefulness in ministry is not based on our abilities but on our willingness to be used by God, no matter our circumstances or season of life. My updates were usually not lengthy. They included information on my health status, things happening in our family (especially Laura's softball team), comments about friends we saw or heard from, and a Bible verse or two with which the Lord blessed me that day. My postings were certainly not great works of literature, but they were anointed and blessed by God and therefore were meaningful and useful to many during that particular season. In case I have aroused your curiosity regarding my CarePage, I selected a sampling of the dozens of entries I wrote and put them in Appendix A at the back of this book.

I did not do a lot of long-term thinking in 2008, as most days were a struggle just to hang on to fight the cancer battle another day. So I did not realize the success of my CarePage was an early sign that God had additional plans for my newfound enjoyment of writing. I would come to consider writing as God's gracious gift of a new tongue.

> *And we know that for those who love God all things work together for*
> *good, for those who are called according to his purpose.*
> —Romans 8:28

I had struggled with speaking for many years due to a long battle with diseased vocal cords, leaving me with an unusually soft voice. As a grateful cancer survivor without a functioning tongue, I was now also unable to make certain sounds necessary for correct pronunciation of many words. I would never again verbally communicate effectively. Yet, by God's grace, newfound writing skills gave me a new tongue and a new voice. Writing, especially when combined with the God-given gift of encouragement, has opened up new avenues for me to share the love of Christ with neighbors, co-workers, and relatives. It has also blessed me by requiring me to meditate more deeply on God's word as I write. God indeed turned my weakness into a strength—for His glory, my good, and hopefully good to many others He puts in my path.

> *Then my tongue shall tell of your righteousness and of your praise all*
> *the day long.*
> —Psalm 35:28

As important as Romans 8:28 was to Candy and me during my cancer journey and beyond, the Lord taught us a couple of critical things regarding that verse. First, we must always have enough faith to allow God to define "good" for us. Secondly, we must not stop reading at the end of the verse.

> *For those whom he foreknew he also predestined to be conformed to*
> *the image of his Son, in order that he might be the firstborn among*
> *many brothers. And those whom he predestined he also called, and*
> *those whom he called he also justified, and those whom he justified*
> *he also glorified.*
> —Romans 8:29-30

The good God does for us is often not what we expect or, admittedly, what we hope for. Yet ultimately, His manner of defining and bringing good to us is always better than what we would have prescribed for ourselves. The ultimate good that God speaks of in verse 28 is described in the following two verses: it is to make us more like Christ. God the Father uses whatever circumstances are necessary to conform us more and more to the image of His Son. He chooses us, He calls us, He redeems us, He justifies us, He sanctifies us, and He glorifies us, making us more like Christ with each step.

We who follow Christ are continually in the process of being sanctified, and God uses various means to do so. He removes our perceived strengths that He regards as weaknesses. He takes our weaknesses and works through them to display His glorious strength. He works through what we may describe as "good times" as well as "bad times." Some of the latter are exceptionally painful yet often necessary to cause us to lay aside worldly attitudes, pleasures, and pursuits. If we remain faithful in trusting God, the resulting joy and peace of being closer to Christ lead to a more purposeful, meaningful, and abundant life, even in challenging times. Praise be to God; that is indeed my testimony.

> *Those who fear you shall see me and rejoice, because I have hoped in your word.*
> *I know, O LORD, that your rules are righteous, and that in faithfulness you have afflicted me.*
> —Psalm 119:74-75

Even though verbal weaknesses have been a struggle for most of my adult life, the Lord has used my afflictions and disabilities to strengthen my relationships with others. The threat of losing my life to cancer did so much to fortify my marriage to Candy. I have always been head-over-heels crazy about her, but in the past, we occasionally were at odds over what we now consider trivial matters. Cancer made us understand and better grasp the truly important things in life and in our marriage. We appreciate each other more and love each other more deeply. It has also made me more appreciative of my relationships with my children, siblings in Christ, neighbors, and other friends. Again, I can take no credit for any of this. It's all grace—God's stunning, glorious, unrelenting grace that works all things for good.

I accept the fact that the Lord has used my unusual health weaknesses as a form of discipline and refinement to help transform me more into the man He desires me to be. I am most certainly a much weaker man physically, but God has made me much stronger spiritually and emotionally. Those who know me well know this is very much still a work in progress. While I wish it was not necessary for God to take such measures, I thank Him for how He has used affliction, suffering, and this unique lifestyle for my good. I rejoice that I have a heavenly Father who loves me enough to discipline me for my own good yet always does so in loving and gracious ways.

And have you forgotten the exhortation that addresses you as sons?
"My son, do not regard lightly the discipline of the Lord, nor be
weary when reproved by him. For the Lord disciplines the one he
loves, and chastises every son whom he receives." It is for discipline
that you have to endure. God is treating you as sons. For what son
is there whom his father does not discipline? If you are left without
discipline, in which all have participated, then you are illegitimate
children and not sons.
—Hebrews 12:5-8

A sick bed often teaches more than a sermon. We can best see
the ugly visage of sin in the glass of affliction. Affliction teaches
us to know ourselves. (Thomas Watson, 1663)[6]

God indeed used my weaknesses to make me a kinder, more
compassionate, more patient, and more God-fearing man. Our Lord did
what was necessary to draw me closer to Him, which has given me more joy
than I ever had as an able-bodied man. I thank the Lord that He has, by His
grace, surrounded me with so many wise, knowledgeable, caring, and godly
people for my good. Out of my weakness, God's strength blessed me in ways
I never dreamed to hope for.

The LORD has disciplined me severely, but he has not given me over
to death.
Open to me the gates of righteousness, that I may enter through them
and give thanks to the LORD.
—Psalm 118:18-19

Come, let us return to the LORD; for he has torn us, that he may heal
us; he has struck us down, and he will bind us up.
—Hosea 6:1

Chapter 8

HE NEVER LETS GO

Be strong and courageous. Do not fear or be in dread of them, for it is the LORD your God who goes with you. He will not leave you or forsake you.
—Deuteronomy 31:6

Looking back on it now, it made little practical sense to attend church services on the morning of January 25, 2009. I was still trying to recover from the chemotherapy, surgeries, and radiation treatments that had battered my body for several months. My mouth, throat, and neck healed significantly in the previous two months, but more healing was still greatly needed. Much of the pain of six weeks of intense radiation and chemo in October and November lingered. My partial tongue often oozed with blood and mucus, and I had painful ulcers on my cheeks and gums more days than not. I was never without some degree of pain in my mouth, and trying to speak only heightened the pain. Lymphedema produced swelling in my neck that would take many more months of therapy to go away. Worst of all, being out in public during cold and flu season was unwise because of the heightened risk of infection due to my low white blood cell levels.

Yet Candy and I were overjoyed that we were only dealing with those issues and no longer in a daily life-or-death struggle with cancer. Many people from our church family spent countless hours praying for us and serving us during this journey, and I longed to see them and worship with them once more. So Candy and I did indeed attend the worship service at Living Hope Church that Sunday morning. I liked to think that my attendance that day resulted from being courageous and tough, although my lovely wife often used what she said was a more accurate term: *hardheaded!*

I remember but a few details from that worship service. I cannot tell you what the sermon was about or recall all the names of the many people I saw and greeted. I remember a song early in the service that was particularly moving because it was based on Isaiah 43:1-3, which includes some of the specific promises of God I desperately clung to in the previous months. Tears filled my eyes as I thanked the Lord for never leaving me or forsaking me and carrying me through the painful battle.

As the sermon wound down, I was in a lot of pain and felt exhausted. However, the most vivid memory from that day was the final song. I weakly rose to my feet with the congregation and began to sing—actually more of a low hum—with Candy to my right and my friend Zack Taylor to my left. The words to the Matt Redman song "You Never Let Go" appeared on the big screen, and I began to mumble them. I'm unsure if I had heard that song before that morning. I probably had, but the details of the lyrics did not sink in before that day. A rush of deep emotion swept through me as we sang the opening stanza. The song lyrics brought to mind several Bible verses as we sang of being close to death during stormy times yet unafraid because of the Lord's presence. He faithfully never lets go of those He calls His own.

Even though I walk through the valley of the shadow of death,
I will fear no evil, for you are with me.
—Psalm 23:4a

There is no fear in love; but perfect love casts out fear.
—1 John 4:18a

Fear not, for I am with you; be not dismayed, for I am your God.
—Isaiah 41:10a

And a great windstorm arose, and the waves were breaking into the boat, so that the boat was already filling. But he [Jesus] was in the stern, asleep on the cushion. And they woke him and said to him, "Teacher, do you not care that we are perishing?" And he awoke and rebuked the wind and said to the sea, "Peace! Be still!" And the wind ceased, and there was a great calm. He said to them, "Why are you so afraid? Have you still no faith?" And they were filled with great fear and said to one another, "Who then is this, that even the wind and the sea obey him?"
—Mark 4:37-41

I immediately thought of how closely the lyrics and the verses related to my stormy battle with cancer. The battle continued, but hopefully the worst of it was behind me, at least for now. The song's lyrics triggered flashbacks from specific scenes in the battle, especially when I was near death yet completely unafraid. By the time we got to the chorus, my emotions were in overdrive. In my heart, I cried out in gratitude to the Lord for never letting go of me through this terrible yet wonderful battle and for making His presence known in such amazing ways. He had used this period of my life to draw me closer—much, much closer—to Him than I ever was before, filling me with great joy, even in the midst of incredible pain.

I had to wipe tears from my eyes to see the words of the second verse. Yet those words about the coming light of Christ triggered even more emotions. They brought to mind one of the peak moments in the battle for my life: the dawning light of sunrise on August 15, 2008. The darkness of enduring pain and the threat of physical death had been genuinely real and continued to be, but the light and love of God were so much greater! The Lord continuously filled me with courage, assurance, and even joy: an abundant God-given joy that adverse circumstances could not deter.

> *The people who walked in darkness have seen a great light;*
> *those who dwelt in a land of deep darkness, on them has light shone.*
> —Isaiah 9:2

> *"These things I have spoken to you, that my joy may be in you, and that your joy may be full."*
> —The words of Jesus in John 15:11

Before that moment, I had never known the feeling of being physically overcome with emotion, but I was rapidly finding out. I felt my knees grow weak, and I knew I was about to collapse. Yet just at that moment, I felt Zack's strong right hand grab my right shoulder as he reached around me. I instinctively leaned my left shoulder into his body to prop myself up and looked at my faithful friend. Zack was not only my excellent gastroenterologist, wise church elder, and faithful friend, but he's also a terrific singer. He is one of those people who can give you a big smile while singing and never miss a note, and smile he did as he glanced at me and again sang the chorus.

As we worshiped, I thought of Zack coming to our house a few weeks before on New Year's Eve to treat me for an excruciating infection in my feeding tube site. Again my heart was full of praise to God for not letting go and using Zack as a conduit of His mighty, unyielding love for me.

My face was a mixture of smiles of gratitude and streaking tears as we finished singing. I said a weak, possibly unintelligible "thank you" to Zack and plopped back down in my seat to pull myself together. I thanked the

Lord for that incredible moment of pure worship and gathered my strength for the walk to the parking lot.

I was physically and emotionally drained when Candy and I arrived home after church. I took some nutrition and medicine through my feeding tube and then went straight to sleep, still singing "You Never Let Go" in my head. When I awoke a couple of hours later, I still had the song on my heart and looked up the lyrics to fill in my memory gaps.

As I pondered the lyrics, several verses from Scripture came to mind, especially one the Lord repeated to me over and over throughout the previous eight months:

> *"Have I not commanded you? Be strong and courageous. Do not be frightened, and do not be dismayed, for the LORD your God is with you wherever you go."*
> —Joshua 1:9

The lyrics of Matt Redman's song and these words of God to Joshua aligned well with what I had experienced. Candy and I had indeed been in a dreadful storm, and the shadow of death was darkly foreboding. Yet the Lord gave us courage when we needed it most. The light of His blessings was abundantly brighter than the darkness of our circumstances, and His presence and promises overcame our fears. We were strengthened daily by His word for whatever challenges arose. The greatest blessing was not that I survived cancer but that we emerged closer to Christ than we ever were before, and our focus on Him took away much of the terror of the painful ordeal. All because God never let go. The Savior of our souls, our loving heavenly Father, the Source of our life on earth and our new life in Him, the Reason for our unshakable joy, the One True God, never, ever let go. And He never will.

> *It is the LORD who goes before you. He will be with you; he will not leave you or forsake you. Do not fear or be dismayed.*
> —Deuteronomy 31:8

> *For all who are led by the Spirit of God are sons of God. For you did not receive the spirit of slavery to fall back into fear, but you have received the Spirit of adoption as sons, by whom we cry, "Abba! Father!"*
> —Romans 8:14-15

THE SHADOW OF THE VALLEY OF DEATH

> *Yea, though I walk through the valley of the shadow of death, I will fear no evil: for thou art with me; thy rod and thy staff they comfort me.*
> —Psalm 23:4 KJV

The above verse from Psalms is one of the verses on which Matt Redman based his song, "You Never Let Go." I dearly love the following comments by Charles Spurgeon on this verse from his commentary on Psalms, *The Treasury of David*. They are meaningful to me because of how close I came to death in August 2008. Yet they are even more meaningful as I consider the deaths of loved ones in the past and dear friends in recent years. I hope they are meaningful to you as well.

This unspeakably delightful verse has been sung on many a dying bed and has helped to make the dark valley bright times out of mind. Every word in it has a wealth of meaning.

"Yea, though I *walk*," as if the believer did not quicken his pace when he came to die, but still calmly *walked* with God. To walk indicates the steady advance of a soul which knows its road, knows its end, resolves to follow the path, feels quite safe, and is therefore perfectly calm and composed. The dying saint is not in a flurry, he does not run as though he were alarmed, nor stand still as though he would go no further; he is not confounded nor ashamed, and therefore keeps to his old pace.

Observe that it is not walking *in* the valley, but *through* the valley. We go through the dark tunnel of death and emerge into the light of immortality. We do not die; we do but sleep to wake in glory. Death is not the house but the porch, not the goal but the passage to it.

The dying article is called a *valley*. The storm breaks on the mountain, but the valley is the place of quietude, and thus full often the last days of the Christian are the most peaceful of his whole career; the mountain is bleak and bare, but the valley is rich with golden sheaves, and many a saint has reaped more joy and knowledge when he came to die than he ever knew while he lived.

And, then, it is not "the valley of death," but "the valley of the shadow of death," for death in its substance has been removed, and only the shadow of it remains. Some one has said that when there is a shadow there must be light somewhere, and so there is. Death stands by the side of the highway in which we have to travel, and the light of heaven shining upon him throws a shadow across our path; let us then rejoice that there is a light beyond.

Nobody is afraid of a shadow, for a shadow cannot stop a man's pathway even for a moment. The shadow of a dog cannot bite; the shadow of a sword cannot kill; the shadow of death cannot destroy us. Let us not, therefore, be afraid. (Charles Haddon Spurgeon)[7]

Amen, and amen! Indeed, I can testify that these are not merely theological, theoretical, eloquent concepts from Pastor Spurgeon; they can be an accurate picture of peaceful reality for those who follow Christ. Because of the presence of the Lord with me during my cancer journey, I was unafraid of death, even during the hours when it seemed so imminent. Oh, what a Savior!

Chapter 9

LAURA'S PLUM

*The righteous has enough to satisfy his appetite,
but the belly of the wicked suffers want.*
—Proverbs 13:25

I grew up eating fresh apples, plums, grapes, muscadines, and blackberries picked straight from the tree or vine. My mom also bought lots of fruit we did not grow, such as peaches, bananas, strawberries, cantaloupes, oranges, lemons, and grapefruit. And, of course, no summer outing was complete without some ice-cold watermelon! I simply loved almost any kind of fresh fruit, as well as juices and desserts made with fresh fruit.

My love of fruit continued unabated into my adulthood. At least it did until 2008, when cancer took away my ability to swallow. The last solid food I had before my second cancer surgery was a few bites of Candy's delicious fresh peach pie, my favorite dessert. My cancer was so advanced by that time that my tongue was barely functional. I knew eating would hurt, but I also knew it would be my last chance to eat in a conventional manner for a long time. Chewing and swallowing the few tiny bites of peach pie was indeed painful, yet oh, so tasty, with a soft and delightful blend of tartness and sweetness. At the time, Candy and I had no idea those would be my last bites of food in this life.

As the summer of 2009 rolled around, I was mighty grateful to be alive. Winning the battle against cancer had been wonderful. Yet there were many casualties, the most significant being the loss of a functional tongue, along with the abilities to speak plainly and swallow. I had hoped to regain the ability to swallow eventually, but by January 2009, it was clear that would never happen. So much of the base of my tongue—that's the part of the tongue in one's throat—was removed during surgery that it left me without a mechanism to protect my windpipe when anything goes down my throat. This predicament meant my feeding tube was not temporary but would be an ongoing part of my everyday life for as long as I live on earth. We had thought my feeding tube would act as a lifeboat to help carry me through the rough waters of cancer and cancer treatments. Alas, my lifeboat became my houseboat. There would be no more peach pie or refreshing iced tea for me, at least not on this side of heaven.

Yet God made His presence known in remarkable ways through my cancer journey, and there was no doubt that I could keep trusting Him to care for me. His word had filled my soul with unparalleled hope and joy, even on the most painful days. Surely He would somehow continue to do so.

I found, however, that summertime can be pretty tough for a fruit lover who can't eat. There are so many delicious fruits in season at that time of year. Oh, how I missed fresh peaches, plums, apples, and grapes! I missed drinking water and iced tea. I missed other foods as well. My sense of smell was still quite keen, and sometimes smelling the good food the rest of the family ate made me desperately wish I could partake. One night I dreamed that I figured out how to swallow safely and ate some baked fish—with a squeeze of lemon juice on it, of course. It was so delicious! I was despondently sad, practically heartbroken when I woke up and realized it was only a dream.

After that dream, the disappointment of being completely reliant on my feeding tube for all nutrition and hydration, not just for a season but for the rest of my life, began to consume more and more of my thoughts. *Can life truly be enjoyed without the ability to enjoy tasty food?* Joyless desires for the delicious foods I could no longer eat became more frequent. Frequently I longed for a drink of cool water while outside in the summer heat. My attention was drawn more and more to what I could not have and could not do.

One day in early summer, I chatted with my seventeen-year-old daughter, Laura, at our kitchen table as she ate a plum. We had plum trees in our yard when I was a boy, and I knew a good plum when I saw one. This particular plum Laura was eating looked oh, so good—perfectly ripe, perfect color, perfect smell, perfect texture—just as a delicious plum should be. I thought, *Oh, how I would love a bite of Laura's plum! Oh, for just one more delicious, satisfying taste of a plum like that. Or a tasty bite of a peach or a grape or other fruit in our kitchen. Oh, if I could have just one more taste, O Lord, just one more taste. Just one more delicious taste. Just one more taste.*

Suddenly a passage of Scripture came to mind:

Oh, taste and see that the LORD is good! Blessed is the man who takes refuge in him!
—Psalm 34:8

This verse came to me so abruptly and clearly that I knew it was the Lord who put it on my heart at that moment. He reminded me of all that I had to be thankful for and all the amazing things He had done in my life, especially in this journey through cancer. God reminded me how blessed I was by my family and to be there enjoying the company of my beloved daughter, something that seemed unlikely a year earlier.

After Laura and I left the table, I hurriedly looked up Psalm 34:8 to be sure I remembered it accurately. As I read, the two verses that followed also deeply moved me:

Oh, fear the LORD, you his saints, for those who fear him have no lack! The young lions suffer want and hunger; but those who seek the LORD lack no good thing.
—Psalm 34:9-10

That also reminded me of Romans 8:28:

And we know that for those who love God all things work together for good, for those who are called according to his purpose.

Wow, those verses sure hit home! They were the voice of God saying that if I genuinely loved and sought Him, I would lack no good thing. He would work all circumstances and situations for my good. However, it was clear that to be blessed by this promise, I would have to allow the Lord to define "good" rather than me. I would have to fully trust Him to know what good things I needed rather than trust myself and dare to define "good" to the Creator of the universe.

I continued to pray and meditate on the Lord's message to me. I was moved to read about the Israelites' time of wandering in the desert after leaving their bondage in Egypt. I read how the Lord miraculously fed His people and provided water to drink. And yet, the people grumbled.

Now the rabble that was among them had a strong craving. And the people of Israel also wept again and said, "Oh that we had meat to eat! We remember the fish we ate in Egypt that cost nothing, the cucumbers, the melons, the leeks, the onions, and the garlic. But now our strength is dried up, and there is nothing at all but this manna to look at.". . . Moses heard the people weeping throughout their

*clans, everyone at the door of his tent. And the anger of the LORD
blazed hotly, and Moses was displeased.*
—Numbers 11:4-6, 10

Almighty God performed miracle after miracle that led to the Israelites' release from slavery in Egypt. He provided a great leader to whom He spoke directly to lead them. He miraculously allowed them to escape Pharaoh's mighty army at the Red Sea. He miraculously provided nutritional, tasty manna in the exact quantities needed by a couple of million people wandering in the desert. And what was their response? "We miss the meat and fish and fruit and vegetables that we had in Egypt. Manna, manna, manna, all we ever get is manna."

Hmmm…did that sound all too familiar? Kind of like, "I miss fish, I miss fruit, I miss vegetables. Formula in a feeding tube, formula in a feeding tube, all I ever have is formula in a feeding tube."

This was a strong wake-up call from the Lord to get my eyes off myself and my wants and place them on Him who wonderfully provides for all my needs. He made me realize how blessed I was to live in a time when feeding tubes are available and easy to use. I was blessed that there are products available that provide excellent nutrition for me in a non-conventional manner. I was amazingly blessed that my health had significantly improved each month since the radiation treatments ended in late November 2008. I was wonderfully blessed to be surrounded by family and friends who poured out their love to me in remarkable ways. I was exceptionally blessed that God used this illness to open Himself and His word to me in ways that drew me closer to Him than ever before. I was delightfully blessed to be able to share His blessings with others, primarily through writing. I was eternally blessed that I could taste the indescribable goodness of the Lord through prayer and through His infallible word at any time, day or night, all because of the sacrifice and all-sufficient grace of Jesus Christ. And in the midst of all this, I whined about being unable to taste a bite of a plum? Oh my…a wake-up call, indeed!

Shame filled my heart for the attitude I had carried, and I thanked God for shaking it out of me. I asked Him to replace my desires for fleeting tastes of food with a constant desire for the eternal taste of His goodness, mercy, and grace. I thanked Him for my greatly improved health and for the blessing of a well-functioning feeding tube that was a primary component of that improvement. I asked God to keep me cancer free and healthy enough to go through several feeding tubes, which, I was told, usually wear out after a few years. I thanked Him for the greatest gift of all, salvation in Christ, the

Bread of Life, the Source of my living water, my Lord, and my God. I prayed that my heart would be so full of joy and peace in Christ that there would be no more room for whining about missing a bite of plum or a belly full of fish and vegetables. I thanked Him for showing me that another bite of fresh peach pie in my mouth would be nice, but that brief temporal pleasure was nothing compared to the unmatched and eternal joy that only my Redeemer can provide, the kind that fills my mouth with praise of Him.

> *Our mouths were filled with laughter, and our tongues with songs of joy.*
> *Then it was said among the nations, "The LORD has done great things for them."*
> *The LORD has done great things for us, and we are filled with joy.*
> —Psalm 126:2-3 (NIV)

As I closed my time of prayer and Bible study that afternoon, I thanked the Lord for the extraordinary work of grace He did in my heart. It was indeed a monumental day, not just in my cancer journey but in my continuing eternal walk with Christ.

I urge you to stay ever aware of the multitude of blessings all around you, thereby cultivating a heart of gratitude, which gives root to genuine contentment in the soul, blossoming into authentic joy in life. I pray that, by the Lord's grace, you will not need as many spiritual wake-up calls as I needed. I pray you will always be fully able to taste both the goodness of the Lord and the goodness of food in your mouth. I pray the Lord will continue to bless you with meaningful relationships with Christian friends and family with whom you can "break bread" in fun fellowship and with whom you nurture your relationship with the Bread of Life. We have had great days, and we have had difficult days, and we will continue to do so. I hope that your good days far exceed the difficult ones. But moreover, I hope that even on the most trying days, our mouths will be filled with laughter and songs of joy in Christ so that it can always be said of us, "The Lord has done great things for them, and they are full of joy."

> *"Blessed are those who hunger and thirst for righteousness, for they shall be satisfied."*
> —The words of Jesus in Matthew 5:6

> *Jesus said to them, "I am the bread of life; whoever comes to me shall not hunger, and whoever believes in me shall never thirst."*
> —John 6:35

Chapter 10

IS THE PLUM LINE STILL PLUMB?

My soul will be satisfied as with fat and rich food,
and my mouth will praise you with joyful lips.
—Psalm 63:5

I spent much of 2009 continuing to heal, slowly regaining some strength, awkwardly struggling with verbal communication, and receiving treatments for the lymphedema in my neck (I rather resembled a bullfrog with its throat inflated). I returned to work in February of that year, and my kind manager at International Paper, Dave Borchardt, was graciously accommodating in allowing me to be flexible in my office hours. I gradually worked more and more as my rehab sessions became less frequent.

By autumn, all cancer and rehabilitation treatments were behind me. I was back in the daily grind of full-time work and home responsibilities and was becoming more socially active. I was still in the early stages of the prolonged process of relearning how to speak, and communication was a constant issue. I also had to remember to always have a pocket full of tissues—actually folded 5"x5" paper towel squares—to constantly wipe the saliva from my mouth since I could not swallow it. I had to learn to live with the heightened risk of aspiration, which limits the positions for sleeping, turns congestion from a simple cold into a viable risk of pneumonia, and skyrockets the risk with any surgery or other medical and dental procedures. But the most significant adjustment was figuring out how to have a somewhat normal life as a tube feeder in a culture not designed to accommodate my disability. Using my tube away from home was always inconvenient and often quite challenging. Most social functions I attended centered around food and often resulted in me missing a feeding tube meal while watching others eat.

Yes, by God's grace, I had found great contentment on that summer afternoon with Laura as she ate her plum. But would it stand the test of time? Would it wilt under the pressure of trying to do normal life in a very abnormal way? I enjoyed writing and sharing my "Laura's Plum" story, but would it hold up as life continued in "the real world?" I had posted Psalm 34:8 on notebooks and journals, on a wall at home, and on my desk at work. But would tasting only of the Lord's goodness be enough as the seasons changed, when some warm hot tea on a cold day would be soothing, when the food-centric holidays rolled around in November and December, and when fruit again began to ripen the following year? Would the contentment found on the day of Laura's Plum stick? Would the plum line stay plumb to God's word and will?

> *Prove me, O LORD, and try me; test my heart and my mind.*
> —Psalm 26:2

Let's face it, folks, we like to eat. Eating is one of our most enjoyable activities because that's how God designed us. He makes food desirable and gives us a hunger for it so we will survive. God also blesses us with an ample supply of discriminating taste buds to enjoy eating and drinking and with keen olfactory nerves in our noses for smelling. Oh, what a gracious and loving God! Almost all our social engagements involve eating or drinking, and usually both. God often talks about food and drink in His word because it is necessary for life. He gave strict commands in the Old Testament on what foods were allowed and how they were to be eaten. All Jewish holy days involved fasts, feasts, or both. And throughout the Old and New Testaments, God uses food and drink metaphorically to teach us spiritual truths.

> *How sweet are Your words to my taste, sweeter than honey to my mouth!*
> —Psalm 119:103

> *So the disciples said to one another, "Has anyone brought him something to eat?" Jesus said to them, "My food is to do the will of him who sent me and to accomplish his work."*
> —John 4:33-34

When we have a temporary or long-term condition that negatively affects how or what we eat, it is an upsetting matter—physically and emotionally—because it is one of our most vital functions. As is the case with almost all good things, excessive eating or drinking can lead to detrimental physical, emotional, spiritual, and cognitive problems. But I think you will agree that in moderation, eating and drinking are pretty fantastic!

You probably enjoy eating so much that you have difficulty relating to someone who can no longer eat or drink by mouth. You likely feel sorry for that person because it seems he is missing one of life's most basic enjoyments. I heartily commend you for your compassion, but I fervently declare that by God's grace, it is indeed possible for such a person to be wonderfully content with his life with a feeding tube. How? To answer that, I offer two of the most beautiful words found in all the Bible: "But God."

> *But Joseph said to them, "Do not fear, for am I in the place of God? As for you, you meant evil against me, **but God** meant it for good, to bring it about that many people should be kept alive, as they are today."*
> —Genesis 50:19-20

> *For while we were still weak, at the right time Christ died for the ungodly. For one will scarcely die for a righteous person—though perhaps for a good person one would dare even to die—**but God** shows His love for us in that while we were still sinners, Christ died for us.*
> —Romans 5:6-8

> ***But God**, being rich in mercy, because of the great love with which He loved us, even when we were dead in our trespasses, made us alive together with Christ.*
> —Ephesians 2:4-5a

In the previous chapter, I described my "but God" epiphany on an early summer day in 2009 as I struggled with the reality of never eating again. The Lord did a mighty work, transforming the state of my heart from discontentment to contentment in a matter of minutes. Because it was a work done by God and not me, it stuck. It did not fade as my overall health improved and other circumstances changed. It did not weaken as I became more involved with activities where my disabilities were more prominent. God simply vanquished my desire for food and drink that summer day, and it has never returned. I assure you, that's not something I could have conjured up on my own. It was all God, all grace, all for His glory.

And my God will supply every need of yours according to his riches in glory in Christ Jesus. To our God and Father be glory forever and ever. Amen.
—Philippians 4:19-20

People often ask if it bothers me to be around food since I cannot eat. Some even say they feel guilty eating and drinking in front of me. By God's grace, it does not bother me in the least. Enjoying fun and meaningful fellowship with others easily surpasses any discomfort I might feel from being unable to eat as everyone else does. But, honestly, I feel no such discomfort. In fact, I enjoy watching people delight themselves with good food, similarly to the way I enjoy watching athletes do things I cannot do. I enjoy hearing people with great voices sing and gifted speakers teach and preach, and I cannot do those things either. Eating and drinking now fall in that same category.

God used Psalm 34:8 to turn my heart around in 2009, and it remains an all-time favorite verse. But the verse that perhaps speaks even more clearly to the ongoing state of my heart is Psalm 63:5: "My soul will be satisfied as with fat and rich food, and my mouth will praise you with joyful lips." Oh, yes! Can anything be more delightful than a contented, satisfied soul?

The essential ingredients in a contented heart are genuine trust in God, a spirit of gratitude, a hunger for the word of God, and prayer. Our trust in God mustn't waver based on our circumstances but must always remain firm. A lack of trust brings worry and anxiousness, but genuine trust brings a contented spirit.

Our soul waits for the LORD; he is our help and our shield.
For our heart is glad in him, because we trust in his holy name.
—Psalm 33:20-21

Such trust was not only the key in dealing with my disabilities but also in living with the ever-present threat of a cancer recurrence. My second cancer diagnosis came only six months after the first. I learned that head and neck cancer historically has an unusually high rate of multiple recurrences, which was the case for most head and neck patients I knew. The doctors told me that effective treatments would be more limited if cancer returned to my head or neck after 2008. My next bout with cancer, which seemed likely within a few years, would be severely debilitating and possibly fatal. The only way to live contently under this continual threat was through a deepening trust in God. The path to a deeper trust could be found only in continuing the process I began during the summer of 2008: drawing ever closer to God and getting to know Him better and better through His word and through prayer.

The LORD is my strength and my shield; in him my heart trusts, and I am helped;
my heart exults, and with my song I give thanks to him.
—Psalm 28:7

Genuine gratitude goes hand-in-hand with trust and stems from gratefully acknowledging all the blessings we have in and from Christ. We mustn't dwell on things that don't go as we want or expect but rather be more attentive and grateful for all the things that do. We must overcome our natural propensity to focus on things we think we want but do not have. We must be joyfully and sincerely grateful for the good God has done and is doing, not crippled and shackled by untrusting worries and doubt. Such gratitude is fortified by a robust daily diet of God's word.

Therefore, as you received Christ Jesus the Lord, so walk in him, rooted and built up in him and established in the faith, just as you were taught, abounding in thanksgiving.
—Colossians 2:6-7

Let the word of Christ dwell in you richly, teaching and admonishing one another in all wisdom, singing psalms and hymns and spiritual songs, with thankfulness in your hearts to God. And whatever you do, in word or deed, do everything in the name of the Lord Jesus, giving thanks to God the Father through him.
—Colossians 3:16-17

Blessed is the one you choose and bring near, to dwell in your courts! We shall be satisfied with the goodness of your house, the holiness of your temple!
—Psalm 65:4

Before I had cancer, I believed in my mind what God's word said about contentment, but I doubt I fully took it to heart because I still selfishly desired many things to bring me pleasure and comfort. One of the pleasures I enjoyed most was food, as my waistline confirmed. Another pleasure was generally good health and the expectation of a long and healthy life. Yet the Lord took those pleasures and confidences away from me. Why? I certainly do not know all of God's reasons, but one was to teach me what contentment is in practice, not just in theory. Cancer taught me to be grateful for today's blessings and to trust God for what He sovereignly wills for tomorrow. I learned that feasting daily on His word as I commune with Him brought infinitely more joy than I ever found in physical food. There is far greater peace in trusting God for His provisions and praising Him for His blessings of the present than in living a life marked by anxiousness and worry about what may come.

*Let them thank the LORD for his steadfast love, for his wondrous
works to the children of man!
For he satisfies the longing soul, and the hungry soul he fills with
good things.*
—Psalm 107:8-9

The only satisfying food for the Lord's people is the favour of
God. (Charles Haddon Spurgeon)[8]

I do not pretend to be anywhere close to the spiritual maturity level of
the apostle Paul, nor have I ever come close to suffering in the ways he did. But
life with cancer and a feeding tube has brought me a deeper understanding
and appreciation of these words the Lord inspired Paul to write:

*Not that I am speaking of being in need, for I have learned in
whatever situation I am to be content. I know how to be brought
low, and I know how to abound. In any and every circumstance, I
have learned the secret of facing plenty and hunger, abundance and
need. I can do all things through him who strengthens me.*
—Philippians 4:11-13

By God's grace, He has strengthened me with true contentment in my
soul. The "plum line" is indeed still plumb. I can honestly say I am genuinely
content with my life as a tube-fed, Christ-redeemed, God-blessed, Spirit-
filled, well-loved, adopted son of the Most High God, and I have no doubt
that I always will be. Praise be to God!

*How precious is your steadfast love, O God! The children of mankind
take refuge in the shadow of your wings. They feast on the abundance
of your house, and you give them drink from the river of your delights.
For with you is the fountain of life; in your light do we see light.*
—Psalm 36:7-9

Happy is the soul that can drink in the sumptuous dainties of
the gospel—nothing can so completely fill the soul....God's
everlasting love bears to us a constant and ample comfort, of
which grace makes us to drink by faith, and then our pleasure is
of the richest kind. (Charles Haddon Spurgeon)[9]

Christian contentment is that sweet, inward, quiet, gracious
frame of spirit, freely submitting to, and delighting in God's
wise and fatherly disposal in every condition. (Jeremiah Burroughs, 1651)[10]

Chapter 11

MY WORSHIP
PREPARATION MEAL

Therefore, since we have been justified by faith, we have peace with God through our Lord Jesus Christ. Through him we have also obtained access by faith into this grace in which we stand, and we rejoice in hope of the glory of God. Not only that, but we rejoice in our sufferings, knowing that suffering produces endurance, and endurance produces character, and character produces hope, and hope does not put us to shame, because God's love has been poured into our hearts through the Holy Spirit who has been given to us.
—Romans 5:1-5

In 2009 God did a gracious work in providing contentment regarding my inability to eat or drink. Yet there were still some aspects of my new lifestyle that were, well, hard to swallow. The most heartbreaking aspect was my inability to take the sacrament of Communion, also known as the Lord's Supper, in church services.

First, I tried to figure out alternative methods to take Communion. I experimented with ways to take a substitute form of the elements through my feeding tube. I quickly determined using my feeding tube in a worship service was not practical. For a couple of months, I partook of my liquid replacement for the bread (feeding tube formula) and cranberry-grape juice after returning home from Communion church services. But taking this meal all alone never felt right because it simply was not what Christ instructed us to do, which is to take Communion together with our fellow worshipers. Therefore, I discontinued doing this as a substitute for the sacrament.

Yet I was very reluctant to completely abandon the practice of taking the formula "bread" and cranberry-grape juice "wine" through my tube. Even though that had proved to be a hollow replacement for the public sacrament of Communion, I found it to be a powerful visual tool of remembrance. As I prayerfully pondered those memories, I thought of taking that Communion-like meal again, but not as a replacement for the Lord's Supper. Instead, I could use it as a special meal early on Sunday mornings to help prepare my heart for worship and dedicate the day to the Lord.

I tried it the following Sunday morning, and indeed the Lord used it in a powerful way. Each stage of the meal was significant to me functionally, visually, and spiritually. Immediately it became part of my Sunday morning routine. My passion for it has only escalated through the years, as this practice is now a beloved personal tradition every Sunday, even when traveling.

> *"Come, everyone who thirsts, come to the waters; and he who has no money, come, buy and eat! Come, buy wine and milk without money and without price. Why do you spend your money for that which is not bread, and your labor for that which does not satisfy? Listen diligently to me, and eat what is good, and delight yourselves in rich food."*
> —Isaiah 55:1-2

Let me share with you how I go about my unique Sunday morning tradition. I hope it will convey the deliberate and weighty process I go through each Sunday morning. The Bible verses and my words cited below are meant to capture my general thoughts and feelings during this meal. They are not memorized or read verbatim as a rote ritual; they often change from one week to another as my knowledge of Scripture grows, as my understanding of doctrine deepens, and as God emphasizes certain truths in the previous six days. My intention in sharing this with you is to praise God for this unique and beloved tradition He has given me.

> *Come and see what God has done: he is awesome in his deeds toward the children of man. . . .*
> *Come and hear, all you who fear God, and I will tell what he has done for my soul.*
> —Psalm 66:5, 16

PREPARE

To begin my Sunday morning preparation meal, I gather the things I need: a clear bottle filled with water, a clear bottle filled with feeding tube formula, a clear bottle filled with cranberry-grape juice, a small container of white vinegar, and a clear sixty-milliliter syringe. I start the meal by opening my feeding tube and inserting the syringe into it.

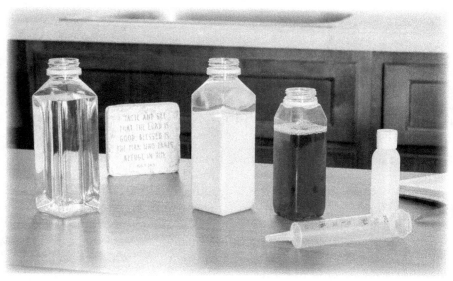

The essential elements of my worship preparation meal.[32]

COME BEFORE THE FATHER WITH A CLEAN HEART

I pour a small amount of clear water into the syringe attached to my feeding tube, then unlock the tube so the contents of the syringe will flow into and through the tube to my stomach. Functionally this bit of water ensures that the tube is flowing properly. This step is especially important when my tube becomes inadvertently unlocked and filled with backwash from my stomach. (Yes, that's as nasty as it sounds.) I pour the fresh water in, and the contents previously in the tube are cleared into my stomach. This reminds me of the need for my heart to be emptied of my nasty self-centeredness and self-focus and to approach the Lord in a "pure and blameless" manner. Even though I pondered this in my quiet time preceding this meal, I pause to ask the Lord to again search my heart and convict me of any unconfessed sin or unforgiveness of others. Following this time of reflection, I ask God to make my heart clean and pure as I approach His throne of grace.

> *Create in me a clean heart, O God, and renew a right spirit within me.*
> *Cast me not away from your presence, and take not your Holy Spirit from me.*
> *Restore to me the joy of your salvation, and uphold me with a willing spirit.*
> —Psalm 51:10-12

Search me, O God, and know my heart! Try me and know my thoughts! And see if there be any grievous way in me, and lead me in the way everlasting!
—Psalm 139:23-24

Let us then with confidence draw near to the throne of grace, that we may receive mercy and find grace to help in time of need.
—Hebrews 4:16

REMEMBER THAT JESUS POURED HIMSELF OUT FOR ME

I pour a portion of the feeding tube formula from the container into the syringe. Functionally, this formula is how I get the vast majority of my nutrition and calories as I consume it multiple times each day. Visually, I watch the formula pour out of the container into the syringe. The syringe starts full of the formula but slowly empties as the formula flows down my feeding tube and into my stomach. Spiritually, I reflect on Isaiah 53 and Philippians 2 as I watch the syringe slowly emptying, which symbolizes the body of Christ being poured out for me.

Therefore I will divide him a portion with the many, and he shall divide the spoil with the strong, because he poured out his soul to death and was numbered with the transgressors;
yet he bore the sin of many, and makes intercession for the transgressors.
—Isaiah 53:12

Have this mind among yourselves, which is yours in Christ Jesus, who, though he was in the form of God, did not count equality with God a thing to be grasped, but emptied himself, by taking the form of a servant, being born in the likeness of men. And being found in human form, he humbled himself by becoming obedient to the point of death, even death on a cross.
—Philippians 2:5-8

This prophecy of Isaiah and the testimony of Paul were both about the Messiah, whom John testified was the Creator of the world, the world that would reject Him when He came to rescue them (see John 1:1-11). This was Christ, who lived a perfect life of righteousness and willingly poured out His life for me as the Lamb of God. That is what I humbly ponder as I watch my syringe slowly empty. The deeper I think on these things, the more in awe of Christ I am.

Because of His unfathomable grace, Jesus, the Messiah, did indeed humble Himself. He left the pure, sinless heaven, where His power and sovereignty were unquestioned. He came to our sinful world as a helpless baby born in a cattle shelter. In doing so, Jesus emptied Himself of His visible Shekinah glory and majesty and His unmistakable identity as the Lord of all. He poured out His enjoyment as a sovereign spiritual being in heaven to live the perfect life of righteousness as a boy, youth, and man on earth. On the cross, Jesus allowed Himself to be poured out, even to death, as He was forsaken by the Father, bearing all my sin and shame. He took the full extent of the Father's wrath so my dead soul could be given life in Him. These are the things I ponder as I watch the formula being slowly emptied.

And this is the testimony, that God gave us eternal life, and this life is in his Son. Whoever has the Son has life; whoever does not have the Son of God does not have life.
—1 John 5:11-12

As I pour another round of formula into the syringe, I ponder the fact that as Jesus poured Himself out on the cross, He poured His life, His light, and His love into me. By emptying Himself of His divine rights, but not His divinity, and living a perfectly righteous life, He pours into me His righteousness (by imputation, not infusion). He pours in the assurance and joy of being declared just before the Father and the desire to pursue a purposeful, fruitful life of righteousness. The feeding tube formula is representative of the bread that He shared at the Last Supper, the bread that represents His sacrificed body. Jesus Christ is my Bread of Life, for I have life only in Him.

"This is the bread that comes down from heaven, so that one may eat of it and not die. I am the living bread that came down from heaven. If anyone eats of this bread, he will live forever. And the bread that I will give for the life of the world is my flesh."
—The words of Jesus in John 6:50-51

As I watch the syringe empty of formula for the last time, I thank the Lord that I am preparing for worship with the wisdom and strength He pours into me and not with that of my own.

I have been crucified with Christ. It is no longer I who live, but Christ who lives in me. And the life I now live in the flesh I live by faith in the Son of God, who loved me and gave himself for me.
—Galatians 2:20

79

As I conclude savoring the rich blessing of Christ presenting His body as the perfect sacrifice, I am reminded that I cannot be alive in Christ without being forgiven of my sins. The penalty for my sins must be paid for my sinful life to be redeemed. And I know there can be no forgiveness or redemption without the shedding of blood (Hebrews 9:22). But rejoice, oh my soul, for there is forgiveness because Jesus Christ poured out His blood for me!

REMEMBER THAT JESUS SHED HIS BLOOD FOR ME

I fill the syringe with cranberry-grape juice. Functionally, this juice provides only a limited amount of nutrition, vitamins, and antioxidants, but it is a vital part of my special Sunday morning meal of preparation. Visually, I watch the blood-red juice pour out of the container into the syringe. When I release the lock on my feeding tube, the syringe empties more rapidly than it did for the thicker formula. Spiritually, I thank the Lord Jesus for His unmatched sacrifice, unfathomable love, grace, and mercy as I think of the Last Supper when He told His disciples that His blood would soon be poured out.

> *And he took a cup, and when he had given thanks he gave it to them, saying, "Drink of it, all of you, for this is my blood of the covenant, which is poured out for many for the forgiveness of sins."*
> —Matthew 26:27-28

As I refill the syringe with juice and watch it empty into me, I am reminded that when the blood of Jesus was shed, it was not in vain. By willingly pouring out His life on the cross, He has transfused spiritual life into me, giving life to my once-dead soul.

> *In him we have redemption through his blood, the forgiveness of our trespasses, according to the riches of his grace, which he lavished upon us, in all wisdom and insight.*
> —Ephesians 1:7-8

As I pour the remainder of the juice into the syringe, I am reminded that I am not my own, for I have been purchased by His outpoured blood in order for Him to be glorified and honored through my worship of Him and my service in His name.

> *Or do you not know that your body is a temple of the Holy Spirit within you, whom you have from God? You are not your own, for you were bought with a price. So glorify God in your body.*
> —1 Corinthians 6:19-20

As I view the now-empty containers of formula and juice on the counter, I am reminded that someday I will actually eat the bread and drink the wine—by mouth!—in the presence of Christ at the wedding feast of the Lamb. On that endless day, the entirety of my being will worship God and praise Christ Jesus for all eternity. I pray that this Lord's Day will be a good warm-up for that day, with grateful, joyous, and undistracted worship.

> *Then I heard what seemed to be the voice of a great multitude, like the roar of many waters and like the sound of mighty peals of thunder, crying out, "Hallelujah! For the Lord our God the Almighty reigns. Let us rejoice and exult and give him the glory, for the marriage of the Lamb has come, and his Bride has made herself ready; it was granted her to clothe herself with fine linen, bright and pure"—for the fine linen is the righteous deeds of the saints. And the angel said to me, "Write this: Blessed are those who are invited to the marriage supper of the Lamb." And he said to me, "These are the true words of God."*
> —Revelation 19:6-9

GRATEFULLY BLESS THE TRIUNE GOD

I pour about half an ounce of water into the syringe. Functionally, each use of my feeding tube must end with at least an ounce of water to make sure the nutritional formula, medicine, or juice is cleared from my tube and is well into my stomach. As I watch the clear water fill the syringe and empty, I pray, "Bless You, Father God, for You have poured into me Your love and the Spirit of adoption as a son. You are my eternal Father, and I am Your chosen child. I commit this day of worship to You."

> *For all who are led by the Spirit of God are sons of God. For you did not receive the spirit of slavery to fall back into fear, but you have received the Spirit of adoption as sons, by whom we cry, "Abba! Father!"*
> —Romans 8:14-15

I pour another half ounce of water into the syringe. Again I watch the syringe empty as I pray, "Bless You, Lord Jesus, for You have poured into me Your redemption, Your word, and Your life. Therefore, I am alive in You and declared righteous and justified in the eyes of the Father. You are my Master and King, and I am Your servant. I commit this day of worship to You, O Lord."

> *And it is my prayer that your love may abound more and more, with knowledge and all discernment, so that you may approve what*

is excellent, and so be pure and blameless for the day of Christ, filled with the fruit of righteousness that comes through Jesus Christ, to the glory and praise of God.
—Philippians 1:9-12

For our sake he made him to be sin who knew no sin, so that in him we might become the righteousness of God.
—2 Corinthians 5:21

I pour a final half ounce of water into the syringe and pray, "Bless You, O Holy Spirit, for You have been poured into me upon my salvation in Christ to abide in me always. You are the seal and evidence of my salvation as You work in me, for me, and through me. You are the strength and wisdom of my worship, learning, and service. Give me ears to hear and eyes to see as I commit this day of worship to You, O Holy Spirit."

"If you love me, you will keep my commandments. And I will ask the Father, and he will give you another Helper, to be with you forever, even the Spirit of truth, whom the world cannot receive, because it neither sees him nor knows him. You know him, for he dwells with you and will be in you."
—The words of Jesus in John 14:15-17

IT IS FINISHED

I finish my meal by pouring a dash of white vinegar into the syringe. Functionally, I end one or two meals each day with a small amount of vinegar because it helps keep my tube clean from bacteria and prevents clogs from forming. Spiritually, I am reminded of Jesus's final moments of life on the cross.

Later, knowing that everything had now been finished, and so that Scripture would be fulfilled, Jesus said, "I am thirsty." A jar of wine vinegar was there, so they soaked a sponge in it, put the sponge on a stalk of the hyssop plant, and lifted it to Jesus' lips. When he had received the drink, Jesus said, "It is finished." With that, he bowed his head and gave up his spirit.
—John 19:28-30 NIV

Yes, having completed His task of living a perfect life of righteousness that I cannot live, Jesus tasted the vinegar wine, announced that His mission was completed, and willingly gave up His life. I ponder this as I ask myself,

What else must the Lord do to save me, make me His own, and give me a hunger and thirst for true worship of Him? As I squirt the dash of vinegar into the syringe, I answer, *Nothing, for it…is…finished."*

Before the vinegar has a chance to clear the feeding tube and go into my stomach, I lock the tube, which traps the vinegar in it. I then remove the syringe from the tube. As I do, I ask myself, *And what is the result of Christ Jesus pouring Himself out and into me?* I pause, look at the now clear syringe, and answer, *A clean vessel, prepared and equipped by Him to worship, serve, and glorify my Savior on this Lord's Day.*

> *Therefore, if anyone cleanses himself from what is dishonorable, he will be a vessel for honorable use, set apart as holy, useful to the master of the house, ready for every good work.*
> —2 Timothy 2:21

> *Bless the Lord, O my soul, and all that is within me, bless his holy name!*
> —Psalm 103:1

My early Sunday morning meal is an intentional act of personal worship. It ignites my feelings of devotion to God by reminding me visually and spiritually of His merciful and gracious acts of love, sacrifice, rescue, and redemption. I pray that this personal act of worship will always glorify and honor God, help prepare my heart for acts of corporate worship of Him, and set the course for a day devoted to worship and Sabbath rest in Him.

> *I will bless the LORD at all times; his praise shall continually be in my mouth.*
> *My soul makes its boast in the LORD; let the humble hear and be glad.*
> *Oh, magnify the LORD with me, and let us exalt his name together!*
> —Psalm 34:1-3

This unique meal is not the only thing I do on the Lord's Day to prepare for worship, but it is the all-important tone-setter for the day. I hope this story has encouraged you, and I pray that some of the life-breathed words of the Lord that I have shared will linger in your heart and be returned to our gracious God with awe, thanksgiving, and praise.

The powerful imagery of my worship preparation meal stirs my heart every Sunday morning.[33]

*This picture and others in this book may be viewed in color by scanning this QR code:

Chapter 12

ONE BREAD, ONE CUP, ONE FLESH

And he took bread, and when he had given thanks, he broke it and gave it to them, saying, "This is my body, which is given for you. Do this in remembrance of me." And likewise the cup after they had eaten, saying, "This cup that is poured out for you is the new covenant in my blood."
—Luke 22:19-20

As discussed in the previous chapter, one of the most hurtful realities of losing the ability to swallow was also losing the ability to take Communion. Not participating in this vital sacrament deeply pained my soul after returning to public worship in 2009. After a few months of sadness and frustration, I discussed the matter with our teaching pastor at Living Hope Church, Greg Gibson (Gib). He suggested I continue to participate in Communion to the extent I could. Even though I could not receive the elements, I could receive a verbal blessing from the elder or pastor to whom we believers approached for the elements. I was overjoyed to do so and quickly found it deeply meaningful. Although I still missed taking and consuming the actual elements, I was very thankful that God graciously used Gib to open this new path of blessing.

You have heard the expression, "Absence makes the heart grow fonder." That certainly became true for me with Communion. For the many years that I was able to take Communion in a normal way, I generally took it seriously. Yet losing the ability to take it made me focus more on the true meaning of this sacrament than I ever had before. God allowed me to lose the ability to eat the bread and drink from the cup, but He replaced it with a much fuller understanding of the meaning and reasons for this sacrament. I was so thankful that I could physically participate in Communion in at least a limited manner. Yet I still sorely missed taking the bread and the juice.

In the summer of 2020, Candy and I began worshiping at Grace Evangelical Church (Grace Evan). Because of Covid precautions, their monthly practice of taking Communion was altered. Traditionally, the church had passed the bread and grape juice down each row but switched to placing the elements on tables within the sanctuary. Participants walked to the tables in an orderly fashion to pick up the elements and returned to their seats with them. This practice at least allowed me to approach the Communion table in a worshipful way, even though there was no verbal blessing involved as there had been at Living Hope. I was grateful I could do something to participate physically, but I longed for something more meaningful.

In April 2021, Grace Evan leadership announced that in May we would return to the practice of passing the elements down the rows during our monthly Communion services. Almost everyone accepted this as good news, as it was another step toward normalcy. But I was deeply dismayed. I could not bear the thought of returning to the days of not participating other than passing the plates of elements down the row after not taking any for myself.

Communion is not simply a ritual we Christians do periodically but a commandment of God: "*Do* this...."

> *For I received from the Lord what I also delivered to you, that the Lord Jesus on the night when he was betrayed took bread, and when he had given thanks, he broke it, and said, "This is my body, which is for you. Do this in remembrance of me." In the same way also he took the cup, after supper, saying, "This cup is the new covenant in my blood. Do this, as often as you drink it, in remembrance of me." For as often as you eat this bread and drink the cup, you proclaim the Lord's death until he comes.*
> —1 Corinthians 11:23-26

Communion is indeed a mental exercise and spiritual act by believers in Christ to remember His sacrifice, but it is also a physical act of doing. Doing what? Partaking of the bread and the cup. Since that is not physically possible for me, I feel it is essential to actively obey the command by participating in some purposeful manner that glorifies God. His word says that such participation in Communion is imperative.

The cup of blessing that we bless, is it not a participation in the blood of Christ? The bread that we break, is it not a participation in the body of Christ? Because there is one bread, we who are many are one body, for we all partake of the one bread.
—1 Corinthians 10:16-17

The Greek word *koinonia* in the first sentence above is translated in the ESV and the NIV as "participation." The NASB and LSB render the word as "sharing" and the KJV and NKJV as "communion." In all cases, it is a word that denotes activity, not passivity. By participating in the blood and body of Christ, we identify with Jesus Christ and with His sacrifice on the cross, for it is only through Him that we have spiritual life. When we take the broken bread, we participate in His body being torn so that we may be eternally reconciled with God. Likewise, we take the cup, participating in His blood being shed so that our dead souls may find life in Him. The Greek word *koinonia* is also translated as "fellowship" in other Scriptures. Hence, we take the Lord's Supper in fellowship with the Holy Trinity: God the Father, God the Son, and God the Holy Spirit. We also take this sacrament in fellowship with others, communally participating as a group of gathered believers in our local churches. We participate in this special sacrament soberly and worshipfully in obedience to God and for the glory of Christ. Therefore, non-participation clearly is not an option. But how could I do so with no ability to eat or drink?

I spoke to my friend Johnathan Todd, the associate pastor at Grace Evan, about my dilemma. He had no immediate solutions but said that he would pray about it. A few days later, Johnathan presented me with an idea that thrilled my soul. He said the idea came to him as he was praying about the issue, so I took that as a word of blessing from the Lord.

On Sunday, May 16, Candy and I put Johnathan's idea into practice: we worked together to take Communion as man and wife who have been made one flesh by the new covenant of Christ and the covenant of our marriage vows before God. While we recognize that our salvation in Christ is as individuals, remembering His salvific sacrifice as a couple proved to be an extraordinary blessing.

He [Jesus] answered, "Have you not read that he who created them from the beginning made them male and female, and said, 'Therefore a man shall leave his father and his mother and hold fast to his wife, and the two shall become one flesh'? So they are no longer two but one flesh. What therefore God has joined together, let not man separate."
—Matthew 19:4-6

As the elders passed the elements to Candy and me, I took one piece of bread for both of us. It had always been our practice to pray silently before eating the bread, and Candy and I continued this practice, except now we held hands as we prayed. After a few minutes of prayer, I took the bread to my lips and momentarily held it there. Oh, how wonderful it was! I thanked Jesus for being our Bread of Life, broken for the salvation of our souls. I felt the texture of the bread and could smell it. This was the first time Communion bread had been on my lips in thirteen years. I praised God with Psalm 63:5: "My soul shall be satisfied as with rich and fat food, and my mouth will praise you with joyful lips." I then passed the bread to my delightful, God-given helpmate, the bone of my bone and flesh of my flesh, who completed taking of the bread for us as she ate it.

When the Communion juice was passed, I again took one cup for the two of us. After a few minutes of prayer, I tilted the cup just enough for the juice to touch my lips. I remembered Psalm 34:8: "Oh, taste and see that the LORD is good! Blessed is the man who takes refuge in him!"—as I passed the cup to Candy. I thanked Jesus for shedding His atoning blood so that Candy and I have new life in Him. After she drank it for us, we again clasped hands.

Our eyes leaked a bit as we pondered the profound way we experienced this long-familiar sacrament in a unique and unforgettable new way. The Lord had provided an exceptionally meaningful way for me to participate in Communion, as Candy and I, as one flesh by the grace of God, took the elements together. As the service closed, Candy and I instinctively held each other tightly as we gave thanks to the Lord.

Our friends Steve and Nadia Alm sat beside us in that Sunday morning worship service. I had previously told Steve that Candy and I were excited about the upcoming Lord's Supper but did not go into detail. During the sacrament, my wise friend wisely focused on Christ rather than on us; but as soon as the service ended, he and Nadia were anxious to hear more of the details of our Communion experience. As Candy and I told Steve and Nadia what we had done, the four of us hugged and cried tears of joy together.

Little did we know then that the event was even more significant than we realized. It was the last worship service that Steve was able to attend. He was struggling with bladder cancer, and his condition took a sharp turn for the worse soon thereafter. My dear friend passed away nine weeks later. While I still grieve Steve's passing, I rejoice that the Communion meal we had at Grace Evan in May 2021 was not the last meal I will share with Steve, for I know that one day we will again eat together at the marriage supper of the Lamb.

And the angel said to me, "Write this: Blessed are those who are invited to the marriage supper of the Lamb."
—Revelation 19:9a

Candy and I have joyfully continued to take Communion together in this manner each month. It never fails to bless us deeply. While I would never recommend that an able-bodied couple follow our example, I am most grateful that the Holy Spirit moved within Johnathan to give us this unique method of taking this sacrament. Possibly Communion would be just as meaningful had the Lord never taken away my ability to swallow, but there is no doubt that my gratitude and focus have been more finely tuned.

You prepare a table before me in the presence of my enemies;
you anoint my head with oil; my cup overflows.
Surely goodness and mercy shall follow me all the days of my life,
and I shall dwell in the house of the LORD forever.
—Psalm 23:5-6

Jesus said to them, "I am the bread of life; whoever comes to me shall not hunger, and whoever believes in me shall never thirst.... This is the bread that came down from heaven, not like the bread the fathers ate, and died. Whoever feeds on this bread will live forever."
—John 6:35, 58

Chapter 13

AS TIME GOES BY

SPOILER ALERT: If you are one of the twenty-seven American adults who have never seen the eighty-some-year-old movie Casablanca, I am about to reveal how it ends.

T he June 29, 2008, entry of my CarePage wished a happy birthday to my lovely bride, Candy, and also commented on my third day with a feeding tube: "After a couple of days, Mr. PEG Tube and I are slowly getting used to each other. I think we'll end up having a great relationship." In hindsight, I wish I had infringed upon the last line of the 1942 movie *Casablanca* and written, "Mr. PEG Tube, I think this is the beginning of a beautiful friendship."

In the movie, the reluctant hero, Rick Blaine (played by Humphrey Bogart), risks his life and well-being to help the Resistance Movement and insists that his lost love, Ilsa Lund (played by Ingrid Bergman), fly to Lisbon with the heroic Victor Laszlo (played by Paul Henreid) to escape the Nazis in Casablanca. Laszlo is a renowned Czech Resistance leader the Nazis desperately want to capture and is secretly married to Ilsa. Ilsa loves Rick more than she does Victor, but Rick knows she is instrumental in helping Victor in Europe's Resistance against Germany. Rick is eventually aided by another reluctant hero, Captain Louis Renault (played by Claude Rains), the corrupt but good-natured prefect of the Casablanca police. Being unable to fly to Lisbon themselves, Rick and Louis plan to join other Free French to fight the Nazis in other parts of Africa.

The moral of the story is that Rick forsook his personal love interest in Ilsa for the greater good of the world. As the film closes, Rick and Louis walk down the airport runway while watching the plane to Lisbon fly safely away. Rick says, "Louis, I think this is the beginning of a beautiful friendship." We are left to wonder if Rick and Ilsa will ever see each other again.

In June 2008, I said goodbye to a dear, dear love of mine, the ability to eat good food and drink refreshing liquids, and said hello to a new friend, my percutaneous endoscopic gastrostomy (PEG) feeding tube. I knew the tube was necessary to keep me alive and believed it was a situation God allowed for the good of something much greater: my spiritual well-being. I did not know if I would survive the battle with cancer, but if I did, by God's grace, I expected to eat and drink by mouth again someday. I did not know when that might be, but I was grateful to have Mr. PEG to help me until that welcomed day.

A year later, I wrote "Laura's Plum," the story of how I dealt with the reality that because my cancer was so extensive, I would never regain the ability to swallow on this side of heaven. The gloom of that reality was overcome by the blessing of God's delicious grace. In that story, I wrote, "I asked God to keep me cancer-free and healthy enough to go through several feeding tubes, which, I was told, usually wear out after a few years." Any guesses on how long my original Mr. PEG Tube lasted? Any guesses on how many additional PEG tubes I've required since then?

Well, to give you a hint, I used my old friend, the original Mr. PEG, for lunch about five minutes ago. As I write this on the first day of 2023, our friendship has lasted 5,300 days and counting, which is about fourteen and a half years. It has indeed been a beautiful friendship.

Medical professionals tell me that a fourteen-year-old feeding tube is utterly unheard of. When my friend and gastroenterologist, Dr. Zack Taylor, installed my PEG tube, I asked how long feeding tubes usually last. He said mine should be good for the several months that I would need it, as most tubes last a couple of years. Zack said, in theory, a feeding tube might possibly last as long as five years if it was cared for exceptionally well.

In 2014 I reminded Zack of that statement, pointing out that my original tube was still intact and functioning. Zack said he did not realize it had been that long and was somewhat shocked. He said he had never heard of a functioning six-year-old PEG tube before mine. Feeding tubes simply do not last that long; within a few years or even a few months, they wear out, stop working, or get accidentally yanked out. Yet mine never has, even after all these years. It's somewhat like getting three hundred thousand miles on a set of automobile tires and still having plenty of tread left. It just doesn't happen. Yet my PEG tube just keeps hanging on, dependably doing its job, five, six, or seven times a day, every day, every week, every year.

As time goes by, my ancient PEG tube's longevity is a continual, visual, and functional reminder of God's blessings upon my life. It often brings to mind how my cancer journey has been stamped with the Lord's attributes, particularly His goodness, grace, and faithfulness. It's a recurring reminder that God does extraordinary things with ordinary people, ordinary events, and ordinary objects. My PEG tube's unspoken message each day is that there are far more important issues in life than my physical comforts and pleasures. There is a greater good taking place. His plans for me are always better than my plans, and His blessings often come in unexpected ways. It is a reminder never to take God's grace for granted and to gratefully lift prayers of thanksgiving and praises to the Lord of my life throughout each day. Oh, what a Savior! How can I not praise Him? How can I not be grateful? How can I be silent about the blessings and grace He pours over me and into me each day?

> *The* LORD *upholds all who are falling and raises up all who are bowed down.*
> *The eyes of all look to you, and you give them their food in due season.*
> *You open your hand; you satisfy the desire of every living thing.*
> *The* LORD *is righteous in all his ways and kind in all his works.*
> —Psalm 145:14-17

Chapter 14

CHARGE OF THE LIGHT BRIGADE

"When can their glory fade?
O the wild charge they made!…
Honor the charge they made!
Honor the Light Brigade!"
—From the "Charge of the Light Brigade"
by Alfred, Lord Tennyson, 1854[11]

M y significant and somewhat uncommon health issues started long before my first bout with cancer in 2007. In these next few chapters, I invite you to go back with me to the mid-1990s when Candy and I lived in Charlotte, North Carolina. I was transferred there with International Paper in the fall of 1989 when our oldest son, Michael, was eight months old. While in Charlotte, our family grew, as Laura was born in 1992 and Joseph in 1993.

> *A friend loves at all times, and a brother is born for adversity.*
> —Proverbs 17:17

> *Light is sown for the righteous, and joy for the upright in heart.*
> —Psalm 97:11

I took a deep breath as I prepared to walk into Jay Ballard's insurance office in Huntersville, North Carolina, on a spring night in 1995. I said one last quick prayer, a continuation of the longer prayer during the twenty-minute drive from my home in north Charlotte, asking the Lord to help me have an upbeat attitude toward my two friends, no matter what happened. I asked God to help me remember my deep affection for these men and how much they had meant to my family and me during our six years in Charlotte. I prayed that my probable frustrations would not make me forget their kind and caring intentions toward me. Even though I was excited to spend some time with these brothers in Christ, a cloud of doubt and low expectations went with me as I approached the office door. The travails and disappointments of the previous six months weighed heavily on me, and I had come to expect any interpersonal communication to be exceedingly difficult and discouraging.

My voice had grown weaker and weaker during the summer of 1994. It stopped functioning completely early in October of that year while reading a bedtime story to my oldest son, five-year-old Michael. From then on, all my in-person communication was done with my ever-present notepad and pen. It was an aggravatingly slow, laborious way to communicate, frustrating both for me and those with whom I tried to communicate.

The following month, my mother was diagnosed with advanced ovarian cancer. Around Thanksgiving, Candy, Michael, two-year-old Laura, and one-year-old Joseph and I traveled from our home in Charlotte to my boyhood hometown, Starkville, Mississippi, to visit Mom in the hospital. I was shocked and heartbroken to see how sick she was. Being unable to speak to Mom at such a critical time amplified my despondency. I desperately prayed that my voice would return before we came back to see her at Christmas.

I never got the chance to talk to Mom again. A nurse from the Starkville hospital, a friend from my childhood, called me on December 20th, only a couple of days before we were scheduled to return. Her news that Mom had died ripped my heart as nothing else ever had. The human light that was the most consistent from my birth until that moment suddenly and shockingly went dark. Besides Candy and our kids, no one in my life meant more to me than my mother. We buried her a few days later and returned to Charlotte for Christmas—a very sad Christmas.

I was named the executor of Mom's estate, a task immensely complicated by my inability to speak. Meanwhile, I continued managing a rather large department at International Paper's Charlotte Accounting Center. At home, I had an unhappy wife and three young children. I was miserably lonely with severely limited ability to converse with others, including Candy, the kids, friends, and co-workers.

The grieving of my mother's passing, the loneliness and frustration of being unable to speak, and the heavy load of responsibilities weighed heavily on me in the first months of 1995. That heaviness eventually led to a degree of dark depression, something I had never experienced before. I begged the Lord to take the lonely darkness away. He did not do so in the manner or timing I hoped, but, as always, God had a better plan.

Before losing my voice, I was in an accountability group with two church friends, Jay Ballard and Jay McGuire, who I collectively referred to as my *Brothers Jay*. Jay Ballard was an exceptionally friendly young man, athletic, tenderhearted, and quick with a smile. His laidback personality masked an inner drive to succeed and make a positive difference in the lives of others. He and I were good friends and co-taught an adult Sunday school class for a season at Derita Baptist Church where we were members.

Jay McGuire had a robust frame with a robust and friendly personality to match. He was a natural leader with an engineer's mind and was purposeful in all he did. Because of his diligent study of God's word, his biblical knowledge eclipsed that of most of his peers, including Jay Ballard and me. Each Jay had a terrific sense of humor, balanced by an unrelenting passion for following and serving Christ. We had met weekly to study the Bible, pray, and hold one another accountable for growing in our faith and faithfully leading our families. I dropped out of our little group when I could no longer speak and was consumed with work for International Paper and my mother's estate.

In the spring of 1995, Jay and Jay came to me and told me it was time to rejoin them. I scrawled on my notepad, *But I cannot talk; I will only be a hindrance.* Jay McGuire rolled his eyes and said, "John, we don't care. Got it? We...do...not...care! We just want you there. And we need you there. You have your pen and notepad, and we both know how to read, so we can make it work."

Jay Ballard added, "And, brother, we're not taking 'no' for an answer. See you Tuesday night."

I tried to hide my uneasiness as I entered Jay Ballard's office the next Tuesday evening. I knew they meant well, but in all likelihood, they would be like everyone else and not have the patience to deal with the uncomfortable silence while I wrote. My apprehensions began to thaw a bit as soon as my Brothers Jay greeted me with smiles and well wishes. Each of them made a humorous remark that made us all laugh. Laughter, even in silence, was good medicine that had been largely missing from my diet for several months.

As we settled into our chairs, Jay Ballard asked how I was doing. I tilted my head to one side with a half-smile and shrug and mouthed the word, *okay.* Jay McGuire wasn't going to let me off that easy. "No, John, we want to know how you are really doing."

I inhaled a deep breath of concern as I took out my pad and pen. My apprehensions were about to get an early test in a big way. I wrote a few short sentences as hurriedly as I could, desperately trying to beat the invisible alarm clock that would sound at the end of their patience in enduring the awkward silence. As I wrote the last word, relieved that I had finished before they started speaking again, I looked up to quickly hand the pad to the nearest Jay. To my surprise, both my friends—men with very busy lives, demanding work careers, families with young children, and significant responsibilities at church—sat with calm, unhurried expressions. Neither had the facial expressions and body language I was accustomed to in such situations: aggravated impatience or restless boredom. Wow! My apprehensions continued to melt.

Jay and Jay read my response with sincere interest, commented, and soon asked another question. Again, they both sat calmly and silently as I wrote, not talking to each other or to me. They just patiently waited. When I finished writing, they read what I wrote, we discussed it, and the conversation went on from there. The faithfulness of these friends obliterated my pent-up worries and apprehensions. Their patience wore down my despondency, and their complete acceptance of my disability brought back some of my old personality, at least for a night. They talked, I listened, I wrote, and they read. We joked and laughed as we had months before. We referenced and read Bible passages. We were serious and direct and confessed weaknesses. We prayed. When I wanted to interject a thought, I quietly raised my pen, and they knew what that meant. And again, they simply sat and patiently waited for me while I wrote—and sometimes I wrote and wrote and wrote as I poured out my heart to them. Waiting in calm silence may seem like a very simple and effortless thing to do. But after rarely experiencing it from anyone else for months, I fully recognized the amount of intentional patience, sacrifice of time, and brotherly love embedded in both the talk and the silence that evening.

I still smile when I recall a humorous incident from that night. One of the Jays silently read what I wrote and passed my notepad to the other Jay for him to read. After this happened a few times, I smiled and inwardly chuckled as I wrote, *Hey guys, how about one of you just read my note out loud instead of passing it around?* Jay McGuire said, "Oh, yeah, that would make a lot more sense. See, that's why we need you here, to figure out things like that!" We all laughed, and I silently thanked the Lord for the warming balm of laughter.

We had a wonderful time that night. Our meeting took much longer than usual because of the long periods of silence that interspersed our discussions. A few hours into our meeting, Candy called Jay's office to be sure we were still there since it was so late. As we finally left the office around eleven that night, I was bursting with gratitude and joy. My Brothers Jay had just given me an invaluable gift from the grace the Lord poured into them. They did something no other adult had been willing to do, at least not to that extent. My brothers had injected much-needed light into my dark circumstances. They accepted my awkward condition with compassion and patience. They refreshingly shared a bountiful and uplifting dose of grace, peace, and joy from the word of God, as well as a burden-lightening time of prayer. As I drove home, I thanked the Lord for my brothers, for they demonstrated what true friendship and *phileo* love of a Christ-follower looks like in real life. They were more than mere church friends. The Brothers Jay were genuine light-bearers of Christ.

> *"In the same way, let your light shine before others, so that they may see your good works and give glory to your Father who is in heaven."*
> —The words of Jesus in Matthew 5:16

> *For at one time you were darkness, but now you are light in the Lord. Walk as children of light (for the fruit of light is found in all that is good and right and true).*
> —Ephesians 5:8-9

> *I thank my God always when I remember you in my prayers,...For I have derived much joy and comfort from your love, my brother, because the hearts of the saints have been refreshed through you.*
> —Philemon 4, 7

The following Tuesday night, we did it all over again. And the next Tuesday after that. And the next and the next and the next. Some people live for the weekend; I lived for Tuesday nights. I gratefully treasured this recurring gift then and have cherished those memories ever since.

Jay McGuire was especially adept at getting to the heart of any issue, especially those related to the consistency of living out our faith in Christ. Jay Ballard and I usually paddled around in the shallow end with easy accountability questions and tame topics before gradually wading deeper into heavier and more personal matters. Jay McGuire, on the other hand, usually dove right into the deep end and asked the hard questions right off the bat. No, it wasn't really like a dive so much as it was like a cannonball; the splash would be too big to ignore, someone's face was going to get showered, and someone's dry towel was going to get soaked. Such was the nature of our relationship. Ballard and I had been accountability partners for several months before asking McGuire to join us. Our visits were like two old friends talking at the kitchen table over coffee or iced tea. When McGuire joined us, he was like the guest who comes into your house and starts opening closets and desk drawers, yet in a charming manner. Ballard and Barton examined each other's life and walk with Christ using our five-dollar Wal-Mart flashlights; McGuire showed up with a five-hundred-watt halogen spotlight. That was, of course, the appropriate role of a loving accountability brother. The other side of accountability was to man up and be transparent and honest with one's brothers about what is being revealed rather than ducking back into the shadows.

> *Faithful are the wounds of a friend,...*
> *Listen to advice and accept instruction, that you may gain wisdom*
> *in the future.*
> —Proverbs 27:6a; 19:20

Therefore, it was not surprising that on one of the first Tuesday evenings after I rejoined the group, Jay McGuire said, "John, the Lord could restore your voice this very minute if He wanted to, but He hasn't. What do you think He's trying to teach you through this?" I confess my initial reaction was one of bristling defensiveness, and I was tempted to give a quick non-answer. Yet because of the bond of brotherly love and trust that was so well established, I knew Jay's question was for my good. He was putting before me the question I should have asked myself a long time ago.

Jay's question cut to the heart of my spiritual condition. My pen was speechless, for I had no good answer. I realized that the focus of my prayers for myself had been limited to asking the Lord for healing and for wisdom in dealing with all my responsibilities. I hadn't given much thought to the idea that God was using this time of difficulty to mold me, discipline me, and mature me in my faith.

I didn't have an answer for Jay that night, but over the course of the ensuing weeks and months, I began to realize that I needed to change some of the attitudes in my heart and priorities in my life. Most of my challenging and sad circumstances remained unchanged, but the Lord used my Brothers Jay to begin to change my outlook on those things and to seek more spiritual maturity. As I did, I felt increasingly more compassionate and sympathetic to Candy's plight. I began to see with more understanding and appreciation all she did to try to help me. I learned to be much more patient with people who seemingly had little concern or understanding of what I was going through and more thankful for those who did. I still had a long road of important and sometimes very hard lessons to learn ahead of me. But the light of Christ was starting to pierce my darkness.

The lessons learned from my Brothers Jay were monumental, although I was still rather slow to fully grasp their impact. These friends did not think what they were doing was any great deed of kindness; they were just being my friends. Yet their investment in my life with their time, patience, kindness, and love had an immediate positive impact on me and an even greater long-term effect.

> *Let love be genuine. Abhor what is evil; hold fast to what is good. Love one another with brotherly affection. Outdo one another in showing honor.*
> —Romans 12:9-10

Had God given Jay and Jay unique spiritual gifts that most people do not have? No. According to God's word, the attributes they displayed are not spiritual gifts but are part of what genuine love and the fruit of the Spirit look like in the real-world lives of light-bearing followers of Christ.

> *Love is patient and kind; love does not envy or boast; it is not arrogant or rude. It does not insist on its own way; it is not irritable or resentful; it does not rejoice at wrongdoing, but rejoices with the truth. Love bears all things, believes all things, hopes all things, endures all things.*
> —1 Corinthians 13:4-7

> *But the fruit of the Spirit is love, joy, peace, patience, kindness, goodness, faithfulness, gentleness, self-control; against such things there is no law.*
> —Galatians 5:22-23

I am not implying that these guys were the only genuine Christ-followers around me. Dozens of friends, relatives, and co-workers in North Carolina, Tennessee, Mississippi, Georgia, Louisiana, and Texas faithfully prayed that the Lord would heal me and help Candy. Other church friends watched our children when Candy and I went to doctor appointments and helped in other ways. I am sure some more perceptive friends prayed for my spiritual strength and well-being. I received insightful teaching and preaching each Sunday. Yet these two men took true friendship and genuine brotherly love to another level as they saw the most pressing short-term need I had and gave of themselves to help meet that need.

The Light Brigade that Tennyson wrote about was a mounted unit of British soldiers in a heroic yet failed military attack against overwhelming odds in the Crimean War of the mid-1850s. The Light Brigade that the Lord sent to battle my darkness—Jay Ballard and Jay McGuire—was no less heroic in my eyes and was quite successful in its mission. These brothers valiantly charged into my quiet darkness, wielding the light of Christ and the sword of the Spirit, which is the word of God. They shared His grace and truth, showed me His love, and lifted my spirits. Like all heroes except One, these are men with observable flaws, weaknesses, and challenges of their own. However, because of their faithful love of Christ and the people He put in their path, the Lord used them as His ambassadors of light in powerfully effective ways.

The unfolding of your words gives light; it imparts understanding to the simple.
—Psalm 119:130

Again Jesus spoke to them, saying, "I am the light of the world. Whoever follows me will not walk in darkness, but will have the light of life."
—John 8:12

I will forever remember Jay and Jay as genuine heroes, my own personal Light Brigade. I pray that the Lord will use those memories to help make me sensitive to the needs of those around me and respond as a light-bearer of Christ as these dear brothers did.

For it is you who light my lamp; the LORD my God lightens my darkness.
—Psalm 18:28

Chapter 15

CHRISTMAS EVE, 1995

And suddenly there was with the angel a multitude of the heavenly host praising God and saying, "Glory to God in the highest, and on earth peace among those with whom He is pleased!"
—Luke 2:13-14

I have been a big fan of Christmas for as long as I can remember. I love celebrating Jesus's nativity, the cheerful Christmas spirit, the festive decorations, the fun get-togethers with friends and family, special Christmas music and events, and exchanging gifts. But the Christmas of 1995 will always have a very special place in my heart.

As I described in the previous chapter, my Brothers Jay proved to be exceptionally faithful friends in the spring of 1995, and they continued to be consistent lights of encouragement in the months that followed. However, as spring turned to summer and then to fall, my voice remained depressingly mute, and the associated darkness and discouragement continued to build. My inability to speak complicated my responsibilities as a department manager for International Paper (IP) in North Carolina and executor of my Mom's estate in Mississippi. I had some great coworkers to help me with the former, but the latter was especially wearing. My stepfather had very little knowledge of financial or insurance matters, and I had to take care of his financial and legal matters for many months after my Mom's passing. Since I couldn't speak on the phone, email was in its infancy, and there was no such thing as smartphones and texting, I had to make numerous trips to Mississippi on weekends and vacation days from work for face-to-face conversations. Those conversations were cumbersome and tiring because they involved me writing on a pad of paper rather than talking. I was glad to help early in the year, but as the months went by, it became increasingly wearisome and discouraging.

In the latter part of the year, I received even more bad news. IP planned to move the Charlotte office operations to Memphis and close our North Carolina office. That transition would begin in 1995 and be completed sometime in 1996. My position would be absorbed in a complete reorganization of accounting functions. If I wanted to continue working for IP, I had to apply for a different position. Without the ability to speak, I had no idea how I could even interview for another job, with IP or another company, much less get one.

To further complicate matters, we had had a long, drawn-out battle with our HMO, who did not have the expertise to diagnose the problem with my vocal cords yet refused to pay for me to go outside their group to find another specialist. I wrote multiple letters, and Candy spent hours on the phone, fighting that battle, seemingly to no avail.

Candy and I worked together well on the insurance wars, but my inability to speak had otherwise strained our marital relationship. Candy felt somewhat like a single mom and was angry about being in such a predicament. I felt heavily burdened by all that was on me and miserably lonely because of my inability to engage in normal conversation with others. I felt horribly inadequate as a husband, dad, and friend. My faith in God through Christ remained intact, yet He seemed as quiet as I was. It was the most depressed and darkest time my soul has ever known.

Thankfully, the Lord provided some scattered beams of light into my dark world, especially on my Tuesday night visits with Jay and Jay. Another light beam was my six-year-old, Michael. He loved to show off his advanced reading skills, so he welcomed the chance to read my notes out loud at home, in church, restaurants, or stores. In such places, he was usually my voice, and the voice of a six-year-old was better than no voice at all. Michael was a big help to me, and he loved feeling so important. The IP employees who reported to me were also a huge help, especially my primary assistant, Gloria Griffin. I doubt I could have kept my job without Gloria's patience and kindness. I was thankful for these beams of light, yet their brightness made me ever more conscious of the depth of my quiet darkness.

Life started to brighten in late fall. We discovered that one of the nation's leading specialists in vocal problems was only seventy-five miles away in Winston-Salem. He literally wrote the book on this specific issue with non-functioning vocal cords. The HMO finally gave in and agreed to pay for his services. Yes, things were looking up!

In the first few minutes of my first appointment with this vocal cord specialist, I recognized that he was exceptionally competent and confident in his ability to diagnose and successfully treat my voiceless predicament. After some tests and examination, he explained the problem stemmed from thick growths caused by the human papillomavirus. The growths, called papillomas, clung to my vocal cords, thickening them to the extent that they could no longer function. Surgery was scheduled for mid-November to remove the papillomas with a laser and confirm they were benign (almost always the case).

After the surgery, the doctor announced it was a success, even though my vocal cords were unable to generate any sound. He assured me that I would be able to speak within a week to ten days but asked me not to do so for five weeks in order for the vocal cords to heal completely. I was so anxious to be healed and no longer be a mute, but another thirty-five days of silence seemed a small price to pay to regain full use of my voice.

When I realized that the five weeks of mandated vocal silence would end just a few days before Christmas, I immediately began making big plans for this exciting event. The previous year, we buried my Mom on December 23rd, and it was an incredibly sad, mournful Christmas. But this Christmas, oh, what a great Christmas it would be! I would give my kids a truly wonderful, spectacular, unforgettable Christmas present: a father who could talk with them. My youngest two children, Laura and Joseph, had no memory of ever hearing me speak, and it was only a vague, fading memory for Michael. On Christmas morning, I would let Candy and the kids go downstairs from our bedrooms before me, then bound down the stairs to them and proclaim in a strong, loud voice, "Merry Christmas!" Oh, I could hardly wait. This was going to be the best Christmas our family had ever had!

A week after surgery, I still had no voice. There was no need to worry, for I was confident that my voice would return in another day or two. Two weeks passed; no voice yet, which seemed odd. Three weeks, still no voice; now I was starting to worry. The specialist in Winston-Salem was baffled why the vocal cords still would not function. He suspected there could be extensive nerve damage within the cords that was not visible from the outside. He wanted to bring in another specialist for a much riskier operation, but I asked for more time before taking that step. Four weeks passed; still no hint of a voice.

The five weeks had come and gone. It was Christmas Eve 1995, and I still couldn't speak. Not one peep. The wonderful Christmas Day I had envisioned wasn't going to happen. The best Christmas present ever for my kids had not shown up. I didn't know if I would ever speak again. I didn't know how much longer I would be able to provide for my family. And, oh, how crushing was the thought that I would have to continue to endure this dark, depressing loneliness around the clock, all the time, except for Tuesday nights with Jay and Jay. Candy and the kids had already gone to bed, but I could not sleep. It was another terribly sad Christmas. I thought that perhaps reading my Bible might help.

As I opened the word of the Lord, I asked Him to help me, guide me, and give me some glimmer of hope. I decided to continue a study of Exodus that I had recently started. No, it was not a very "Christmassy" passage of Scripture, but that was perfectly fine because I was not feeling very Christmassy. Not in the least.

I began to read about God's call to Moses and Moses' responses. The Lord performed various miraculous signs to demonstrate the power that would be with Moses when he confronted Pharaoh. Yet Moses told the Lord he didn't think he could be His man in Egypt because he was a poor speaker. The Lord's response to Moses was powerful:

> *The LORD said to him, "Who gave man his mouth? Who makes him deaf or mute? Who gives him sight or makes him blind? Is it not I, the LORD? Now go; I will help you speak and will teach you what to say."*
> —Exodus 4:11-12 NIV84

As I read, I knew God said those words to Moses about thirty-five hundred years ago, but in my heart, it felt as though He were shouting them to John Barton on this Christmas Eve. I was immediately filled with both crushing conviction and unimaginable joy. I was overcome with the realization that I had fully trusted in the word and promise of an overly self-confident doctor. I had built up my expectations and planned my Christmas day based on what the doctor said would happen. I had not heard any such promises from God but assumed He was on board with my plans. I sank to my knees and pleaded for forgiveness.

As the weight of this conviction sank in, I also realized the issue was much larger than my poor attitude on this night. For fifteen months, I was focused almost entirely on what I could *not* do, not on what the Lord *could* do. Jay McGuire challenged me months earlier to consider what God was trying to teach me. I obviously had not yet made a passing grade in that class! I had failed to acknowledge that the holy and sovereign Lord of all, Jehovah Raphe, our Great Physician, was in complete control of the situation. He would decide if and when my vocal cords would function again. It was the Lord who allowed my voice to leave, and it was Him and only Him who would bring it back—

and it would be in His perfect timing. He was Jehovah Elohim, the Creator who knit together my vocal cords, and He knew precisely what was going on with them. My faith must rest fully in El Shaddai, Almighty God, who was sovereign over this and all situations. I could fully trust Jehovah Jireh, the One, would provide for my family; it wasn't up to me, and it never had been. He would provide me a job when and where He willed and do so in His perfect timing. Jehovah Rohi, our Good Shepherd, had a path forward for me—a good path, one that He would define and use for His glory and for the good of my family and me. He was the author of my faith and the source of all genuine joy. The Lord had a plan for me to serve Him in ways that were to be based not on what I could do but on what He could do through me. My job was to trust Him, and it was high time I started doing that with all my heart, soul, mind, and strength.

> *"And you shall love the Lord your God with all your heart and with all your soul and with all your mind and with all your strength."*
> —The words of Jesus in Mark 12:30

The resulting relief and joy in my soul were at levels I had never before experienced. The heaviness of my self-centered grief, depression, and loneliness was eviscerated, and the new lightness of my heart acted as a helium balloon, springing me off the floor to my feet. I spent another couple of hours in praise, worship, and study of the word. I gratefully turned from Exodus to Matthew and Luke and read the story of the first Christmas, for my spirit had been catapulted to very "Christmassy" levels! I wept, I laughed, I called out gleefully and confidently to God. I sang, I praised, I danced with delight. My vocal cords didn't join in this very special Christmas Eve service, but even that was a blessing, for there was no risk of waking Candy and the kids!

> *Bless the LORD, O my soul, and all that is within me, bless his holy name!*
> *Bless the LORD, O my soul, and forget not all his benefits,*
> *who forgives all your iniquity, who heals all your diseases,*
> *who redeems your life from the pit, who crowns you with steadfast love and mercy,*
> *who satisfies you with good so that your youth is renewed like the eagle's.*
> —Psalm 103:1-5

It turned out to be a wonderful Christmas Day indeed, not because of the conditions and plans I had set forth earlier, but with the renewed joy of a closer relationship with my Savior. I hugged Candy more often and more passionately than I had in a long time. I hugged our children with more selfless love than I had in a while. They sensed my newfound joy and responded with joy of their own. We had a grand time playing with their new toys, listening to Candy and Michael read the Christmas story to us, singing Christmas songs, and simply enjoying each other on an exceedingly happy holiday. It was the brightest day I had known in a very, very long time.

> *As a father shows compassion to his children, so the LORD shows compassion to those who fear him.*
> —Psalm 103:13

Chapter 16

MICHAEL'S BIRTHDAY, 1996

"Now go; I will help you speak and will teach you what to say."
—Exodus 4:12 (NIV84)

F our weeks after the wonderful Christmas of 1995, I teamed with Jay McGuire to visit people in our community who had recently attended our church for the first time. Yes, you are right: it was quite strange that I participated in this event with no ability to speak. But based on the word of the Lord on Christmas Eve to "go," along with Jay's encouragement, I knew this service activity was something I needed to do. Jay advised that it was vital not to let my circumstances keep me from being involved in our church's ministry and mission work. He reminded me of a lesson I had shared with him a couple of years earlier: always actively serve God rather than allow ourselves to sit, soak, and sour on the sidelines. I knew Jay was right and joined him as his silent but active visitation partner that evening. As we visited a handful of families, Jay did what he did so well: engage with others in friendly, meaningful conversation. I did what I could do well: pray, smile, encourage Jay, and listen.

While Jay and I were out, we received a message that a member of our church, Mary Jane, requested that we go to her house after visitation. She said the Lord gave her a clear word that she was to pray over me before my next doctor's appointment. Upon learning from Candy that my appointment in Winston-Salem was the next morning, she urged us to stop by her house, no matter the hour. Jay and I did as she requested. As I knelt, Mary Jane, her husband, Sam, and Jay put their hands on my shoulders and prayed over me for healing. After the final "amen," we hugged, and I used sign language and a smile to thank them as we left.

> *And the prayer of faith will save the one who is sick, and the Lord will raise him up. And if he has committed sins, he will be forgiven. Therefore, confess your sins to one another and pray for one another, that you may be healed. The prayer of a righteous person has great power as it is working.*
> —James 5:15-16

The following morning, Tuesday, January 23, 1996—Michael's seventh birthday—Candy and I went to Winston-Salem and met with one of the vocal cord specialists. After examining my vocal cords, he asked me to try to make the sound, *eeeeeee*. I opened my mouth and made a sound for the first time in sixteen months! It wasn't thunderous by any means, but it was certainly loud enough for the doctor and Candy to hear. Candy almost fell out of her chair in shock. I excitedly yet cautiously added a few actual words. I could talk! The doctor patiently waited as Candy and I instinctively hugged each other with inexpressible joy. The doctor asked me a few questions, and I responded with short answers, feeling a need to be frugal with my words. These sounds from my mouth felt like valuable pieces of a long-lost treasure, and I was reluctant to let go of them too quickly. As the appointment continued, I gradually felt more confident to speak and did so reasonably well. After a few minutes, we gratefully accepted the doctor's news that no follow-up appointments were necessary unless complications arose. Our prayers were answered, and in a delightful way that we would never forget. Hallelujah!

> *Great is the LORD, and greatly to be praised, and his greatness is unsearchable.*
> *One generation shall commend your works to another, and shall declare your mighty acts.*
> *On the glorious splendor of your majesty, and on your wondrous works, I will meditate.*
> —Psalm 145:3-5

It was indeed a jubilant birthday celebration at the Barton home that night. Michael had enjoyed a fun birthday party on Saturday, so he didn't mind sharing the spotlight with me during this special family time.

He had enjoyed occasionally being his dad's voice but was overjoyed that we could finally converse without a notepad. Two-year-old Joseph kept his wide blue eyes attentively on me most of the evening, fascinated to hear my voice. Three-year-old Laura was perhaps the most excited, as she repeatedly exclaimed, "My daddy can talk! My daddy can talk!" She gladly heralded the good news to whomever she encountered for several days.

Candy and I were thrilled, yet our exuberance was measured by humble gratitude. We were tremendously relieved that the exhausting sixteen-month battle was over and thankful that we emerged victorious. Yet the Lord had made it clear that victory came only on His terms, not ours. Along the way, He had allowed us to be decisively humbled for His glory and our good. Hopefully the lessons He taught were learned well.

> *Oh come, let us sing to the LORD; let us make a joyful noise to the rock of our salvation!*
> *Let us come into his presence with thanksgiving; let us make a joyful noise to him with songs of praise!*
> —Psalm 95:1-2

I tried not to overuse my voice for a few days after that, but it was hard not to share my joy with everyone I saw. My co-workers at International Paper were thrilled that I could finally converse with them in a normal way. Our church friends were overjoyed, especially my Brothers Jay. Jay McGuire later told me it was an important faith-building process for him, as it encouraged him not to give up hope nor give up praying, even if our prayers seem to go unanswered for a long time. We must always trust that God's timing and means of answering our prayers will be perfect for Him to be most glorified in our lives.

Two weeks after my voice returned, I interviewed in Memphis for a job opening with International Paper. I met with several people, including an old friend and former fellow supervisor in Charlotte, Don Mathison. He had transferred to Memphis several months before but faithfully stayed in touch with me. In early January, when I still had no idea if I would ever speak again, Don convinced me to sign up for this February interview for a position on the team he led. I also met with Dave Borchardt, an exceptionally bright and focused man I had interacted with on several occasions during our International Paper careers. It was such a blessing to be able to speak with these men and others that day. The Lord soon blessed me again when Dave informed me that the job in Memphis was mine. Dave became my new manager, the best I had ever had, and I again had the pleasure of working with my good friend Don. Once again, the Lord demonstrated His faithfulness to provide for my family and me in His perfect timing and in ways that displayed His gracious love.

> *"Therefore I tell you, do not be anxious about your life, what you will eat or what you will drink, nor about your body, what you will put on. Is not life more than food, and the body more than clothing? Look at the birds of the air: they neither sow nor reap nor gather into barns, and yet your heavenly Father feeds them. Are you not of more value than they? And which of you by being anxious can add a single hour to his span of life? And why are you anxious about clothing? Consider the lilies of the field, how they grow: they neither toil nor spin, yet I tell you, even Solomon in all his glory was not arrayed like one of these. But if God so clothes the grass of the field, which today is alive and tomorrow is thrown into the oven, will he not much more clothe you, O you of little faith? . . . But seek first the kingdom of God and his righteousness, and all these things will be added to you."*
> —The words of Jesus in Matthew 6:25-30, 33

I wish my testimony included the fact that I never again had any problems with my voice. The specialist in Winston-Salem told us there was a 95% chance the growths would return. His prognosis was spot on, and I lost my voice again within a couple of years. By God's grace, there was an ENT in Memphis with the expertise to identify the problem and do the corrective surgery. The cycle of recurring papillomas continued, however, for several years. Thankfully they were never painful but always made my voice considerably less functional. Each surgery left scar tissue, gradually reducing the ongoing strength of my vocal cords. Sometimes the growths came back quickly, within a few months of the previous surgery. Other times they grew more slowly, taking up to two years to become problematic.

My ENT in Memphis eventually moved to Florida, but God provided two successive ENTs with papilloma expertise in Little Rock. The second was Dr. Felicia Johnson, who performed my twelfth and last papilloma surgery in December 2006.

In August 2007, I saw Dr. Johnson for a regular check-up on my vocal cords. While there, I asked her about another issue: I had a painful ulcer on the right side of my tongue that wouldn't go away. You know where the story went from there.

Even though my bouts with tongue cancer were excruciating and life-threatening, I still consider the first fifteen months of voicelessness in 1994–

95 as the most difficult time of my life. The dark loneliness was the only time I have experienced any level of actual depression, probably because it was also the low point in my marriage to Candy. Neither of us handled the situation as we should have. We thought we were pretty spiritually mature, but when tested, we found that we were not. We learned some hard but important lessons—mostly from our mistakes—that have served us well ever since.

I am very grateful for the testing of our faith during those years, for I firmly believe I would not have survived Stage 4 tongue cancer without the lessons learned from this earlier health crisis. The Lord taught us that our faith in Him must grow, not waver, in trying circumstances. He underscored the importance of our marriage and the care needed to nurture it. He used my Brothers Jay to illustrate true Christian friendship. We experienced a practical application of the truth that salvation and sanctification in Christ are not to make us good people with comfortable lives but believers who genuinely trust God to care for us in all situations as we grow in Christlikeness. We learned that we are to be thankful for good earthly physicians, but our ultimate trust for healing must rest solely in God. And the Lord mercifully demonstrated the power of fervent and faithful prayer.

I pray these crucial lessons will always be remembered and practiced with increasing trust, gratitude, joy, and hope.

> *Trust in the LORD with all your heart, and do not lean on your own understanding.*
> *In all your ways acknowledge him, and he will make straight your paths.*
> —Proverbs 3:5-6

Chapter 17

HEALING OF MY
GREATEST AFFLICTION

I am severely afflicted;
give me life, O LORD, according to Your word!
—Psalm 119:107

Sing for joy, O heavens, and exult, O earth; break forth, O mountains, into
singing! For the LORD has comforted his people and will have compassion on his
afflicted.
—Isaiah 49:13

Most of this book centers around my afflictions, the related physical suffering, and the ongoing aftereffects. I have joyfully described how God has blessed me through these trials and used them to teach, mold, and use me for His glory. Yet I must not neglect to tell you of my greatest affliction: my sin.

I sin every day because I have been a sinner since I was born. It is crucial to make that distinction: I am not a sinner because I sin; I sin because I am a sinner. Sin was in my nature at birth—and in yours too. I yearn not to sin and strive to live in a righteous and holy manner to honor and glorify God. Yet I struggle against sinful attitudes and desires every single day. I cannot bear to think of how many times I have sinned against Almighty, Holy God, the eternal Sovereign Judge. I sinned yesterday, and I sinned today. As much as I do not want to, I will undoubtedly sin tomorrow. Many sins I notice and ask God to forgive me and help me to truly repent. But sometimes I sin and do not even notice because I am so sinful.

> *Behold, I was brought forth in iniquity, and in sin did my mother conceive me.*
> —Psalm 51:5

> *For I know that nothing good dwells in me, that is, in my flesh. For I have the desire to do what is right, but not the ability to carry it out. For I do not do the good I want, but the evil I do not want is what I keep on doing. Now if I do what I do not want, it is no longer I who do it, but sin that dwells within me.*
> —Romans 7:18-20

What are the consequences of my sin? God is a Holy God who cannot tolerate even the slightest bit of impurity with Him in heaven. He cannot have fellowship with anyone who has any sin in their lives, even with people we consider magnanimous who only have what we consider trivial or inconsequential sins. We might even refer to them as "weaknesses," "mistakes," "shortcomings," or "poor choices" rather than "sins." But sin is any disobedience or nonconformity to God's word. R. C. Sproul said sin is "cosmic treason."[12] The bottom line is sin is sin, and we can't dress it up enough or justify it enough to make it acceptable to God.

But hold on just a minute! What about all those good things I've done? How about all those people I helped and made happy? How about all the righteous living I've done as an upright and honest man? Here is God's reply:

> *We have all become like one who is unclean, and all our righteous deeds are like a polluted garment. We all fade like a leaf, and our iniquities, like the wind, take us away.*
> —Isaiah 64:6

> *As it is written: "None is righteous, no, not one; no one understands; no one seeks for God. All have turned aside; together they have become worthless; no one does good, not even one."… [F]or all have sinned and fall short of the glory of God.*
> —Romans 3:10-12, 23

We all agree that God is perfectly good, and if He is good, He must be just. In His perfect justice, God cannot overlook sin in anyone. Sin must always be punished. There are no exceptions. Anyone who God looks upon and sees unrighteousness and sin cannot be with Him; that person must be punished by the full extent of God's wrath for all eternity. God's wrath is not something people even like to think about, much less discuss. But we must clearly understand the punishment that awaits all whom God sees as sinful and unrighteous.

> *"The Son of Man will send his angels, and they will gather out of his kingdom all causes of sin and all law-breakers, and throw them into the fiery furnace. In that place there will be weeping and gnashing of teeth."*
> —The words of Jesus in Matthew 13:41-42

> *Then Death and Hades were thrown into the lake of fire. This is the second death, the lake of fire. And if anyone's name was not found written in the book of life, he was thrown into the lake of fire.*
> —Revelation 20:14-15

What might such a lake of fire be like? Will it be like gasoline burning as it floats on water? I don't think so. I think it will be more like being thrown into the mouth of an active volcano filled with choking lethal gases and blinding temperatures over two thousand degrees Fahrenheit. The molten lava is thick and engulfs anything in its path. What would it be like to be thrown into such a dark place with a body impervious to destruction but not impervious to pain? There are no words to describe such a thing other than *God's wrath*. Yet I know His wrath is not like that because it will be worse than anything I can imagine.

My goodness, this story is certainly not a fun read so far, is it? No, not fun, but accurate, whether we like to think about it or not. I must think about it because, at one time, I was on the broad road of sin, heading to that destination. The wonderful news, however, is that it is not the end of the story!

Because of God's great love and mercy, He sent His Son, Jesus Christ, to earth in the form of a human to live a perfect, sinless life of righteousness. No big sins, no little sins, no hidden sins, no sins in His heart, mind, or body; none whatsoever. He and He alone lived a life of perfect obedience to God the Father, a life of pure righteousness that is necessary for one to have fellowship with God. On what appeared to be the final day of Jesus's life on earth, He was beaten, flogged, and crucified on a cross, a torturous means of slow-motion execution favored by the Romans and, in the case of Jesus, encouraged by the Jewish leaders who despised Him. Yet the physical cruelty was not the worst thing Jesus suffered. During His final three hours on the cross, as inexplicable darkness covered the earth, the impossible was done: the Son was forsaken by His Father as He bore the cumulative wrath of God and died the substitutionary death for all who would ever trust in Him. At the end of the three hours, Jesus looked to heaven and declared, "It is finished," and breathed His last. God's wrath was fully absorbed. The life of righteousness and atoning death were complete. Jesus was buried in a sealed tomb late on a Friday afternoon, and on the third day—Sunday morning— He rose from the grave. Sin and death were defeated!

God has mercifully allowed me to share in this victory. He brought my dead soul to life and gave me the greatest gift of all: faith in Jesus Christ. By faith, I know that Jesus lived a substitutionary life and died a substitutionary death, and God looks upon me and sees the righteousness of Christ. He looks upon Christ and sees my sins and the full payment for them. By His grace and through the faith God gave me, my soul has been redeemed, and the life I live, I now live in Christ, with Christ, and for Christ. I have been forever reconciled to God the Father, who has adopted me as one of His children.

> *"For God so loved the world, that He gave His only Son, that whoever believes in Him should not perish but have eternal life. For God did not send His Son into the world to condemn the world, but in order that the world might be saved through Him."*
> —The words of Jesus in John 3:16-17

> *Jesus said to him, "I am the way, and the truth, and the life. No one comes to the Father except through Me."*
> —John 14:6

> *I have been crucified with Christ. It is no longer I who live, but Christ who lives in me. And the life I now live in the flesh I live by faith in the Son of God, who loved me and gave himself for me.*
> —Galatians 2:20

> *But when the fullness of time had come, God sent forth his Son, born of woman, born under the law, to redeem those who were under the law, so that we might receive adoption as sons. And because you are sons, God has sent the Spirit of his Son into our hearts, crying, "Abba! Father!"*
> —Galatians 4:4-6

I said earlier that hell would be worse than anything we can imagine. So what will the new heaven and the new earth, our eventual eternal home, be like? God gave John a glimpse of it, and the old apostle used the best descriptive words he knew to paint us a picture. Yet we know that there are no words to fully describe its beauty and glory, nor are our minds sufficient to imagine how glorious it will be.

> *Then I saw a new heaven and a new earth, for the first heaven and the first earth had passed away, and the sea was no more. And I saw the holy city, new Jerusalem, coming down out of heaven from God, prepared as a bride adorned for her husband. And I heard a loud voice from the throne saying, "Behold, the dwelling place of God is with man. He will dwell with them, and they will be his people, and God himself will be with them as their God. He will wipe away every tear from their eyes, and death shall be no more, neither shall there be mourning, nor crying, nor pain anymore, for the former things have passed away.". . . The wall was built of jasper, while the city was pure gold, like clear glass. The foundations of the wall of the city were adorned with every kind of jewel. . . . And the twelve gates were twelve pearls, each of the gates made of a single pearl, and the street of the city was pure gold, like transparent glass. And I saw no temple in the city, for its temple is the Lord God the Almighty and the Lamb. And the city has no need of sun or moon to shine on it, for the glory of God gives it light, and its lamp is the Lamb.*
> —Revelation 21:1-4, 18-19a, 21-23

You know by now that I love to tell stories, especially those about the extraordinary ways God has blessed me and continues to bless me in unique ways. But when all is said and done, all those stories would not matter a bit without this one. I was a sinner destined to suffer eternally in hell because of my sin. But my dead soul was made alive by the Holy Spirit, and I trusted in Christ for salvation. My life is no longer my own but is Christ's and His alone, for He has purchased it with His blood. I live for the glory of Christ, to proclaim His name, to share His light and His love, and to serve in His name. And that, my friends, is the best story of all.

> *And you were dead in the trespasses and sins in which you once walked, following the course of this world, following the prince of the power of the air, the spirit that is now at work in the sons of disobedience—among whom we all once lived in the passions of our flesh, carrying out the desires of the body and the mind, and were by nature children of wrath, like the rest of mankind. But God, being rich in mercy, because of the great love with which he loved us, even when we were dead in our trespasses, made us alive together with Christ— . . . For by grace you have been saved through faith. And*

this is not your own doing; it is the gift of God, not a result of works, so that no one may boast. For we are his workmanship, created in Christ Jesus for good works, which God prepared beforehand, that we should walk in them.
—Ephesians 2:1-5a, 8-10

Chapter 18

THE FIRST,
MAYBE SECOND STAGE

*May the God of endurance and encouragement grant you to live in such
harmony with one another, in accord with Christ Jesus, that together you may
with one voice glorify the God and Father of our Lord Jesus Christ. Therefore
welcome one another as Christ has welcomed you, for the glory of God.*
—Romans 15:5-7

Nothing perhaps affects man's character more than the company he keeps.
(J. C. Ryle)[13]

I grew up in the 1960s and 1970s, and like many in those times, I was
fascinated by the space race. I fondly remember our elementary school
teachers bringing portable televisions to school so we could crowd around
and watch the NASA missions lift off or splash down. Of course, the apex
of the space race was the moon landing by Apollo 11 on July 20, 1969.
I will never forget the tense excitement of watching the fuzzy black-and-
white image of astronaut Neil Armstrong climbing down the ladder of the
Eagle (the mission's Lunar Excursion Module). It was thrilling to witness
science fiction become reality when Commander Armstrong stepped onto
the moon's gray, dusty surface and announced to the watching world, "That's
one small step for man, one giant leap for mankind."

I was mesmerized then as a boy and possibly even more so as an
adult after reading more about the complex engineering, the courageous
astronauts, and the internal and external politics that made the United States'

space program such a soaring success. Therefore, I was overjoyed when my oldest son, Michael, decided to major in aerospace engineering at Mississippi State. He then received a master's degree in astrodynamics from Purdue and made aerospace engineering his career.

Michael's knowledge of rocket science exceeds mine by many light-years, but I do understand some of the elementary concepts of rocketry. A multistage rocket is essentially a launch vehicle comprised of two or more booster rockets stacked, or staged, on top of each other. Each stage has its own booster engines and fuel supply. The first stage of a rocket is responsible for getting it off the ground. As it runs out of fuel, the first stage is jettisoned, and the second stage booster engines are fired. The rockets that took men out of Earth's orbit in NASA's Apollo program all had three stages. The engine design and fuel chosen for each stage are based on the environment (composition of the layer of atmosphere or outer space) that stage is expected to be used in.

As I look back at my salvation and ongoing sanctification in Christ, there have been a few monumental times that remind me of booster rockets firing as they propelled me to another level of spiritual maturity. You have read about the boosting effect that afflictions had on my faith as an adult. Those stories prompted some to ask when the first stage of my faith in Christ first launched. That's a question not easily answered.

A few months before Apollo 11's historic moon landing, I made a profession of faith in Christ as a ten-year-old boy. I was gripped by the nightly messages of a visiting pastor during a revival week at our church. After the Wednesday night service, my mom and I had a long talk about trusting Christ as my Savior. I understood the decision to follow Christ as much as a child could, and that night in April 1969, I knelt with Mom beside my bed and asked Jesus to forgive me of my sins and be my Savior.

I was a good church boy for a number of years, but in my late teens and early twenties, I began to stray. Badly. I worked most weekends, so my church attendance became increasingly less frequent. Predictably my faith suffered severely, and, accordingly, I did some very foolish and sinful things.

After successful academic achievements in high school and college, I graduated from Mississippi State in 1981 and immediately moved to Memphis to begin a career in public accounting. I moved to a one-bedroom apartment in Whispering Oaks, an apartment complex in east Memphis popular with young adults, upon the recommendation of two friends and fraternity brothers, Collins Hewes and George Ramsey, who had moved there the year before.

At the time, I was dating an attractive and personable young lady I had met at Mississippi State. Sarah and I got along wonderfully and rapidly became very committed to one another. She was still in college and transferred to Southwestern at Memphis (later renamed Rhodes College), a school known for its high academic standards. She lived on campus, but we saw each other often, going out on dates or studying together—she for her classes and me for the CPA exam.

In 1982, I moved into a three-bedroom apartment in Whispering Oaks with George and another recent State graduate, Dan Craig. All three of us grew up in Starkville, and being with these friends was a continual reminder of the values that were instilled in us as we were growing up. My roommates were good men, and living with them was a blessing.

Collins and I had befriended a sweet young school teacher, Susan Gracy, the year before at a Whispering Oaks pool party. By God's grace, she and two of her friends, Karen Keeney and Sandra Symes, moved into the apartment directly across the sidewalk from George, Dan, and me. Another friend, Leigh Ann Jones, was a school teacher in Jackson, Tennessee, but became the girls' fourth roommate during the summer months. The seven of us quickly became close friends, although none of us were romantically linked. We visited one another almost daily and became like a family of brothers and sisters, except with no sibling rivalries.

We jokingly referred to our group as "The Commune" because we shared our provisions, knowledge, feelings, and time. And usually we shared lots of laughter and fun, although we shared our heartaches as well. Most importantly, we shared a common set of ethics and morals. We were blessed to be young adults in an era that didn't have the distractions of today's electronic culture, and we relished our face-to-face conversations. We soon met each other's families and friends. My parents were thrilled that I was surrounded by such good influences. And when I met the parents of my Commune sisters, they graciously made me feel like a favored and beloved son right away. I could not have dreamed of a better situation.

One of the major effects of living in the Commune was getting back to more regular church attendance with my neighbors. As I heard the word of God preached every Sunday, I became increasingly aware of the poor state of my spiritual well-being.

The gradual change in my spiritual outlook was jolted and hastened in 1983 by four major events. The first came early in the year. As our group of friends grew closer, I came to admire, appreciate, and love them more and more. Yet there was one person who did not fit in so well with our group: my girlfriend, Sarah. She and I moved to Memphis with the understanding that we would become officially engaged in 1983 and would marry in 1984 after her graduation. I loved Sarah and was firmly committed to our relationship, but I increasingly realized that she did not share some of the character traits I most admired in my Commune sisters. As Sarah and I matured, our interests and core values seemed to grow in different directions. I agonized over how to reconcile these differences but eventually realized that we were more committed to our commitment than to each other. I was confident that my path of life was much better than it had been a year earlier, and I did not think it was a path that would bring Sarah the things in life she wanted. So after a long talk, we agreed to end our relationship.

The second major event happened in June of that year when our roommate Dan married his longtime fiancé, Laurie. George and I were thrilled for our two longtime friends but also needed a new roommate. Around that same time, our neighbor Karen told us of a friend from her high school who had recently returned to Memphis. She asked if we would be willing to take him in as our new third roommate. George and I agreed that any friend of Karen's was a friend of ours, so we welcomed Jack Edmands as our new roommate the first time we met him. Because Jack didn't have a job yet, I paid his rent until he got on his feet again. I confess that made me rather proud of myself, but I soon discovered that I, not Jack, was the primary recipient of God's grace in this new relationship.

Jack was unlike anyone I had ever known. He had a humble, unassuming, and pleasant personality, making him exceptionally likable. Jack had been an outstanding and very popular student, star athlete, and class president at Ridgeway High School in Memphis before going to UCLA to play baseball. He also had a terrific sense of humor and could be downright hilarious. Jack, George, and I got along great as roomies and had lots of fun times. Going to sporting events with Jack was incredibly fun, as his expertise allowed him to see details I could not, especially in baseball. I could distinguish a fastball from a breaking ball, but Jack would identify what kind of breaking ball it was. I was fascinated! No matter what we did, I almost always learned something useful from Jack.

But the most striking thing about Jack was his love of God's word. I had never shared a roof with any man who read and studied the Bible as much or as passionately as Jack, nor with anyone so dedicated to living what he learned. I quickly realized that Jack and I professed the same faith in Christ, but his life looked uncomfortably different than mine. He truly lived what I believed, which was deeply convicting. Jack would later say that he shuddered at the thought of being held up as an example for anyone because he felt his life was such a mess at the time. But God knew our new friend was exactly what George and I needed. Oh, what a gracious God is ours!

The third major event happened soon after Jack's arrival. Like many weekends, some friends and I went to our favorite bar on Saturday night and were in church the next morning for worship. One of my neighbors and I were sitting on the steps outside my apartment that Sunday afternoon, talking about the people we saw the previous night and about the church service that morning. After we talked awhile, she said, "You know, JB, we've got it good. We can party with the party people on Saturday night and worship with the church folks on Sunday morning. We're right there in the middle, sitting on the fence between them." I knew she meant that we could enjoy being with friends at parties and bars and not let it affect our Christian faith; we were in the world but not of the world. But her words cut me to the quick, for they exposed my divided heart. I realized that while I had been convicted to live a more godly life, I still harbored too much affection for certain things of the world. My ears heard my friend's words, but my soul heard, *JB, if you're neither hot nor cold, but only lukewarm, I will spit you out of my mouth*—a paraphrase of the words of Jesus in Revelation 3:15-16. Within a few minutes, I made up a reason to cut our visit short and go inside.

As soon as the apartment door shut behind me, I fell to my knees and prayed to God for mercy: "O Lord, I know I have not been living the life You want me to live. Everybody thinks I'm a nice, friendly, good guy, but You see me as I really am. Lord Jesus, I prayed to receive You as my Savior and Lord fourteen years ago, but You know the awful things I have done since then. Lord, I don't know if I was saved then and became terribly backslidden or if I was never truly saved. Whatever the case, I beg You to forgive me, cleanse me, save me, and give me an undivided heart. I don't want to be on the fence anymore. I only want to be on Your side. I want to be like Jack because Jack wants to be like You."

> *My soul melts away for sorrow; strengthen me according to your word!*
> *Put false ways far from me and graciously teach me your law!*
> *I have chosen the way of faithfulness; I set your rules before me.*
> —Psalm 119:28-30

> *One thing have I asked of the LORD, that will I seek after:*
> *that I may dwell in the house of the LORD all the days of my life,*
> *to gaze upon the beauty of the LORD and to inquire in his temple.*
> —Psalm 27:4

"One thing:" Divided aims tend to distraction, weakness, disappointment. The man of one book is eminent, the man of one pursuit is successful. Let all our affections be bound up in one affection, and that affection set upon heavenly things. (Charles Haddon Spurgeon)[14]

After my prayer, I got out my Bible and began reading with a newfound hunger. God's word immediately became a more important part of my life, and Jack became my first Bible commentary when I had questions. He was my first and most influential spiritual mentor, a relationship that endured for the remaining years of his life. He also became one of the best friends a man could ever hope for. Even though we were roommates for only a couple of years, our strong friendship remained intact, no matter where we lived or what circumstances we encountered. I could always, always, always depend on Jack.

Be not wise in your own eyes; fear the LORD, and turn away from evil. It will be healing to your flesh and refreshment to your bones.
—Proverbs 3:7-8

My rare friendship with Jack was abruptly paused on Monday, September 19, 2022. He had never allowed himself to get out of shape; he exercised regularly and was exceedingly careful about what he put in his body. Yet Jack passed away suddenly from a massive heart attack that Monday evening, shortly after returning home from the gym and before going to a Bible study. I was shocked and deeply grieved for months. Yet I know, by grace through faith, that my friendship with Jack has not ended. We will see each other again, and together we will praise our Lord Jesus for all eternity. I thank the Lord for Jack Edmands! Only two other people have had such an enormous impact on my life. One is my mom, and the other is the subject of the fourth life-changing event of 1983.

After being without a girlfriend for several months, I began to yearn for another serious relationship, but this time with a young lady who was serious about her faith in Christ. I began to pray for the Lord to bring a special Christian girl into my life. Within a couple of weeks, one of my fellow CPAs at work began to catch my eye as never before. I had casually known Candy Levitch since she joined the accounting firm in 1982 but never paid much attention to her since we never worked together on the same project. I knew she was very friendly and smart, but I suddenly noticed how cute she was! Why did I never notice that before? I began to make small talk with her occasionally, which made me want to know her even better. I knew Candy was a solid Christian, and I still felt so immature in my faith that I feared I wasn't good enough for her. She and I had a mutual friend in Anita Arnold, one of Candy's friends in the singles ministry at Bellevue Baptist, and a coworker and good friend of my neighbor Karen. So acting somewhat like a shy school kid, I asked Anita if she thought Candy would go out with me. When Anita said she would definitely be open to a date with me, I called Candy right away before she could change her mind!

On September 3, 1983, Candy and I had a delightful and memorable first date. We weren't strangers since we had been together multiple times in large group settings at work. Yet we thoroughly enjoyed getting to know one another much better. I liked almost everything about Candy and was especially impressed by the genuineness of her faith in Christ. We soon went on a second date, which quickly led to dating regularly. I was very excited to introduce Candy to my friends in the Whispering Oaks Commune. As I hoped, she fit in well with everyone, which was a welcomed confirmation that Candy was indeed the Lord's answer to my prayers.

Recently Karen, Susan, and I were reminiscing about the many significant life changes that took place in those years, including my falling for Candy. I told them that I think I knew after our second date that Candy was the girl I had prayed and hoped for. Karen laughed and said, "Well, maybe you didn't know it until then, but we all knew it after the first date. It was written all over your face!" My Commune siblings knew me well, sometimes even better than I knew myself.

Dating Candy was a tremendous boost to my walk with Christ. She was far more advanced than me in her knowledge of the Bible and grounded in spiritual disciplines of study and prayer. She constantly motivated me to seek more biblical knowledge and wisdom, read other books about growing in Christ, and listen to Christian music. It was an exciting time, as I was filled more than ever with the peace and joy of Christ.

Another indirect boost to my spiritual development came from my mom. For too many years, I hid some things in my life from her, which should have blared warning signals to me. But now I was becoming much more of an open book with Mom when we would talk by phone or when I would visit her and my stepdad. She was thrilled to meet and host my friends when I took them to Starkville for ball games or a visit. She had always loved my roommates George and Dan and their families, and now she got to meet and know my other Commune friends. Of course, she adored Jack, as most people did. Mom and Candy hit it off from the start. I didn't realize it then, but this tight community of friends and their effect on me were answers to Mom's many years of praying for me.

Were these major events of 1983 the booster engines of the launching stage of my salvation and life with Christ, or were they the long-delayed second stage of the rocket launched in 1969? I cannot tell you for sure. Jesus said to Nicodemus (and to us), "For God so loved the world, that he gave his only Son, that whoever believes in him should not perish but have eternal life" (John 3:16). He later said, "Truly, truly, I say to you, whoever hears my word and believes him who sent me has eternal life. He does not come into judgment, but has passed from death to life" (John 5:24). As a young boy, I heard, understood, and believed the gospel of Christ, and, at least for a few years, tried to live obediently. Wasn't I saved then? But Jesus also said to Nicodemus, "Truly, truly, I say to you, unless one is born again he cannot see the kingdom of God" (John 3:3), and later said, "Whoever has my commandments and keeps them, he it is who loves me. And he who loves me will be loved by my Father, and I will love him and manifest myself to him" (John 14:21). I certainly had years of blatant disobedience in my life. Does that mean I was not born again as a boy?

Paul's epistles were written to Christian churches, and he often urged them to put off their old worldly ways and put on the ways of Christ. He explicitly named many of the sinful things they were doing and urged them to repent.

> *Do this, knowing the time, that it is already the hour for you to awaken from sleep; for now salvation is nearer to us than when we first believed. The night is almost gone, and the day is near. Therefore let's rid ourselves of the deeds of darkness and put on the armor of light. Let's behave properly as in the day, not in carousing and drunkenness, not in sexual promiscuity and debauchery, not in strife and jealousy. But put on the Lord Jesus Christ, and make no provision for the flesh in regard to its lusts.*
> —Romans 13:11-14 NASB

We would typically associate some of those things only with unbelievers, but Paul said that believers were doing them and must repent, or it would be evidence that they were never saved. Through Paul, God called these early Christians to be changed as they were being sanctified. Martyn-Lloyd Jones once said,

> Sanctification is that which separates us from sin unto God, whereas sin, ultimately, is to forget God. The essence of sin does not reside in the particular thing that I do, but rather in refusing to glorify God as he should be glorified. And all these sinful ac-

tions of ours are the manifestations of that central disease which is forgetfulness of God.[15]

"Forgetfulness of God" seems to be a good description of me during my rebellious years. Does that mean I was not saved until 1983 when I knew for sure my heart had been changed? Or was I on an agonizingly slow road of sanctification? That question haunted me for a long time. In recent years, however, I have come to simply rejoice that for four decades, I have been assured that, by His grace, I am an adopted son of the Most High God. I know that my heart was made alive in Christ, and my soul is inhabited by Him in the form of the Holy Spirit. The Spirit's work in me and through me is evidence that I am truly saved by God's grace through the faith He has graciously given me. I was saved by the completed life, work, and resurrection of Jesus Christ, not by something I did in 1969 or 1983 or anytime between or after. Because God is the Founder and Perfector of my faith, I am completely at peace with God alone knowing the date of my rebirth.

> *Blessed is the one whose transgression is forgiven, whose sin is covered. Blessed is the man against whom the LORD counts no iniquity, and in whose spirit there is no deceit.*
> —Psalm 32:1-2

> *For by grace you have been saved through faith. And this is not your own doing; it is the gift of God, not a result of works, so that no one may boast.*
> —Ephesians 2:8-9

I will never forget how God transformed my life during those Commune years. He providentially and graciously connected me to friends, old and new, in a unique situation during those few years for His glory and my good. I did nothing to deserve, seek, or orchestrate those delightful and meaningful friendships. It was all the grace of God. Grace upon grace upon grace. I will be forever grateful for the life and love we friends shared. The Lord used those "booster rockets" to send me on the best trajectory my life had ever been on and set the course for the rest of my life. I am grateful that the Spirit continued with the imperative work of my sanctification, although more major booster stages have been needed, as the chapters before this one have chronicled. The chapter that follows continues with the theme of sanctification, God's continual renewing and transforming work that makes us more like His Son as He prepares us for our eternal home.

Therefore, since we are surrounded by so great a cloud of witnesses, let us also lay aside every weight, and sin which clings so closely, and let us run with endurance the race that is set before us, looking to Jesus, the founder and perfecter of our faith, who for the joy that was set before him endured the cross, despising the shame, and is seated at the right hand of the throne of God.
—Hebrews 12:1-2

Chapter 19

ALL THINGS NEW

In the beginning, God created the heavens and the earth.
—Genesis 1:1

And he who was seated on the throne said, "Behold, I am making all things new." Also he said, "Write this down, for these words are trustworthy and true."
—Revelation 21:5

From start to finish, we see in Scripture that God creates new things and makes all things new. There is evidence all around us that God is still in the business of making new things and making things new, whether we look up, out, or in.

Let's first look up—up to the new masterpieces God paints with each sunrise and sunset. Look up to the stars at night. Or at least try to. One of the disadvantages of our modern civilization is the "light pollution" many of us have that prevents us from seeing the night sky clearly and the incredible display of God's awesome work. But when we can clearly see the stars at night, oh, how glorious it is! Astronomists estimate there are over one hundred billion stars in our galaxy, the Milky Way—one of the billions of galaxies in the universe—and new stars are formed each year. Yes, God is still declaring His omnipotence and glory in the heavens!

> *The heavens declare the glory of God, and the sky above proclaims his handiwork.*
> *Day to day pours out speech, and night to night reveals knowledge.*
> —Psalm 19:1-2

Now let's look out to where there is an abundance of new works by the Lord. Take a look at crops growing in a field or flowers in a garden, and you'll see amazing examples of new things made and things made new. Plants flower in order to produce new seeds, and seeds are sown to bring new plants. I have always been amazed by seeds. They appear to be hard, lifeless objects, but by the power of the Creator, new life can burst from within them.

> Blessed be the LORD, the God of Israel, who alone does wondrous things. Blessed be his glorious name forever; may the whole earth be filled with his glory! Amen and Amen!
> —Psalm 72:18-19

> And he [Jesus] said, "With what can we compare the kingdom of God, or what parable shall we use for it? It is like a grain of mustard seed, which, when sown on the ground, is the smallest of all the seeds on earth, yet when it is sown it grows up and becomes larger than all the garden plants and puts out large branches, so that the birds of the air can make nests in its shade."
> —Mark 4:30-32

Let's take a look at our own bodies. I am baffled how anyone can deny that we are, as Psalm 139:14 says, "fearfully and wonderfully made" by God. Are you aware of how often cells in the human body are renewed? Different organs are renewed at different rates. Some cells in the stomach replace themselves every two or three days. Taste buds regenerate in ten to fourteen days. Skin cells are replaced every two or three weeks. Other cells take much longer. Of course, the body does not replace entire limbs and other major body parts that are removed, including, unfortunately, the tongue. For existing body parts, however, all the cells in one's body are renewed every seven to ten years. Therefore, God doesn't just fearfully and wonderfully make us; He is constantly remaking us! Yes, our God is definitely in the business of making all things new.

But let's look more closely at that passage from Psalm 139:14: "I praise you, for I am fearfully and wonderfully made. Wonderful are your works; my soul knows it very well." Yes, not only does my mind know of the Lord's new physical works, but my soul knows of it to an even greater extent. By His grace, Christ Jesus brought salvation to my soul for all eternity by living the life I could not before dying the death I deserve. God's ultimate purpose in saving me is to glorify Himself by transforming me into Jesus Christ's image.

And I will give you a new heart, and a new spirit I will put within you. And I will remove the heart of stone from your flesh and give you a heart of flesh. And I will put my Spirit within you, and cause you to walk in my statutes and be careful to obey my rules.
—Ezekiel 36:26-27

I appeal to you therefore, brothers, by the mercies of God, to present your bodies as a living sacrifice, holy and acceptable to God, which is your spiritual worship. Do not be conformed to this world, but be transformed by the renewal of your mind, that by testing you may discern what is the will of God, what is good and acceptable and perfect.
—Romans 12:1-2

In the previous chapter of this book, I wrote about the transformative new things God did in my life during my days as a young bachelor in Memphis. Since then, God has continued His work to renew and transform my soul. He continually works for me, in me, and through me and commands that I live in obedience to Him. His commandments are neither burdensome nor heavy but become my delight as they powerfully teach me truth and lovingly guide me in righteousness. As I read, study, and meditate on the word of God, the Holy Spirit teaches me how to prayerfully seek and rely on God's wisdom and strength, not my own. Too often, I am a very slow and stubborn learner, but God is mercifully patient. He uses His word to renew my mind and the desires of my heart. God's sanctifying power progressively frees me from the power of sin in my life. When I actively and consistently seek a life of righteousness as God commands, I continue to sin, but its grip on me loosens more and more as I am sanctified. Although this process will never be perfected in this life, striving for it brings increasing joy and peace.

Everyone who believes that Jesus is the Christ has been born of God, and everyone who loves the Father loves whoever has been born of him. By this we know that we love the children of God, when we love God and obey his commandments. For this is the love of God, that we keep his commandments. And his commandments are not burdensome.
—1 John 5:1-3

But now that you have been set free from sin and have become slaves of God, the fruit you get leads to sanctification and its end, eternal life.
—Romans 6:22

Yet my sin nature is never fully eradicated on this side of heaven. It still amazes me how easily my attitude sours when I fail to start the day in prayer and Bible study. Have you ever noticed how quickly the leaves on a tree limb wilt when the branch is cut off from the tree? That's what happens to my heart if I don't start my day communing with God. It wilts quickly without the nutrition of a hearty breakfast from God's word and fellowship with Him. In its weakened condition, it is much more vulnerable to temptations. The eyes of my heart are dependent on being refocused each morning by the truth and grace of Scripture; without that sight adjustment, I see people and events differently. I'm not as nice to Candy or anyone else, and I fall into temptations to sin much easier. My sanctification is dependent on the power of the abiding Holy Spirit, but I have to do my part as well. I must choose to seek God throughout each day or deal with the negative consequences in my attitude and behavior.

How can a young man keep his way pure? By guarding it according to your word.
With my whole heart I seek you; let me not wander from your commandments!
I have stored up your word in my heart, that I might not sin against you.
—Psalm 119:9-11

God also providentially uses circumstances to loosen sin's grip and sanctify Christians. Such circumstances are often in the form of hardships, such as affliction, hurtful and harmful relationships, and persecution. The Lord has used His word to effectively grow Candy and me in our faith, but He also has used afflictions and disabilities to transform us. The cancer journey forced us to a critical fork in the road of our sanctification process: we could either blame God for our troubles and trust Him less, or we could draw ever closer to Him with deepening trust and expanding dependence. By His grace, we took the latter path, which has had a transformative effect on our lives, as we have experienced God's renewing power in many ways.

In all this you greatly rejoice, though now for a little while you may have had to suffer grief in all kinds of trials. These have come so that the proven genuineness of your faith—of greater worth than gold, which perishes even though refined by fire—may result in praise, glory and honor when Jesus Christ is revealed.
—1 Peter 1:6-7 (NIV)

God blessed me in ways during and after the turbulent year of 2008 that are difficult to describe fully. The Lord's faithfulness during those first hours in the MD Anderson ICU deepened my faith and strengthened my assurance of salvation as nothing else has. It is hard to conceive of anything else that could have impacted me in such a profound way. God's faithfulness during the radiation treatments drove the pillars of my faith deeper yet. I still shake my head in wonder at how God moved so powerfully in my life during that entire year.

For the moment all discipline seems painful rather than pleasant, but later it yields the peaceful fruit of righteousness to those who have been trained by it.
—Hebrews 12:11

God sweetens outward pain with inward peace. (Thomas Watson)[16]

I welcomed a return to much more normalcy in 2009, although I had to do life differently in many respects. Yet it was evident that much more than my physical body had been changed, for the Lord did a significant work of renewal in my heart and mind as well. I had a greater sense of gratitude and contentment. I was more keenly aware of the many blessings in my life each day. I was more filled with praise of God and had a quicker trigger finger on prayers of thanksgiving throughout each day. My soul was more at peace and more joyful. I found myself to be more patient and empathetic with others. The fuse on my temper was much, much, much longer. I grieved more over my sin. I have no medical evidence to back it up, but it seemed my mind worked a bit differently than before. I was not as sharp in processing technical matters but much more creative. That required me to work harder to do my job at International Paper but opened up many more avenues to creatively use my gift of encouragement. I was still the same person, but in some ways, I felt notably different than I was two years earlier. It seemed God had used my afflictions to fast-forward some of His sanctifying renewal work!

Therefore, my beloved, as you have always obeyed, so now, not only as in my presence but much more in my absence, work out your own salvation with fear and trembling, for it is God who works in you, both to will and to work for his good pleasure.
—Philippians 2:12-13

But the fruit of the Spirit is love, joy, peace, patience, kindness, goodness, faithfulness, gentleness, self-control; against such things there is no law. And those who belong to Christ Jesus have crucified

the flesh with its passions and desires. If we live by the Spirit, let us
also keep in step with the Spirit.
—Galatians 5:22-25

The effect of the Lord's fast-forwarding in 2008 put me on a much more steady and effective path of renewal in the years afterward. There was far more consistency in my pursuit of the Lord's truth and grace in His word, in my application of it, and in my demeanor.

The Lord's cumulative renewal efforts were and continue to be most visible in my marriage to dear Candy. God transformed a good, solid marriage into a wonderfully strong marriage. We both had our hearts softened and our priorities rearranged. Our love and appreciation for one another now seem to grow continuously. God also has expanded my appreciation for genuine friendships as existing relationships have been deepened, and I am more proactive in seeking new friendships. The Lord made me much more sensitive to opportunities to encourage others and more resolved to follow through on those opportunities.

I know, O LORD, that your rules are righteous, and that in faithfulness
you have afflicted me.
—Psalm 119:75

God's transformative work also changed how I go about my day. My morning quiet times with the Lord have become more valued and fruitful. I am more prayerful and more desirous to pray for others. My newfound love of writing led to keeping a daily journal in which I record praises, prayers, specific Bible verses, and lessons learned. I have always been a visual learner. I jokingly say that part of my brain is in my fingertips because writing about something is the best way for me to ponder it deeply and remember it. By starting each morning this way, my heart has become more apt to be worshipful and thankful throughout the day rather than anxious and selfish.

Rejoice in the Lord always; again I will say, rejoice. Let your
reasonableness be known to everyone. The Lord is at hand; do
not be anxious about anything, but in everything by prayer and
supplication with thanksgiving let your requests be made known to
God. And the peace of God, which surpasses all understanding, will
guard your hearts and your minds in Christ Jesus.
—Philippians 4:4-7

By making me more compassionate and thoughtful, the Lord has altered my perspective on my life and surroundings. I am more reflective, prayerful, and creative. I write about many of those observations to help form and sift through my thoughts. Sometimes I feel led to share things I write with others in hopes that it will encourage and benefit them. The chapters that follow are examples of such things.

For we are His workmanship, created in Christ Jesus for good works, which God prepared beforehand, that we should walk in them.
—Ephesians 2:10

And I am sure of this, that he who began a good work in you will bring it to completion at the day of Jesus Christ.
—Philippians 1:6

I am still very much a work in progress. Some days I stumble terribly and am reminded of how much dark and nasty worldliness still needs to be vanquished from my heart. Yet God never ceases to lovingly carry on His renewal work to make me more and more Christ-like all for His glory and my good. I will be forever thankful to the Lord for using my afflictions and disabilities to awaken my soul, spurring me to employ His gifting to encourage others.

But this I call to mind, and therefore I have hope: The steadfast love of the LORD never ceases; His mercies never come to an end; they are new every morning; great is your faithfulness. "The LORD is my portion," says my soul, "therefore I will hope in him."
—Lamentations 3:21-24

The holy life is a walk, a steady progress, a quiet advance, a lasting continuance....Good men always long to be better, and hence they go forward. Good men are never idle, and hence they do not lie down or loiter, but they are still walking onward to their desired end. They are not hurried, and worried, and flurried, and so they keep the even tenor of their way, walking steadily towards heaven; and they are not in perplexity as to how to conduct themselves, for they have a perfect rule, which they are happy to walk by. The law of the Lord is not irksome to them; its commandments are not grievous, and its restrictions are not slavish in their esteem. It does not appear to them to be an impossible law, theoretically admirable but practically absurd, but they walk by it and in it. They do not consult it now and then as a sort of rectifier of their wanderings, but they use it as a chart for their daily sailing, a map of the road for their life-journey. (Charles Haddon Spurgeon)[17]

Lead me in the path of your commandments, for I delight in it.
—Psalm 119:35

Did Christ finish his work for us? Then there can be no doubt, but he will also finish his work in us....And indeed the finishing of his own work of redemption without us, gives full evidence that he will finish his work of sanctification within us; and that because these two works of Christ have a respect and relation to each other; and such a relation, that the work he finished by his own death, resurrection, and ascension, would be in vain to us, if the work of sanctification in us should not in like manner be finished. (John Flavel, 1672)[18]

Chapter 20

RINGING TRUE

"He who has ears to hear, let him hear."
—The words of Jesus in Matthew 11:15

Now we have received not the spirit of the world, but the Spirit who is from God, that we might understand the things freely given us by God.
—1 Corinthians 2:12

I retired from International Paper in 2019 to focus more on my unique health needs, enabling me to be a much more diligent student of God's word, theology, and doctrinal matters. As I did, my knowledge and understanding of some aspects of theology and doctrine were solidified, others were sharpened, some were tweaked, and a few underwent wholesale change. I also became progressively more aware of a sensation that I describe as a "ringing true" in my heart and soul as I heard or read sound doctrine preached or taught that aligned with Scripture. I do not think this phenomenon is simply an emotion I feel but a work of God's grace in my soul.

> *Beloved, do not believe every spirit, but test the spirits to see whether they are from God, for many false prophets have gone out into the world.*
> —1 John 4:1

It is vitally important that my theology and doctrine be based entirely on the word of God, not on how I feel about a particular matter. I must be an assiduous student of the word as the people encountered by Paul and Silas in Berea were.

The brothers immediately sent Paul and Silas away by night to Berea, and when they arrived they went into the Jewish synagogue. Now these Jews were more noble than those in Thessalonica; they received the word with all eagerness, examining the Scriptures daily to see if these things were so. Many of them therefore believed, with not a few Greek women of high standing as well as men.
—Acts 17:10-12

Yet this is not solely a scholastic endeavor. The Holy Spirit plays a crucial role in our understanding of Scripture.

"These things I have spoken to you while I am still with you. But the Helper, the Holy Spirit, whom the Father will send in my name, he will teach you all things and bring to your remembrance all that I have said to you."
—The words of Jesus in John 14:25-26

How does the Holy Spirit accomplish this? I am in no position to explain the mysteries of the thrice holy God, the Creator, Sustainer, and Sovereign Lord over all that has ever been and all that will ever be. But recently, a fairly simple analogy came to mind that helped me to understand a bit better.

Are you familiar with the term *sympathetic resonance?* That's what happens when the vibrations of one object, perhaps a musical instrument or even the human voice, cause another object to vibrate when the two objects are in harmonic likeness. For example, a standard A440 tuning fork—440-hertz frequency for the A note above middle C—at rest will vibrate when a nearby piano or guitar plays that same A note at the same frequency. The tuning fork's ringing is sympathetic resonance. Conversely, when that same tuning fork is struck and an A note of a different frequency is played or voiced, dissonance occurs as the two frequencies clash.

I am not a musician, so I visited with my friend Jim Umlauf to help me better understand the concept of sympathetic resonance. Jim is the minister of worship at Grace Evangelical Church, where Candy and I are members, and is an accomplished musician and outstanding teacher of God's word. He demonstrated sympathetic resonance in action as he tuned one of his acoustic guitars with an A440 tuning fork. After striking the tuning fork on his knee to make it ring, he mounted it on the bridge of the guitar. The immediate effect was that the guitar acted like an amplifier, making the fork's ring much louder. I was intrigued already! Jim then played the untuned A string on his guitar. Because the two frequencies were not in sync, there was an oscillation in the sound waves, or dissonance, in what we heard. As Jim adjusted the string's tuning peg, the oscillating waves slowed as the dissonance lessened. When the string was perfectly tuned, there was no more oscillation, only a single, resonating note. Jim also showed me how he could sing a specific note or play it with a different instrument and cause a guitar mounted on his wall to ring in sympathy. As a musical novice, I was thoroughly fascinated!

Jim also explained other uses for sympathetic resonance in music. Some violins, guitars, and other stringed instruments are constructed with sympathy strings under the fingerboard in addition to the regular strings. As a particular note or chord is strummed or plucked on the regular strings, one or more of the untouched under strings will ring in sympathy, giving the music a much fuller sound. Oh, the things we non-musicians never knew!

Jim and I also discussed my idea of sympathetic resonance as an analogy for the work of the Holy Spirit, who abides and works in the soul of believers in Christ. It is the Spirit who gives us "ears to hear" truth as it is proclaimed in ways that lead to understanding. When Jesus promised the Holy Spirit to His followers, He described Him as "the Spirit of truth."

> "And I will ask the Father, and he will give you another Helper, to be with you forever, even the Spirit of truth, whom the world cannot receive, because it neither sees him nor knows him. You know him, for he dwells with you and will be in you."
> —The words of Jesus in John 14:16-17

When solid theology or doctrine is read or heard, God, in the form of the Spirit of Truth, resonates in the soul of a believer like a tuning fork with no oscillation of sound waves. That is the internal feeling I describe as "ringing true." This work of the Holy Spirit gives me "eyes to see and ears to hear" the truth of God's word in an understandable way.

> Deal bountifully with your servant, that I may live and keep your word.
> Open my eyes, that I may behold wondrous things out of your law.
> —Psalm 119:17-18

> "But when the Helper comes, whom I will send to you from the Father, the Spirit of truth, who proceeds from the Father, he will bear witness about me."
> —The words of Jesus in John 15:26

What a joy it is to experience God the Holy Spirit consistently resonating within me during times of private and corporate worship. His resonance brings joy and confidence while reading some of my favorite authors and Bible commentators, such as Thomas Watson, Matthew Henry, Charles Spurgeon, and Martyn Lloyd-Jones, as their words ring clearly of truth in my soul.

Conversely, when I hear or read unsound doctrine, I feel dissonance in my soul. I have often felt this dissonance, even though I can't put my finger on precisely what was out of alignment with God's word. The dissonance serves as a red flag, a warning that I should further investigate the information and claims being presented. Repeated dissonance is often a signal to take corrective action or perhaps steer clear of the source in the future.

Lastly, sometimes there is neither resonance nor dissonance. If a worship song contains neither solid biblical truths nor clear untruths, it will not resonate in my soul, even if the music is beautiful. Even if I emotionally respond to the music, my soul will have an empty response. Likewise, a sermon may be entertaining or emotionally uplifting, but if it is void of doctrine, there will be no response by the Holy Spirit.

The sympathetic resonance analogy also applies to my thoughts, words, or actions, which can cause dissonance within my soul if they conflict with the truth of God's word. Since I am a believer and therefore have the Holy Spirit abiding in me, sin will invoke a feeling of oscillation in my soul, just as Jim and I heard oscillating sound waves from the tuning fork and out-of-tune guitar. The biblical expression for that is being "out of step" with the Holy Spirit. Getting back in step with the Spirit and halting the oscillation requires recognizing my sin, repenting, seeking the Lord's forgiveness, and making a course correction.

> *If we say we have no sin, we deceive ourselves, and the truth is not in us. If we confess our sins, he is faithful and just to forgive us our sins and to cleanse us from all unrighteousness.*
> —1 John 1:8-9

> The more a man prizes holiness and the more earnestly he strives after it, the more will he be driven towards God for help therein, for he will plainly perceive that his own strength is insufficient, and that he cannot even so much as live without the bounteous assistance of the Lord his God. (Charles Haddon Spurgeon)[19]

I must learn, however, how to distinguish between emotions generated within my mind and resonance or dissonance generated by the Holy Spirit in my soul. I must recognize the difference between genuine joy and mere giddiness and between God-sent conviction and emotional remorse. Doing so comes by deepening my relationship with the Holy Spirit through diligent and consistent pursuit of truth in God's word. Everything must be weighed against Scripture. It helps tremendously to surround myself with trusted, wise, knowledgeable, and well-equipped preachers, teachers, mentors, and siblings in Christ. These saints help me study and understand God's word, identify truth from error, and untangle emotions from reality. I need such people to point out the blind spots I have.

> *"When the Spirit of truth comes, he will guide you into all the truth, for he will not speak on his own authority, but whatever he hears he will speak, and he will declare to you the things that are to come. He will glorify me, for he will take what is mine and declare it to you."*
> —The words of Jesus in John 16:13-14

Similarly, Christians often "resonate" with one another in fellowship and service. The Holy Spirit is at work as I fellowship, study, and pray with other "Bereans," genuine Christ-followers who seek, know, and practice sound doctrine. I believe God uses the "ringing true" sensation to connect Christ-followers with one another in meaningful and pleasant friendships. This resonance with others is also essential to steadily strengthen our bond in Christ as we serve together. Just as violas, violins, or guitars equipped with sympathy strings have a fuller, richer sound, our service to Christ is more fruitful when we work in unison with other believers. May the Holy Spirit always resonate among us as we worship and serve together for the glory of God!

> *Only let your manner of life be worthy of the gospel of Christ, so that whether I come and see you or am absent, I may hear of you that you are standing firm in one spirit, with one mind striving side by side for the faith of the gospel.*
> —Philippians 1:27

Chapter 21

MY MORNING COFFEE

The LORD is my chosen portion and my cup; you hold my lot.
—Psalm 16:5

Like most people I know, I start my day with a cup of piping hot, delicious coffee to get me going. My coffee is different than the coffee my neighbor drinks, but it also has a lot of similarities. Like his coffee, mine jumpstarts my brain and awakens my senses to help me prepare to take on the day. Like his, mine takes some preparation and planning, but over the years, my neighbor and I have developed efficient routines so that a great cup of morning coffee greets each of us soon after waking. My neighbor's coffee and mine are both beneficial to the health of our hearts. Like my neighbor, I deliberately drink my coffee slowly, savoring its captivating aroma and energizing taste. It is indeed a delicious, invigorating start to our day and has become a morning essential for both of us. Like my neighbor, I have become somewhat of a connoisseur of great coffee and studied the intricacies and nuances of the many types of coffee. I have developed strong preferences for some over others, but the truth is I've never had a bad cup because all coffee is useful for starting my day. Like my neighbor, I have also developed close ties to some favorite coffee shops over the years and forged friendly relationships with other regular patrons and favorite baristas.

Yet there are some clear differences between my neighbor's coffee and mine. His coffee comes from beans; my coffee proceeds from the mouth of God. His is processed through a grinder and coffee brewer; mine was spoken through King David, Asaph, sons of Korah, and other writers, was translated into English in the sixteenth century, and is found in the middle of my Bible.

His coffee loses its appeal when it gets cold and stale; mine never loses its freshness or flavor. His coffee has a definitive shelf life; mine is eternal. His is colloquially referred to as "a cup of joe"; mine is called "The Psalms."

What has made the Psalms my top of the morning essential for thirty years? The Psalms are the first-person cries of the psalmists to God—cries of praise, thanksgiving, anguish, frustration, weariness, and righteous anger. They are so prayerful in nature that they immediately set my heart and mind into a mode of prayer. The Psalms are words of God given to me to be prayerfully spoken or sung back to Him. They set the course of my mind on the Lord rather than on myself, my responsibilities and activities, or the news of the day. Those things are not unimportant but are secondary to this highest priority. The Psalms set my heart on praising God and thanking God first rather than immediately lifting my petitions of the day. After my heart has been seeped in the praise and gratitude of the Psalms, my petitions often have a different flavor. The Psalms always seem to capture my current emotions—my joys, my sorrows, my complaints, my thrills, my frustrations—and put them in a right or at least better perspective. The book of Psalms is my beautiful morning sunrise, even on the cloudiest of days.

I not only find God in the Psalms—I find myself. I find God's blessings in my life, and I find my sins. I find God's desires, and I find my shortcomings. I find my history and my future. I find my thoughts and feelings expressed in righteous ways that are pleasing to God. The Psalms draw praises, confessions, and desires out of me that I didn't have before I opened my Bible that morning. They lead me to write out the cries of my heart in my morning journal, and that task takes me even deeper into meditating on the word. Intercessional requests for others are almost always brought to mind as I read, and I use God's own words to pray to Him on behalf of friends and family. After the Psalms have enlivened my heart and mind, my appetite is whetted for more nourishment from other parts of God's word. The Psalms never change the events of the day that await me, but they never fail to change my perspective on them.

My neighbor has some excellent flavors and styles of coffee, but I am more than content to stick with mine. My neighbor is also my friend, and he cares about me. He wishes I could drink coffee each morning as he does. But oh, how much more do I wish that he would know the glorious wonder of the coffee I drink and know its Maker. May the Lord provide me opportunities this day to share a cup with my neighbor.

Awake, my glory! Awake, O harp and lyre! I will awake the dawn!
—Psalm 57:8

"Awake my glory," that is, my tongue (our tongue is our glory, and never more so than when it is employed in praising God), or my soul, that must be first awakened; dull and sleepy devotions will never be acceptable to God. We must stir up ourselves, and all that is within us, to praise God. (Matthew Henry ~1706)[20]

In my case, Pastor Henry's comments would apply to my new tongue, my writing, as I prayerfully write early morning praises to God in my journal.

I rise before dawn and cry for help; I hope in your words.
—Psalm 119:147

Sing praises to the LORD, O you his saints, and give thanks to his holy name.
For his anger is but for a moment, and his favor is for a lifetime.
Weeping may tarry for the night, but joy comes with the morning.
—Psalm 30:4-5

Satisfy us in the morning with your steadfast love, that we may rejoice and be glad all our days.
—Psalm 90:14

The LORD is near to all who call on him, to all who call on him in truth.
—Psalm 145:18

But for me it is good to be near God;
I have made the Lord GOD my refuge, that I may tell of all your works.
—Psalm 73:28

Your word is a lamp to my feet and a light to my path.
—Psalm 119:105

O God, you are my God; earnestly I seek you; my soul thirsts for you; my flesh faints for you, as in a dry and weary land where there is no water.
So I have looked upon you in the sanctuary, beholding your power and glory.
—Psalm 63:1-3

This book is filled with dozens of other Scripture references to Psalms. I pray they will stir you to become a connoisseur of the Psalms also!

Chapter 22

TRUST YOU YET MORE

Let me hear in the morning of your steadfast love,
for in you I trust.
Make me know the way I should go,
for to you I lift up my soul.
—Psalm 143:8

One of my favorite books is *The Treasury of David* by Charles Spurgeon. It is his personal commentary on all one hundred fifty psalms and also includes the insights of other notable theologians and pastors from the seventeenth, eighteenth, and nineteenth centuries. Spurgeon gradually released these commentaries in his monthly magazine, *The Sword and the Trowel,* as he completed work on batches of psalms. He released the first batch in 1865 and the final one in 1888. The completed work, originally released as a seven-volume set, is available today in three volumes. Those three volumes are among my most treasured possessions. The Lord uses Pastor Spurgeon's decades-long diligence to bless me more days than not, as I often refer to it as I begin my day in the Psalms.

On a spring morning a few years ago, my "morning coffee" consisted of a favorite, Psalm 145:

> *David's Psalm of praise.*
> *I will extol thee, my God, O king; and I will bless thy name for ever and ever.*
> *Every day will I bless thee; and I will praise thy name for ever and ever.*
> —Psalm 145:1-2 Authorized KJV

After reading and praying through all twenty-one verses, I turned to Pastor Spurgeon's insights.

> DAVID'S PSALM OF PRAISE. It is David's, David's very own, David's favourite. It is David's Praise just as another (Psalm 86:1-17) is David's Prayer. It is altogether praise, and praise pitched in a high key. David had blessed God many a time in other psalms, but this he regarded as his peculiar, his crown jewel of praise. Certainly David's praise is the best of praise, for it is that of a man of experience, of sincerity, of calm deliberation, and of intense warmth of the heart. It is not for any one of us to render David's praise, for David only could do that, but we may take David's psalm as a model, and aim at making our own personal adoration as much, like it as possible: we shall be long before we equal our model. Let each Christian reader present his own praise unto the Lord, and call it by his own name. What a wealth of varied praise will thus be presented through Christ Jesus![21]

I took Pastor Spurgeon's words as a challenge to try to write my own psalm of praise. Even though I love to write, I rarely try my hand at poetry, so I knew the task would not be easy. Yet I found the labor sweet, as it caused me to focus deeply on God's attributes and blessings and rely on the leading of the Holy Spirit to put my thoughts on paper clearly and somewhat poetically.

The finished product was a three-stanza poem with the same two-line refrain after each: "I trust You, O Lord, with all that I am this morn; when next the sun rises, may I trust You yet more." If I fully trust the Lord this morning, the only way I can trust Him more tomorrow morning is by my trust growing today. If I fear God rightly, get to know Him better through His word and prayer, and exercise my faith muscles by fully trusting Him in all situations, God is faithful to strengthen my soul, enlarge my heart, and increase my knowledge and faith in Him. The better I know God today, the more I trust Him tomorrow.

On the day I called, You answered me; my strength of soul You increased.
—Psalm 138:3

I will run in the way of Your commandments when You enlarge my heart!
—Psalm 119:32

And we know that the Son of God has come and has given us understanding, so that we may know Him who is true; and we are

in Him who is true, in His Son Jesus Christ. He is the true God and eternal life.
—1 John 5:20

So let's learn, let's press on to know the LORD. His appearance is as sure as the dawn;
And He will come to us like the rain, as the spring rain waters the earth.
—Hosea 6:3 NASB

I shared my completed psalm with a few friends, one of which was Tony Edwards, a godly man, a gifted musician, and a guy who has a habit of taking something and making it better. Tony felt inspired to write and record a song, "Trust You Yet More," based on my psalm, and received help from another excellent musician, Carl Casperson. Tony was gracious enough to sing the song, along with "You Never Let Go," at my "5,000 Amazing Days of Grace" celebration in March 2022.

My Morning Psalm of Praise

I praise You, Father God, on this new day dawning;
it's Your presence, Lord, my hungry soul is wanting.
I run to You and Your word with great joy and haste,
for it is Your goodness that I desire to taste.
Before You alone this morning I humbly bow,
You alone to whom I eagerly listen now.
For You are perfectly holy, perfectly just;
in You is life and without You I am but dust.

I trust You, O Lord, with all that I am this morn;
when next the sun rises, may I trust You yet more.

You are indeed the Almighty God on High,
yet delight to hear my every plea and sigh.
Thank You, Good Father, for choosing me as Your own,
for redeeming me and never leaving me alone.
Thank You, Lord, for my every heartbeat and breath,
thank You for living my life and dying my death.
You alone, Holy God, will I worship and fear,
You above all, O Lord, I adore and revere.

I trust You, O Lord, with all that I am this morn;
when next the sun rises, may I trust You yet more.

All good works on earth spring from Your gracious hand;
please use me to serve You, Lord, and my fellow man.
May my words and actions magnify Your great name,
flowing from a repentant heart that does the same.
Please fill my soul with Your truth and grace so dear,
and spill over from me and bless all who are near.
Help me, O Lord, to faithfully trust and obey,
to reflect the reign of Christ in my life today.

I trust You, O Lord, with all that I am this morn;
when next the sun rises, may I trust You yet more.

—*John Barton, May 4, 2019*

I'm not much of a poet yet, but it was a meaningful exercise. How about you? What words of adoration, praise, and thanksgiving would be included in your psalm? How would writing original thoughts of praise, either as prose or poetry, to start your morning impact your outlook on the day? How can you glorify the Lord today with the gifts and talents He has given you?

Chapter 23

GOD'S TWO BOOKS

Come and see what God has done:
he is awesome in his deeds toward the children of man.
—Psalm 66:5

W hen Candy and I go on vacation, we usually head to a national or
state park. We love seeing God's beautiful creation displayed in
majestic mountains, rolling hills, mighty waterfalls, and vast oceans. We feel
a closeness to our Creator when we explore beautiful mountain meadows,
gentle streams, and sandy or rocky beaches. We marvel at His handiwork
when we see colorful canyons, mysterious caves, spewing geysers, and wildlife
in their natural habitat. So far, we have visited and thoroughly enjoyed
fourteen national parks and numerous state parks.

When we are not on vacation, we are active sky-watchers, reveling
in any opportunity to gaze upon beautiful sunrises, sunsets, rainbows, full
moons, and as many stars as our suburban life allows. Even a trip a few steps
from our front door reveals beautiful flowers whose anatomy amazes me;
they look so fragile yet are tough enough to survive a thunderstorm. The
beauty of God's creation surrounds us, but we can take it for granted or get
so wrapped up in the cares of the world that we pay it little attention.

Candy and I marvel at God's artistic creativity. We are awed by the way
He displays His unmatched beauty and sovereignty in nature. How can we gaze
at the Rocky Mountains or the Grand Tetons and not see their proclamation
of their Creator's majesty? How can we not be mesmerized by God's artistry in
the Grand Canyon? How can I see mighty waterfalls in Tennessee state parks
and not get a sense of God's power? How can anyone witness a hurricane,

a tornado, or even a thunderstorm and not feel the vast superiority of our Maker? How can people get these incredible glimpses of God's character and not become curious to know more? Psalm 19 describes how God uses His creation to reveal certain things about Himself and His character.

The heavens declare the glory of God, and the sky above proclaims his handiwork.
Day to day pours out speech, and night to night reveals knowledge.
There is no speech, nor are there words, whose voice is not heard.
Their voice goes out through all the earth, and their words to the end of the world.
—Psalm 19:1-4a

Yes, even though nature does not use words, it "speaks" eloquently through its grandeur, intricacy, and power. Nature does not proclaim its own glory but God's glory. Theologians refer to this as God's "general revelation."

Continuing the theme of general revelation of nature, the psalmist then describes the daily journey of the sun. Of course, we know it is Earth, not the sun, that does the journeying, but the psalmist is speaking from the vantage point of how it looks to us:

In them [the heavens] he [God] has set a tent for the sun,
which comes out like a bridegroom leaving his chamber,
and, like a strong man, runs its course with joy.
Its rising is from the end of the heavens, and its circuit to the end of them,
and there is nothing hidden from its heat.
—Psalm 19:4b-6

There can be no life on Earth without the sun. It is a daily reminder that the Giver of all life is He who created and maintains the star of the solar system. Its glorious repetitive warmth and light speak to us of the glory, life-giving power, regenerative faithfulness, and steadfast love of the Lord.

No other creature yields such joy to the earth as her bridegroom the sun; and none, whether they be horse or eagle, can for an instant compare in swiftness with that heavenly champion. But all his glory is but the glory of God; even the sun shines in light borrowed from the Great Father of Lights. (Charles Haddon Spurgeon)[22]

Psalm 139:14 tells us that our human bodies are "fearfully and wonderfully made." I contend that can be said of Earth as well. God placed our planet ninety-three million miles from the sun (with a variation of a million and a half because of our elliptical orbit), precisely the distance range for life to exist: not too hot, not too cold. He tilted the axis of Earth 23.5 degrees, the precise angle needed to provide seasons but not unlivable extremes that other planets have. He gave us a single beautiful night light, the moon, and positioned it at just the precise distance, close enough to provide ocean tides but not so close as to cause constant tidal flooding. He provided the precise chemicals needed for life to be sustained and the mechanisms for these chemicals to be maintained in proper balance.

It was not necessary for life, but God graciously chose to make our planet grandly beautiful, with a kaleidoscopic array of stunning colors and an assortment of disparate landscapes. In the 1960s, satellites began to photograph portions of Earth from space for the first time, displaying how beautiful it is from above. In 1972, the crew of Apollo 17 took the first photo of our entire planet from eighteen thousand miles away. The iconic *Blue Marble* photograph became an instant hit worldwide. It was a stunning display of God's handiwork.

Yet beauty is also found in the most petite flowers, as well as in a vast array of mammals, birds, fish, reptiles, amphibians, and insects. By God's grace, beauty is also found in those He chose to make in His own image: people. Our gracious and good God chose to give us a beautiful planet to reflect His beauty and majesty and, through this "general revelation," invites us to know Him better.

The Holy Spirit inspired Paul to write about the clarity of general revelation in his letter to the Romans:

> *For the wrath of God is revealed from heaven against all ungodliness and unrighteousness of men, who by their unrighteousness suppress the truth. For what can be known about God is plain to them, because God has shown it to them. For his invisible attributes, namely, his eternal power and divine nature, have been clearly perceived, ever since the creation of the world, in the things that have been made. So they are without excuse.*
> —Romans 1:18-20

And yet Paul's letter to the Romans goes on to say that some people see these things but still deny the sovereignty of God over their lives. Such is the power of our sinful nature.

> *For although they knew God, they did not honor him as God or give thanks to him, but they became futile in their thinking, and their*

foolish hearts were darkened. Claiming to be wise, they became fools,
and exchanged the glory of the immortal God for images resembling
mortal man and birds and animals and creeping things.
—Romans 1:21-23

All nature, all the time, shouts out the existence, power, and splendor of God. Sinners can close their eyes and stop their ears, but general revelation remains plain all around them. Only when the unrighteous actively suppress this plain truth can the testimony of general revelation be denied. (Dr. Robert Godfrey)[23]

Oh, that I may never be so blind that I fail to see the beauty and majesty of God's glory all around me!

All God's works do praise him, as the beautiful building praises the builder or the well-drawn picture praises the painter; but. . . . of all God's works, his saints, the workmanship of his grace, the first-fruits of his creatures, have most reason to bless him. (Matthew Henry)[24]

As we return to Psalm 19, David, the psalmist, suddenly makes what seems an abrupt twist as he turns from describing nature to characterizing God's holy word.

The law of the LORD is perfect, reviving the soul;
the testimony of the LORD is sure, making wise the simple;
the precepts of the LORD are right, rejoicing the heart;
the commandment of the LORD is pure, enlightening the eyes;
the fear of the LORD is clean, enduring forever;
the rules of the LORD are true, and righteous altogether.
More to be desired are they than gold, even much fine gold;
sweeter also than honey and drippings of the honeycomb.
—Psalm 19:7-10

While at first glance it may appear that the psalmist is mixing two different topics into a single psalm, these four verses continue the theme of God's revelation about Himself to man but at a much deeper level. We see and get to know our Creator in His holy Scripture. Theologians refer to this as "special revelation." After beautifully describing the attributes of the word, which reflect the attributes of God, David uses verse 11 to state the purpose of special revelation: to conform us to be more and more repentant, holy, righteous, wise, worshipful, and acceptable to God.

Moreover, by them is your servant warned; in keeping them there is great reward.
—Psalm 19:11

In the three verses that follow, David, having been introduced to God through nature and engaged in close relationship through Scripture, then prays in response. He asks for the Lord's strength and grace to help him obey that Scripture and please God. How can I not respond in the same manner?

Who can discern his errors? Declare me innocent from hidden faults.
Keep back your servant also from presumptuous sins; let them not have dominion over me!
Then I shall be blameless, and innocent of great transgression.
Let the words of my mouth and the meditation of my heart be acceptable in your sight,
O LORD, my rock and my redeemer.
—Psalm 19:12-14

I think of these two books, nature and the Bible, as a book of introduction and a book of insights. The former is like the Lord's beautiful front lawn and inviting front porch, the latter like His personal parsonage. From the former, He beckons us to enter the latter, to commune with Him in His warm parlor, expansive study, bountiful dining room, and soul-stirring music studio. Visits to each draw us to the adjoining chapel, where we cannot help but bless our Host, Creator, and Redeemer. To bless God means to praise Him with personal affection and gratitude, and both books evoke such a response.

All your works shall give thanks to you, O LORD, and all your saints shall bless you!
They shall speak of the glory of your kingdom and tell of your power,
to make known to the children of man your mighty deeds, and the glorious splendor of your kingdom.
—Psalm 145:10-12

One of my great joys is to occasionally enjoy God's books simultaneously. How inspiring it is to have my morning quiet time with my Bible in my lap with the mountains, ocean waves, or a beautiful lake immediately before me. Nature provides inspiring background music as I listen to God's voice through His written word: God's two marvelous books in stereo!

Yet I don't have to travel from my suburban Collierville home to dial in to God's first book, for it is all around us every day in the skies, trees, and gardens. I usually have my morning time of prayer and Bible study in a room with limited sight lines of the sky, but some days I go upstairs, where I have a much broader vista. From there, I have a much clearer view of the eastern sky, where each day is a unique display of beautiful and colorful skies that constantly change as the rising sun approaches, finally breaks, and begins to rise above the horizon. The most colorful days are those with just enough clouds to reflect the rising sun's rays but are not too low or too thick to block my view of the eastern horizon. The clouds of varying shapes, sizes, densities, and heights reflect the sun with different colors and hues, making for stunning morning masterpieces. These "first book" soundtracks are incredibly inspiring as I dive into God's "second book."

> *From the rising of the sun to its setting, the name of the LORD is to be praised!*
> —Psalm 113:3

> *Light dawns in the darkness for the upright; He is gracious, merciful, and righteous.*
> —Psalm 112:4

> *How lovely is your dwelling place, O LORD of hosts!*
> *My soul longs, yes, faints for the courts of the LORD;*
> *my heart and flesh sing for joy to the living God.*
> —Psalm 84:1-2

These two great books of God have been critically important to Candy and me since our courtship began nearly forty years ago. We love to see, hear, and read God's majesty, glory, power, and beauty in His general book, His beautiful creation. We pray that this beauty will always lead us to desire to know God better and draw us to His remarkable book, His holy word. And we pray that His word will always lead us to more praise of His creation. Oh, that we may continue to be worthy students of both books!

> True understanding of doctrine should always lead to adoration, to praise, and to utter humbling ourselves in wonder before God. (Martyn Lloyd-Jones)[25]

Like David the psalmist, Candy and I pray for strength, wisdom, and grace to live out what we learn in ways that are pleasing and acceptable to God. We pray that our love for the Lord will continuously grow, uniting our hearts to fear His name and serve Him well. We pray that as we have traveled as a family to many beautiful places, we have done an effective job as parents in teaching our children the priceless value of these two God-given volumes.

> *Teach me your way, O LORD, that I may walk in your truth; unite my heart to fear your name.*
> *I give thanks to you, O LORD my God, with my whole heart, and I will glorify your name forever.*
> —Psalm 86:11-12

> *Great are the works of the LORD; they are pondered by all who delight in them.*
> *Glorious and majestic are his deeds, and his righteousness endures forever.*
> *He has caused his wonders to be remembered; the LORD is gracious and compassionate.*
> —Psalm 111:2-4 NIV

Chapter 24

FERTILE SOIL, FRUITFUL HARVEST

Keep your heart with all vigilance,
for from it flow the springs of life.
—Proverbs 4:23

S everal years ago, I asked a local businessman about the construction of their new facility, which seemed to be behind schedule. He explained that the project was delayed and had become much more expensive than planned because of the poor quality of the soil at the construction site. After engineers determined the soil was unsuitable for construction, the company spent millions of dollars removing the old soil and trucking in higher-quality soil. The initially planned completion date for the summer of that year was delayed for at least six months and possibly longer.

That conversation brought to mind the parable of the sower, the soil, and the seed.

That same day Jesus went out of the house and sat beside the sea. And great crowds gathered about him, so that he got into a boat and sat down. And the whole crowd stood on the beach. And he told them many things in parables, saying: "A sower went out to sow. And as he sowed, some seeds fell along the path, and the birds came and devoured them. Other seeds fell on rocky ground, where they did not have much soil, and immediately they sprang up, since they had no depth of soil, but when the sun rose they were scorched. And since

they had no root, they withered away. Other seeds fell among thorns,
and the thorns grew up and choked them. Other seeds fell on good
soil and produced grain, some a hundredfold, some sixty, some thirty.
He who has ears, let him hear."
—Matthew 13:1-9

The seed is the word of God. The sower is the one preaching and teaching the word. The soil is the heart of those who hear the word preached and taught. Jesus explains that there are four different categories of hearts: those with hard hearts (the beaten soil on the path), where the word cannot penetrate at all; those with shallow hearts (the rocky ground), where the word sprouts with emotion at first but fails to grow; those with crowded hearts (the thorny ground) that try to fit in the word along with the worldliness that they continue to grasp and which eventually chokes out any good growth; and the fertile, teachable hearts (the good soil), where the word takes firm root, sprouts, grows, and is evidenced by a spiritually fruitful life that glorifies God.

So who is responsible for the hardness or fertility of our hearts? That question can lead to some fiery theological debates, and I hope not to light the match. For help in this subject, I turned to the book of Exodus and the story of God freeing His people from slavery in Egypt. I found three times when the word says that Pharaoh hardened his own heart. Ten times it says God hardened Pharaoh's heart, and six times it simply says Pharaoh's heart "was hardened," without clearly identifying the one doing the hardening. The explanation that makes sense to me is that Pharaoh was responsible for the hardness of his heart, just as I am responsible for mine. God did not intervene to prevent Pharaoh from hardening his own heart, thereby following through with His statement to Moses that He would harden Pharaoh's heart.

My heart was as hard as Pharaoh's at one time. It was so hard and dead that God's word describes it as "a heart of stone." But God, by His grace, intervened to give me a new heart, one with life, one with good, fertile soil, one that is firm yet soft, pliable, moldable, and receptive to God's word. Had God not done that, I would not even be alive to tell this story, for I am thoroughly convinced that I would have succumbed to cancer had I battled it without Christ. Yet my heart is still in the process of being changed to the way God ultimately wants it to be. He gives me perfect instructions on how to care for it, yet I am not perfect at following them. God sovereignly chose to give me new life in Christ and a new heart, and I am responsible for seeking His power and wisdom to maintain my heart in good condition.

And I will give you a new heart, and a new spirit I will put within you. And I will remove the heart of stone from your flesh and give you a heart of flesh.
—Ezekiel 36:26

You may or may not fully agree with all I wrote in the previous two paragraphs, but I hope you will agree that we bear the responsibility of being good managers of the good soil God has put in our hearts. To get some ideas on how to do that, I asked my friend Collins Hewes for help. Collins spent his youth on a farm in south Mississippi, his adult working career in agricultural management of farmland throughout the south, and now spends his retirement days doing one of the things he loves best: working with soil to make it fertile and useful. The man knows what he's talking about! Collins graciously gave me the following list of a dozen tips for managing good soil for agriculture:

1. Select a good site and make sure the drainage is adequate.
2. Till the soil.
3. Plant good seed at the proper depth (select a good variety).
4. Add the right amount of fertilizer and nutrients.
5. Provide water by irrigation if rain is inadequate (but not too much water!).
6. Control the growth and spread of weeds.
7. Protect from insects and diseases.
8. Pray a lot.
9. Harvest in a timely manner.
10. Praise God for a good (or not-so-good) harvest.
11. Till for next year's planting.
12. Repeat next year.

That list could easily turn into a twelve-week sermon series, but I will keep my list of practical application points simple. The goal of good management of farm soil is to have consistently good crops. The goal of maintaining good soil in my heart is to be a fruitful man who is in Christ, consistently walks with Christ, lives for Christ, loves the word of Christ, and shares the good news about Christ with others, all for the glory of Christ.

Blessed is the man who walks not in the counsel of the wicked,
Nor stands in the way of sinners, nor sits in the seat of scoffers;

but his delight is in the law of the LORD, and on his law he meditates day and night.
He is like a tree planted by streams of water that yields its fruit in its season,
and its leaf does not wither. In all that he does, he prospers.
The wicked are not so, but are like chaff that the wind drives away.
—Psalm 1:1-4

Select a good site and make sure the drainage is adequate: I must put myself in a position for God's word to penetrate my heart. Spending time in the word must be a daily priority. I must surround myself with godly people in a church where the word of God is clearly and boldly proclaimed and sound doctrine is taught, implanted, and nourished. I must establish strong fellowship with other believers to facilitate my spiritual maturity.

Till the soil: A fertile heart is an active heart, always remaining teachable and not content to limit myself to the knowledge I have now. A fertile heart is one that not only learns but is active in applying and sharing what I learn in ways that stretch and grow me.

Plant good seed at the proper depth (select a good variety): I must deeply study and meditate on God's word. I must be wise to seek out and learn from more than one trusted source for assistance in understanding the Bible. I can't be satisfied with only a few minutes of reading a verse or two, just enough to check the box for today. On the other hand, I can't get so buried in the academic study of the word that I never take time to live it out and share it with others.

Add the right amount of fertilizer and nutrients; provide water by irrigation if rain is inadequate (but not too much water!): I love reading good commentaries on the word, as I find them very helpful in facilitating my understanding. Certain podcasts or recorded teachings can be helpful also. On the other hand, I must not put myself in a position of learning primarily from those writers, speakers, and teachers rather than directly from the word of God by the power of the Holy Spirit.

Control the growth and spread of weeds: Oh, how important it is not to let worldliness or the cares of this world crowd out or infringe on my love of and reliance on the word of God! I must be in the world, for now, but never of the world. Being surrounded by genuine friends who love me enough to hold me accountable is a needed boost to controlling worldly weeds.

Protect from insects and diseases: I must be ever aware that the enemy is always lurking about, tempting me with "not so bad" or "mostly good" things that distract me from the word of God and a godly life. I must be sensitive to detect any sign of bitterness, jealousy, contempt, or envy that grows within me. Again, friendships with godly people can help me see my blind spots so I can be vigilant to protect myself from these joy-robbing, ministry-retarding enemies of spiritual growth and contentment.

Pray a lot: There is nothing more important than steadfast prayer. I can do nothing on my own without the power and wisdom of the Lord at work. I can never forget that God is sovereign over the hardness or fertility of my heart. All that I do must be covered and immersed in prayer.

Harvest in a timely manner: Godly living is not all input and no output. I am commanded to be fruitful in ministering to others and in sharing the gospel of Jesus with those the Lord puts in my path. It is wise to periodically take an inventory of my fruitfulness. Am I pursuing holiness and righteousness in my everyday life? Am I using my spiritual gifts for God's glory and the good of others? Am I making a difference in the lives of others? Is someone other than me benefiting from my spiritual growth?

Praise God for a good (or not-so-good) harvest: My praise of our immutable God must be based on who He is, not on how satisfied I am with my life at the present time. I thank Him for all He graciously provides, for I deserve nothing. I should have a worshipful and grateful spirit in plentiful times and in lean times. I must trust God to provide and never let go of the assured hope He provides.

Till for next year's planting; repeat next year: The Christian walk is not something we do for a few years and then take off for a while. I need to be forward-thinking to maintain the good soil of my heart on an ongoing basis. The godly, fruitful life designed by God in His word doesn't include a retirement plan.

> *The righteous flourish like the palm tree and grow like a cedar in Lebanon.*
> *They are planted in the house of the LORD; they flourish in the courts of our God.*
> *They still bear fruit in old age; they are ever full of sap and green,*
> *to declare that the LORD is upright; he is my rock, and there is no unrighteousness in him.*
> —Psalm 92:12-15

The business mentioned at the start of this story spent incredible amounts of time and money to get suitable soil upon which to build. Collins testifies that agricultural soil management is usually costly and time-consuming as well. Like the businessman, farmers pray their investment in good soil will be well worth the toil and expense when crops and revenues come rolling in. We Christians have a distinct advantage over these from whom I have drawn these analogies: our usefulness in God's kingdom work is assured if we stay diligent in maintaining healthy hearts, even when we don't immediately see results. The business person and farmer are dependent on market demand and prices to determine if they make or lose money. Conversely, the joy of drawing ever closer to Christ through our heart maintenance efforts brings eternal spiritual wealth in abundance, blessings of fruit of the Spirit, and contentment that defies our circumstances.

> *But the fruit of the Spirit is love, joy, peace, patience, kindness, goodness, faithfulness, gentleness, self-control; against such things there is no law.*
> —Galatians 5:22-23

"O Lord, I pray that by Your wisdom, strength, and grace, I will increasingly be a better soil manager and live an ever more fruitful life for Your glory."

Chapter 25

TRUE COLORS

The grass withers, the flower fades,
but the word of our God will stand forever.
—Isaiah 40:8

D on't you just love the colors of autumn? One of the things people enjoy most about fall is the changing leaf colors in trees.

I am no botanist, but my understanding is that the change in the leaves is primarily due to the decrease in hours of sunlight. As the days grow shorter, the production of chlorophyll slows and eventually stops. Chlorophyll, the pigment that makes leaves appear green, is constantly produced by most plants in the spring and summer months. As chlorophyll production ceases, the green coloring fades from the leaves. What remains are the colors that have been in the leaves all along but have been covered by the green from the chlorophyll. The leaves have various combinations of yellow pigments called xanthophylls, orange pigments called carotenoids, and red and purple pigments called anthocyanins. These pigments have been masked most of the year by the abundance of chlorophyll.

I am reminded of these scientific facts each autumn as I admire the spectacular array of colors displayed by various types of trees. As I thank the Lord for creating such beauty, I am reminded that the colors have been there all along but are only now revealed. Some trees have leaves of brilliant yellow; others are magnificent orange, stunning red, or majestic purple. Other trees are more nondescript, as their shades of brown are quite dull compared to the extravagant show of color elsewhere.

Likewise, I think a person's true colors are usually revealed as the seasons of life change. When things are good for us—our body is healthy, our relationships are good, our finances are sound, our surroundings are secure—we can look green and full of happiness and vitality. But when the "chlorophyll" of good things begins to fade, our true colors are revealed.

The ultimate example of a change in circumstances is Job. He had a tremendous fortune, a big family, good friends, and sound health, only to lose it all in a calamitous manner in an incredibly short amount of time. Yet Job's faith in God remained intact:

Though he slay me, I will hope in him.
—Job 13:15a

Most of us don't have such tragic events in all facets of our life as Job did. My eighteen-month battle with cancer was painfully difficult, but I still had a delightful marriage, wonderful children, dear friends, a good job, and solid finances. Yet things were rough enough that I felt a good bit of "chlorophyll" seeping out of me as I fought for my life. Hopefully that allowed people to see some of my true colors, those that come from the beauty of Christ whose Spirit, by His grace, resided in me. I hope they saw through the ugliness of my disease and its devastating effects on my withering body to see the Lord's beauty as He strengthened my soul daily.

On the day I called, you answered me; my strength of soul you increased.
—Psalm 138:3

That was also an exceptionally difficult season of life for my faithful wife, Candy, as she was my primary caretaker while still working as much as she could and parenting our teenage children. Yet her true colors shone brightly even on the darkest days. I often felt terrible about all she had to do because of my situation and the many tasks she had to continuously juggle each day. One day I asked Candy how she managed to do it all. She said that it was purely the strength of the Lord working in her and through her; she knew full well that she was incapable of doing all that on her own.

During our cancer journey, Candy and I met many other cancer patients and their caretakers and could not help but notice a distinct difference in the "coloring" of those who followed Christ closely and those who did not. We were active members in Jim and Cyndi Siegfried's f.a.i.t.H. ("facing an illness through Him") group, the local faith-based support group for people suffering from long-term illnesses and their primary caretakers. There was no shortage of intense physical suffering within the group, and many of our members did not live very long. Yet our meetings were characterized primarily by joy. Yes, there were plenty of tears, but there were also endless hugs and smiles and howls of laughter. There were cries of petition lifted to the Lord, but those were interspersed among prayers of praise and thanksgiving. Perhaps even more remarkable was that every afflicted person professed they were thankful for their illness, even those with terminal cancer, because it deepened their faith and brought them to a closer relationship with Christ. At least that was the testimony of those who knew Jesus intimately. The occasional non-Christian visitors with us were horrified at our attitudes and were convinced we were all crazy! Oh, but for me, it was a beautiful and inspiring experience to see the genuine joy of the Lord on the faces of people whose bodies were wracked with pain and agony. Their true colors shone through brilliantly, even along dark and stormy paths.

> *So we do not lose heart. Though our outer self is wasting away, our inner self is being renewed day by day. For this light momentary affliction is preparing for us an eternal weight of glory beyond all comparison, as we look not to the things that are seen but to the things that are unseen. For the things that are seen are transient, but the things that are unseen are eternal.*
> —2 Corinthians 4:16-18

> *Rejoice in hope, be patient in tribulation, be constant in prayer.*
> —Romans 12:12

> The glory of Christ often comes into greater focus when we find ourselves in the darkest valleys. (Dustin Benge)[26]

I've also noticed quite a contrast in the true colors—the overall demeanor, attitudes, and disposition—displayed among people who walk with Christ compared with those who do not, especially among the elderly. As their bodies increasingly break down and the reality of the brevity of life here on earth sinks in, older adults generally seem to become better or bitter. Those with Christ keep getting better in spirit as they continue to mature in their walk with the Lord. Those with no hope in Christ become bitter, as they have nothing to look forward to but death. It has been my honor to know many who have a delightful relationship with Christ as they walk with Him through their final years on earth. Even when in great physical agony, they remain beautiful in their countenance and spirit. The marvelous beauty of Christ, their true color, continues to shine brightly through them, even as the last of their "chlorophyll" seeps out. The true colors of their lives reflect the peace, joy, and grace of the Lord, for their lives have been beautifully dedicated to walking with Christ in spirit and in truth.

> *But I will hope continually and will praise you yet more and more.*
> *My mouth will tell of your righteous acts, of your deeds of salvation all the day,*
> *for their number is past my knowledge.*
> *With the mighty deeds of the Lord GOD I will come;*
> *I will remind them of your righteousness, yours alone.*
> *O God, from my youth you have taught me, and I still proclaim your wondrous deeds.*
> *So even to old age and gray hairs, O God, do not forsake me,*
> *until I proclaim your might to another generation, your power to all those to come.*
> —Psalm 71:14-18

> *But he [Jesus] said, "Blessed rather are those who hear the word of God and keep it!"*
> —Luke 11:28

> *I have fought the good fight, I have finished the race, I have kept the faith.*
> —2 Timothy 4:7

Our true colors are constantly developed inside us. For those who have a vibrant and growing faith in Christ, the true colors of their souls get brighter and brighter. The souls of people who do not yet know Christ are like the fallen leaves of late November: brown, brittle, and lifeless. But praise be to God, it's never too late for one to be transformed from a dying, colorless soul to a living and colorful soul in Christ. Oh, what a joy it is when a person, especially an older adult, turns to Christ in faith!

All of us have experienced tragedies, health crises, breaks in close relationships, or other hardships, and we will do so again and again as we age. As the "chlorophyll" of good times seeps away, what colors are displayed from within us? Do the beautiful colors of Christ shine in the darkness on those days? God develops those yellow, orange, red, and purple pigments in us as we mature in our walk with Him through diligent prayer and study of His word. Just as He knows the true color of all those green leaves we see in the summer, He knows the true colors in our souls. When they are displayed during challenging times, God is glorified, and others are encouraged.

The most brilliant autumn colors are usually on healthy trees. The amount of water, nutrients, and sunlight a tree gets largely determines its health. Likewise, the nutrients and care given to the human body dramatically affect its physical health. This also holds true for our souls: our spiritual health is determined by what we feed our soul and our diligence in caring for it. Let us be wise in the way we take care of our physical bodies, yet be even wiser in taking care of the part of us that will last forever—our souls. Let's water and feed our souls with healthy doses of God's word and daily prayer. Let's gather with other believers for these tasks and to encourage and help one another. Let's take care of our souls with repentance, obedience, and appropriately responding to God's discipline. And let's be sure to get lots of Son-light! As we do, we will keep building pigments of faith and allow the true colors of Christ to shine brilliantly inside and out!

> *For while bodily training is of some value, godliness is of value in every way, as it holds promise for the present life and also for the life to come.*
> —1 Timothy 4:8

> *Do all things without grumbling or disputing, that you may be blameless and innocent, children of God without blemish in the midst of a crooked and twisted generation, among whom you shine as lights in the world, holding fast to the word of life.*
> —Philippians 2:14-16a

Of course, this analogy isn't perfect; those beautiful autumn leaves will soon fall to the ground, turn brown, and rot away. However, for those who know Christ, the God-given true colors of their soul will never fade away, fall, or die, but will last for all eternity.

> *"For God so loved the world, that he gave his only Son, that whoever believes in him should not perish but have eternal life."*
> —The words of Jesus in John 3:16

I often enjoy sharing this story with others in autumn. If you read this in autumn, I hope you will pause to ponder the true colors of your life as you see the beauty of the colorful trees around you. If winter, let the barrenness of the deciduous trees be a grim reminder of the hopelessness of life without Jesus, yet let the evergreen trees remind you that our peace and joy in Christ abound in all seasons of life. If spring, let the new signs of life in the budding deciduous trees remind you of the ongoing renewal work of the Holy Spirit in the hearts of believers and the new life in Christ that is available for those who put their trust in Him. If it's summer, let the green leaves remind you of the importance of being thankful for God's bountiful blessings and storing God's word in your heart during pleasant seasons of life. In all seasons, let us allow the beauty of God's creation to remind us of His sovereignty, majesty, and power.

> *Then shall all the trees of the forest sing for joy before the LORD,*
> *for he comes, for he comes to judge the earth.*
> *He will judge the world in righteousness, and the peoples in his*
> *faithfulness.*
> —Psalm 96:12b-13

Chapter 26

ASPENS

I appeal to you, brothers, by the name of our Lord Jesus Christ, that all of you agree, and that there be no divisions among you, but that you be united in the same mind and the same judgment.
—1 Corinthians 1:10

S ome of you may be familiar with aspen trees, which grow primarily in the Great Lakes states, New England, Canada, Alaska, and upper elevations of the Mountain states. Aspens are quite fascinating because they grow in clusters from a shared root system. These unique root systems are protected from many environmental risks, including fire, and therefore grow to be large and very old. In fact, some aspen root systems are among the oldest known organisms on the planet. The shared root system is also why all aspen trees in a single stand have the same DNA.

The Lord has blessed me with delightful friendships with Christians who live in multiple states, cities, and neighborhoods. These friends are from a wide range of ages and churches. They have different hobbies and cheer for an assortment of sports teams. Yet, like aspen trees, we are all connected with the same root—Jesus Christ—who has saved us by grace through faith. Blood tests would reveal that one's DNA is similar only to his family members, but all believers in Christ have the same spiritual DNA. We have the same Father in heaven, the same Savior through whom we have been reborn, and the same Holy Spirit abiding in us. We may not be genetic siblings, but we are absolutely related by blood, for we have become children of God because of the blood sacrifice and substitutionary atonement of Jesus Christ. He is the vine, the root, from which our new life in Christ was sprung and by which we are nourished for spiritual growth and fruitfulness.

> *But to all who did receive him, who believed in his name, he gave the right to become children of God, who were born, not of blood nor of the will of the flesh nor of the will of man, but of God.*
> —John 1:12-13

> *"I do not ask for these only, but also for those who will believe in me through their word, that they may all be one, just as you, Father, are in me, and I in you, that they also may be in us, so that the world may believe that you have sent me."*
> —From the prayer of Jesus in John 17:20-21

Another unusual trait of the aspen tree is that even though it is a deciduous tree that loses its leaves in winter, its bark is photosynthetic, meaning it continues to produce its own sugars during the winter, so the tree continues to grow. Its bark is also an important food source for many animals.

Likewise, each of us is called to be fruitful in all seasons of life by staying connected to Christ, the Vine, by the power of the Holy Spirit working in and through us. We are part of a larger living organism: the church, comprised of all followers of Jesus, which God's word calls the body of Christ. We partner with other Christians by being active members of local churches, where we pool our various gifts and talents for effective ministries and missions. We are not saved to be isolated from the community around us but to be the hands and feet of Christ as we work together to show the love of Christ.

> *"Abide in me, and I in you. As the branch cannot bear fruit by itself, unless it abides in the vine, neither can you, unless you abide in me. I am the vine; you are the branches. Whoever abides in me and I in him, he it is that bears much fruit, for apart from me you can do nothing."*
> —The words of Jesus in John 15:4-5

> *For just as the body is one and has many members, and all the members of the body, though many, are one body, so it is with Christ. For in one Spirit we were all baptized into one body—Jews or Greeks, slaves or free—and all were made to drink of one Spirit.*
> —1 Corinthians 12:12-13

Forest fire is a significant risk factor for most trees, including aspen trees. But because their underground root system is protected, the aspen organism continues to grow, and aspens are usually the first trees to regrow after a major fire.

Christianity is under attack around the world and in our culture. Those who thought North American Christians, churches, and pastors would always be protected from persecution have probably been shocked by certain events of the last few years. The erosion of the stability of the United States directly correlates with the national demise of morals and the shrinking of freedoms. No one should be shocked that anti-Christian views are on the rise. Christians are violently persecuted in many parts of the world, and persecution seems to be escalating globally. A brief look at history tells us that this is nothing new. The world has been trying to rid itself of Christianity since its infancy, yet those efforts always fail. Just as the united root system of aspen trees is impervious to forest fires, the church of Jesus Christ continues to strengthen during the fires of persecution because our root is the unconquerable eternal King, Christ Jesus.

For the sake of Christ, then, I am content with weaknesses, insults, hardships, persecutions, and calamities. For when I am weak, then I am strong.
—2 Corinthians 12:10

Who shall separate us from the love of Christ? Shall tribulation, or distress, or persecution, or famine, or nakedness, or danger, or sword? As it is written, "For your sake we are being killed all the day long; we are regarded as sheep to be slaughtered." No, in all these things we are more than conquerors through him who loved us.
—Romans 8:35-37

As I reflect on the many things Candy and I have encountered over the years, there have been many marvelously good times and some trying hard times. Yet in all of these, we could always count on two things: blessings from our heavenly Father, often in unexpected forms, and loving encouragement and gracious support from friends. We have some of the best friendships we could ever imagine, and we are exceedingly grateful. I hope we are never guilty of taking our friends and siblings in Christ for granted because each is a treasured blessing from the Lord. To our many genuine friends, we say thank you for your kindness and faithfulness; you are indeed fellow "aspens," true siblings in Christ with whom we share the DNA of Christ.

Now the full number of those who believed were of one heart and soul, and no one said that any of the things that belonged to him was his own, but they had everything in common.
—Acts 4:32

Bear one another's burdens, and so fulfill the law of Christ.
—Galatians 6:2

So if there is any encouragement in Christ, any comfort from love, any participation in the Spirit, any affection and sympathy, complete my joy by being of the same mind, having the same love, being in full accord and of one mind. Do nothing from selfish ambition or conceit, but in humility count others more significant than yourselves.
—Philippians 2:1-3

Chapter 27

GIVING AND RECEIVING

Let each of you look not only to his own interests, but also to the interests of others.
—Philippians 2:4

Our journey through my battle with cancer heightened Candy's and my awareness of just how valuable true friendships are. My physical needs were monumental, but physical battles are always affected by the quantity and quality of emotional and spiritual support received. By God's grace, we received endless waves of helpful, heart-warming, and encouraging support during that eighteen-month battle.

In hindsight, we now see that before that particular season of hardship, we were sometimes guilty of wrongfully not accepting help offered to us. But during our cancer journey, we were so overwhelmed with needs that we were in no position to decline many offers to help. As people helped us, we realized that our previous prideful refusal to accept the assistance offered by friends had withheld blessings from them and from us. We came to understand more clearly that the willingness to give and to receive is the basis of healthy friendships. The blessings from friends flowed freely and regularly during that season of our life, as God used them to teach us this valuable lesson about friendship.

Throughout the cancer journey, Candy and I were constantly encouraged by the host of people who reached out to help us. My co-workers at International Paper arranged to have a bake sale to help offset the cost of our many trips between Collierville and Houston. When my manager and friend, Dave Borchardt, came to our house to give us a check for the proceeds, our jaws dropped in amazement. In my CarePage entry that evening, I wrote that I didn't know what they were selling, but it must have been loaves and fish! We were overwhelmed by the kindness of that gift, but they didn't stop with one bake sale; they held another one the following week. And the week after that. And the next week. And the next and next and next, and I eventually lost count. Their financial help was most welcomed, but the thought that those dear folks were willing to do so much for us was even more valuable, for it constantly boosted our spirits.

Friends from our small group at church helped take care of our yard. Multiple people helped by giving me rides to treatments when Candy could not or sometimes just to give her a needed break. Another friend helped Laura get her driving hours required to obtain a license. People brought delicious meals for Candy and the kids. We were constantly buoyed by encouraging messages on my CarePage, in cards, and through emails. Among the most meaningful gifts was the investment of time of four friends who visited me almost every week when we were not in Houston. I will never forget the faithfulness of Steve Alm, Brad Cummins, Jack Edmands, and Pete DeMoss. Sometimes I was too sick to speak, but having one of them there to visit, even for only a few minutes, meant the world to me. All these dear people were willing to give, and we were willing to receive. Blessings were received on both ends of the transaction.

> *But if we walk in the light, as he is in the light, we have fellowship with one another, and the blood of Jesus his Son cleanses us from all sin.*
> —1 John 1:7

We need friendships not only in trying times but at all times. Genuine friendships—the ongoing exchange of heartfelt care and concern actively displayed in purposeful, meaningful ways—are needed in our everyday lives for our emotional and spiritual well-being. It is a great irony that in an age when technology has made communication more effortless than ever before, person-to-person communication skills of our society are declining, and relationships are becoming more shallow. Although smartphones and social media platforms give us more acquaintances than ever, there seems to be a scarcity of genuine friendships.

> *Therefore encourage one another and build one another up, just as you are doing.*
> —1 Thessalonians 5:11

We Christians should be setting an example to others by actively investing ourselves in meaningful friendships. God designed none of us to be lone wolves, nor does His word command or encourage us to go it alone. He designed us to use our uniqueness in harmony with others for good purposes. We are commanded to join with others in local churches to worship together, serve together in missions and ministries, and fellowship together.

Behold, how good and pleasant it is when brothers dwell in unity!
—Psalm 133:1

For as in one body we have many members, and the members do not all have the same function, so we, though many, are one body in Christ, and individually members one of another.
—Romans 12:4-5

Most women have a natural bent toward making and interacting with friends. It's usually more challenging for us guys, but it is vital for our spiritual and emotional well-being to have healthy friendships with other men. Friendships with men help us in ways that women, even our wives, cannot. We help each other in our responsibilities at home, at church, and in the community. More importantly, we help one another grow in our faith. We need men to hold us accountable for doing the right thing, staying grounded in the word of God, and maturing in biblical manhood.

Be watchful, stand firm in the faith, act like men, be strong.
—1 Corinthians 16:13

Establishing and maintaining friendships requires us to give generously of our most valuable commodity: our time. We must selflessly invest ourselves into the lives of others in ways that build trust and genuine compassion for one another. We should be willing to let our guard down enough to honestly show our weaknesses, admit our struggles, and seek the help of others. None of that is easy for most of us, but the benefits of doing so can significantly enrich our lives. The rewards we reap sometimes come quickly but more often take time to harvest. Yet their value is incalculable, as genuine Christian friendships always draw us nearer to our Lord, Christ Jesus.

Two are better than one, because they have a good reward for their toil. For if they fall, one will lift up his fellow. But woe to him who is alone when he falls and has not another to lift him up!
—Ecclesiastes 4:9-10

Do not neglect to do good and to share what you have, for such sacrifices are pleasing to God.
—Hebrews 13:16

I am exceptionally blessed to have many good friends. One of the best is Steven Lee White. He has willingly invested himself and his time into our friendship for many years, consistently proving himself to be a trustworthy and faithful brother in Christ. Steven Lee and I know we can discuss any topic, and there is never a concern about confidentiality or lack of concern. We encourage one another with truth and grace, not meaningless flattery. We use God's word to challenge and counsel one another. We pray for one another regularly and with one another often. Our long conversations, short calls, or abbreviated texts almost always result in an infusion of joy from the Lord. Such a friendship is truly invaluable. I hope each of you, dear reader, has such a friend.

Iron sharpens iron, and one man sharpens another.
—Proverbs 27:17

The Lord has blessed me with many other meaningful friendships over the years, and I am eternally thankful for each one. I won't try to name all of them, for I would surely leave off someone. But you know who you are, and I thank you.

I pray that the Lord will continue to teach me to be a good friend, always willing to help and be helped, that Christ may be glorified in our lives.

Chapter 28

CAMPBELL AND BRANDON

But Jesus called them to him, saying, "Let the children come to me, and do not hinder them, for to such belongs the kingdom of God."
—Luke 18:16

The year 2015 was most memorable. Candy and I moved into our newly-built home in July of that year, and it was and has continued to be a tremendous blessing for a variety of reasons. It has served us well as a place to host friends and family, is in a great neighborhood, and was designed with a room tailored to meet my unique needs associated with using my permanent feeding tube. I will also remember 2015 as the year my heart was captured by two little boys I did not know personally: Campbell and Brandon.

Campbell and his twin sister, Avery,[27] were born on September 29, 2009. Five days later, Brandon was born. Campbell was born to a wonderful mom and dad who lived in Madison, Mississippi, an upscale suburban town near Jackson. Brandon was born to a teenage mom who lived in Hernando, Mississippi, in the Memphis metropolitan area. Campbell had four and a half happy years before cancer invaded his small body, and then he put up a valiant fight for another year and a half. Brandon had three happy years before a mostly-absentee father fatally abused his small body in the final few torturous days of Brandon's life. The two boys' lives were radically different in so many ways. Yet both boys had people who loved them deeply and cared for them wonderfully. Both endured things we never want any child to experience. And today, I believe Campbell and Brandon have something else in common: both are in heaven.

In a society dominated by social media and instant communication, people can develop emotional ties with others they don't personally know. But doing so is quite unusual for me. I am challenged to keep up with all the prayer needs of people I know and those on our church prayer list without adding people with whom I have no direct connection. I usually feel I haven't the time or emotional reserves to get involved with people I don't know. Yet in 2015, Campbell Dale and his family became an exception to that rule.

I first saw a few retweets about Campbell in 2014. He was a little boy from a Mississippi State family, and he had cancer. Being a cancer survivor, a lifelong Mississippi State Bulldog, and a dad with a soft spot in my heart for kids, I always stopped and said a quick prayer for healing for the little fellow and strength for his parents. In March 2015, however, the retweets began to get more and more of my attention, and I began to follow the Twitter account for Campbell's journey myself. I read some older tweets and read his story, as written by his mom, Jill, on a link to her CaringBridge blog. As much as the photos of Campbell, his twin sister, Avery, and their parents, David and Jill, brought smiles to my face, the story of his cancer brought sorrow. Campbell had Rhabdomyosarcoma, a rare type of cancer. As a general rule, the rarer the type of cancer, the less research energy and funding are given to find cures. The outlook for Campbell seemed less than promising. Yet Jill's story was about so much more than Campbell's illness. It was the story of her unwavering and unshrinking faith in Christ. It was about Jill and David constantly relying on God's grace to carry them through such a challenging time and on His strength to bravely face the unknowns ahead of them. It was a story of their great love for the Savior who first loved them and their great love for Campbell.

After reading Jill's story and posts, Campbell was never far from my heart or mind, and he and his family became regulars on my prayer list. I even shocked Candy one day by tearing up after reading an extremely disappointing report from one of Campbell's scans. I don't know if she had ever seen me cry like that for someone who wasn't a close relative or friend.

Most of Campbell's treatments were at Batson Children's Hospital in Jackson. I longed to get a chance to see this family for whom I prayed so often, even though I knew it might be awkward. In late July, the Dales brought Campbell to St. Jude in Memphis for a few weeks, and I felt this was the opportunity for which I had prayed. Candy agreed that we could not let this opportunity pass by. When we met David and Jill at St. Jude, I was not surprised to find that they were gracious, friendly, and welcoming. We spent most of our visit talking to them but also briefly met Campbell, who seemed quite frail yet joyful and playful. The visit only intensified my daily prayers for Campbell and the Dales.

In mid-August, I reported for jury duty at 157 Poplar in Memphis. I had been summoned for jury duty a few times before but never actually served on a jury. As I drove to the courthouse that morning, I was confident that this would be like my previous jury duty experiences: I would likely sit in the large jury pool room for a couple of days, never hear my name called, and then be excused to go home. Or if I was selected as a potential juror on a case, I had a relatively low chance of being chosen as an actual jury member. Even if I were chosen, it would probably be a civil case that would get wrapped up in a couple of days. I was confident there was little chance of being selected as a potential juror on a criminal case, especially not one that required the jury to be sequestered. And even if I did make it that far in the process, it was highly improbable that I would be selected as a juror, given my unusual health situation.

Early that Monday morning, two lists of randomly chosen names were called as potential jurors for criminal cases. Mine was the eleventh name called on a list of fifty. After filling out information cards, we were led across the street to 201 Poplar and up to the sixth floor to report to Judge Lee Coffee's Criminal Court Division VII. We waited in the hallway outside. Then we moved to the waiting room, which I soon found was aptly named. Around noon we were given a lunch break, and I returned to my car in a nearby parking garage to take my meal via my feeding tube. We came back to the waiting area and waited some more. Finally, around 3:00, we were called into court.

As number eleven, I was one of the first twenty potential jurors in the jury box for questioning. Judge Coffee questioned us first. One of his questions was, "Is there any reason why you may not be able to serve on a sequestered jury?" When my turn came, I told the judge that I was a cancer survivor and was unable to eat or drink by mouth. My difficulty in speaking was readily apparent, so that required no explanation. Judge Coffee said that he thought the court could make reasonable accommodations for me, but he was not in a position to determine if serving would compromise my health. "So, Mr. Barton," he said, "I leave that up to you. Do you want to serve on this jury, or do you need to step down?"

Most people I know dread the thought of being called for jury duty. Most would have counseled me to take full advantage of this chance to get out of it. I knew I could tell Judge Coffee about my brief hospitalization two days earlier after passing out from dehydration and use that as evidence that my health situation was too precarious to serve. By that time, however, I knew the nature of the case. A father, who was sitting in the courtroom, had been indicted for killing his three-year-old son in 2013. The young man certainly didn't look like someone who could do such a thing. I saw the family of the child's mother and the deep hurt on their faces. I had no idea who might be innocent or guilty. I felt strongly, however, that if any of those people were my loved ones, I would want someone like me on the jury: someone who would have no preconceived ideas regarding the guilt or innocence of the defendant; someone who would intently listen to the testimony and view the evidence; someone who would try to follow the judge's instructions to the letter; someone who would stand up for what he felt was right even if it was a minority opinion; someone with a Christian worldview; someone who loved children and deeply desired justice if this child was wrongly killed, yet who also had a heart for young men in our community and wanted no part of sending yet another young Memphis man to prison unless the facts of the case and the related law demanded it. I felt that I was in that specific courtroom at that specific time for that specific case for a reason. Did the Lord want me to serve on this jury? I knew the decision was His to make, not mine. So I silently prayed, "Lord, may Your will be done for me to serve or not serve on this jury. You will soon have ample opportunity to take me off through the attorney's challenges. I know it is not my place to go ahead of You and remove myself now." So I answered Judge Coffee, "I would like to serve, your honor."

Following the judge's inquiries and dismissal of a couple of potential jurors, there were three or four rounds of attorney challenges. All the challenges were finally completed around 9:00 p.m. I had not moved from my seat as number eleven, one of only four of the original twenty still sitting in the box. We were joined by ten others who were chosen from the remaining thirty potential jurors. So there it was. The most unlikely of the scenarios I pondered on my drive downtown that morning had come to be. I was a sequestered juror on the State of Tennessee's case against Chris Denley regarding the 2013 death of three-year-old Brandon Parks. [Note: The actual names of the accused and the victim have been changed to fictitious names in this story to respect the privacy of the families involved.]

The five days of sequestered jury duty were quite strange in many ways. We lived in an exclusive community with a population of eighteen: fourteen jurors (two of which would later be chosen at random as alternate jurors) and four county deputies. Our phones were taken from us shortly after we arrived Tuesday morning and were not returned until the trial's conclusion. We had no access to internet, television, radio, or newspapers. We always traveled together by private bus and stayed on a hotel floor that had no other guests. We ate breakfast and dinner in restaurants large enough to segregate us from the other patrons. The deputies went out of their way to be extra accommodating to me, and I guessed that was on the orders of Judge Coffee. Twelve jurors had roommates in the hotel, but two of us had private rooms because of my unique needs. Lunch was delivered to and eaten in the jury room, but I had a private room two doors down to feed myself with my feeding tube. Thankfully, all my fellow jurors and the deputies treated me with great understanding, kindness, and respect.

While in the courtroom, we heard the testimony of many witnesses and saw mounds of evidence. We saw "before" and "after" photos—a happy, healthy Brandon and a battered, lifeless body. We saw images of internal organs that were damaged. What we saw and heard was heartbreaking and gruesome, to say the least. We heard the testimonies of the family members who cared for and deeply loved Brandon during his short life. We heard the detailed medical reports and the testimonies of medical doctors, nurses, examiners, and law enforcement officers. Some details were so horrid that it was tempting to turn away, but only a couple of jurors did. Had I been home and seen those things on a television show, I would have changed the channel immediately. But this was my job for a week, and it was my responsibility to intently listen to everything said and view all the evidence shown.

Even in this strange little world of being a sequestered juror, young Campbell Dale was never far from my thoughts. From our jury room on the sixth floor of 201 Poplar, we could see the top portion of St. Jude Hospital and the Tri-Delta Place—the short-term lodging facility for St. Jude patients and families—where Candy and I had visited the Dales. Looking at those buildings several times a day was a constant reminder to pray for Campbell and his family. I prayed for healing and comfort for Campbell. I prayed that even when he received cancer treatments, he would have the strength and energy to enjoy doing things that little boys like to do. I prayed for the Lord's inner strength, peace, and wisdom to fill David and Jill. I prayed for Avery to be cared for well and feel her parents' love even when they were away. I prayed that the Lord would continue to use the Dale family as a mighty testimony of unwavering faith during tremendous adversity and pain. I also prayed for such faith for the family members involved with this court case, the Parks and Denley families, that they would turn more and more to God for strength and comfort in their pain, just as David and Jill Dale were doing.

Until we returned to the jury room after hearing Judge Coffee's final instructions on Saturday, we were not allowed to discuss the case with anyone, including our fellow jurors. Before then, we had to try to bottle up any emotions we carried from the courtroom to the jury room during breaks. We used card games to escape the reality of the weighty matter upon us. We visited with each other about our families, our jobs, and our likes and dislikes. None of us had ever met before Monday, and we came from very diverse neighborhoods, experiences, and worldviews. As the long days wore on, we grew closer and closer. We learned how to deal with the uniqueness of each person's personality. Within a few days, we were strangers no more. Yet we could not discuss the one thing we had most in common: this court case.

As the days passed, our desire to unbottle some pent-up emotions and growing opinions continued to build, yet we resisted. After hearing some of the most gut-wrenching testimonies, some people just needed to be given some space and left alone, and we all understood. Yes, the five days in this strange world made for a rather surreal experience, yet I felt there was also a growing sense among us jurors that we were doing something fundamentally important. A child who should be a happy, healthy five-year-old had been dead for over two years. The case had finally meandered through the legal channels and into the courtroom. Now it was our job to decide if his father was responsible for his son's death. Our decision would have an extreme impact on the lives of Chris Denley and the two families involved, and the weight of that decision grew heavier with each passing hour.

For many of the jurors, Thursday was the worst day. In a lengthy presentation, the medical examiner gave the graphic details of the autopsy and the extent of the external and internal injuries to Brandon's small body. We saw many gruesome photos of the dozens and dozens and dozens of injuries on and inside his body. It was gut-wrenching to keep watching and listening, but we had to. For some, the most difficult part of the trial was the heart-ripping testimony of Brandon's auntie, who treated the boy as her own child since his birth so his mother could return to high school. Her love for Brandon was evident in her testimony and even more so by the pain on her face. For me, however, it was the unexpected witness brought by the defense late Thursday morning: the soft-spoken defendant himself, Chris Denley, who was not required by law to give any testimony.

Chris talked about the things he confessed as wrongs and the things in which he professed innocence. He spoke of his love for Brandon and for his two daughters. As Chris spoke, I thought of the image of little healthy, happy Brandon and wondered how anyone could intentionally hurt him regardless of the circumstances. I thought about the incredible trauma and pain Brandon endured, and it broke my heart. Of course, I thought of my own children when they were that age and how vulnerable they were. And I thought of Campbell Dale and how vastly different David's love for him looked from Chris's professed love for Brandon. I wondered about Chris's childhood and wondered what things he may have endured himself. I couldn't help but wonder if he had had any positive male role models to show what authentic manhood and fathering look like. Shortly after Chris's testimony, we broke for lunch.

I was so thankful that I had a private room for my meal and did not have to return immediately to the jury room. I went into my private chamber, shut the door, sat at the desk, and buried my face in my hands. My palms were soon damp as I wept deeply for several minutes. I had braced myself for the earlier testimonies that morning, but this last one—the one from Chris—caught me by surprise and ripped my heart out. How could he have abused his young son so horrendously yet still exhibit some level of compassion for him? How could we as a community allow this thin, soft-spoken young man to grow up with such a misguided sense of responsibility and such a distorted sense of right and wrong? How can we, the body of Christ, take more responsibility for reaching young men like Chris?

On Saturday morning, August 22, we heard the attorneys' final arguments and the judge's final instructions to the jury. Two jurors were to be randomly chosen as alternates and dismissed. I prayed the Lord would allow me to continue to serve. We had invested too much of ourselves in the case to walk away, and I wanted to finish the task to which I was called. Two names other than mine were called. I thanked the Lord and pleaded for His guidance for the discussions and decisions that would soon take place.

The other eleven jurors went to the jury room for lunch while I had an abbreviated version of a meal in my room. I quickly rejoined the others, and we began our deliberations. We reviewed all the facts that had been presented to us. We recalled the gruesome reports and photos we had seen. We considered the credibility of the testimony given by Chris, other family members, and law enforcement officers in light of the evidence. We reviewed the legal requirements for a conviction for each charge against Chris. For certain testimony, we asked for transcripts to firm up our memory of them. We were not all on the same page initially, but the more we talked and studied the testimony and evidence, the more we came together in agreement. About four hours later, we returned to court with our verdict. Chris Denley was guilty of felony murder in the perpetration of aggravated child abuse, felony murder in the perpetration of aggravated child neglect, aggravated child abuse, and aggravated child neglect. There was a tremendous heaviness in the verdict we brought, but we were confident it was just. We had been given an intensely difficult job, and we did it well.

After Judge Coffee officially adjourned the trial, he briefly spoke to us after we returned to the jury room. I gained so much respect for him that week that I had already started internally composing the thank you letter I would send the following week. After the judge's gracious comments, we twelve jurors went our separate ways, back to the diverse worlds and lives we had come from Monday morning. Yet none of us returned there unchanged.

For the next few days, the emotional trauma from the case lingered. It was like a time of deep grieving combined with PTSD symptoms. I often found myself at the point of tears—quite unusual for me. My energy levels seemed drained. I had flashbacks of the graphic photos from the medical examiner. Worse yet were the images of happy, healthy Brandon. It simply broke my heart that he was gone. I grieved for Chris Denley also, despite the horrific crimes he committed.

Eventually, I grew out of my melancholy by focusing on praying for Chris and his salvation and rejoicing about Brandon being fully and wholly united with Christ in heaven. I studied the topic of the eternal fate of infants and young children after they die. I tried very hard to study the associated theological principles without allowing my emotions to sway me. *Safe in the Arms of God,* a book by John MacArthur, was an excellent resource. As a result, I became more convinced than ever that children who die before they are capable of understanding faith in Christ or comprehending willful unbelief in Him are eternally with the Lord. They, like me, are saved by grace alone.

My spirits were significantly bolstered the following Wednesday by the news and images of the Dale family spending a memorable day on the Mississippi State campus in Starkville. Campbell, Avery, David, and Jill had been invited to spend the day meeting and interacting with many of Campbell's heroes—Bulldog players and coaches from the football, baseball, and basketball teams. With great pride, I read how my alma mater and its athletics department poured attention and affection over Campbell and his family. My heart warmed hearing and reading the kind words Wes Rae, Dak Prescott, Malik Newman, Ben Howland, Dan Mullen, and others said to and about Campbell. A few days later, I was thrilled to read that after their stop at Mississippi State, the Dales headed to Disney World thanks to the Make-A-Wish Foundation.

My gratitude for Campbell's special days intensified a few weeks later as I read Jill's updates on Campbell. First was the sad news that he seemed to be losing ground quickly. Not long afterward, on September 18, 2015, Jill posted the news that Campbell was fully healed, sitting at the feet of Jesus. Again I prayed through tears—tears of grief but also tears of thankfulness that Mississippi State's little hero was no longer in pain and would never be sick again. He was with our Savior in heaven, with the assurance that one day his cancer-ridden body will be fully restored, and he will live eternally on the new earth God has promised after Christ's triumphant return. I share the belief of David and Jill that one day they will be reunited with Campbell, as will all other believers in Christ, and together we will eternally proclaim His praises face-to-face. I praised our Savior that because of His willingness to be the perfect sacrificial Lamb of God, only Campbell's earthly body and not his eternal soul would taste death. "Thank You, Lord Jesus. Thank You, and praise You!"

As I prayed for Campbell and the Dale family that evening, I could not help but think of Brandon Parks being there with Campbell. I believe that both little boys are forever with our Savior. One day Brandon will also have a fully restored body. He will no longer bear the 116 wounds and bruises the medical examiner found in the autopsy, the images of which were shown to us jurors in the courtroom. I prayed that the Lord would continue to comfort the Parks family and for salvation for Chris Denley.

I thank the Lord for the honor of serving as a juror, as challenging as it was, on a case where the American justice system worked. I thank the Lord for the chance to meet Campbell, David, and Jill. I am thankful that I was able to join so many others in following their journey and praying for them. I thank the Lord for these two little boys, for the reminders they were of the fragility of life in this sin-burdened world. I thank Him for using this experience to show the necessity of caring deeply for people, even those we don't know personally. I am thankful for the grace of God that covers anyone who turns to Him, even those in exceedingly great trials and circumstances. I thank God for His forgiveness and cleansing of all who yield their lives to Christ, no matter how heinous their sins. And I thank our gracious Lord Jesus that someday I, too, will have a fully restored body and voice, and indeed I will join with Campbell and Brandon at the Great Wedding Feast of the Lamb. Together we will gather around the throne of God, singing His praises for all eternity.

Then I looked, and I heard around the throne and the living creatures and the elders the voice of many angels, numbering myriads of myriads and thousands of thousands, saying with a loud voice, "Worthy is the Lamb who was slain, to receive power and wealth and wisdom and might and honor and glory and blessing!" And I heard every creature in heaven and on earth and under the earth and in the sea, and all that is in them, saying, "To him who

sits on the throne and to the Lamb be blessing and honor and glory and might forever and ever!"
—Revelation 5:11-13

On December 14, 2015, the court held the sentencing hearing for Chris Denley. In addition to the automatic life sentence for his felony murder conviction, Chris was sentenced to an additional twenty-five years of imprisonment. Chris will likely never again be a free man on earth. I thank the Lord that we jury members did not know the sentencing guidelines during our deliberations, for that would have made our task even more difficult. As I read about Chris's sentence, I prayed that the Lord would send someone to him within those prison walls to share the truth and love of the gospel so that he may know the freedom of salvation in Christ.

Reading of Chris's sentencing renewed my feelings of grief about the deaths of Brandon and Campbell, especially as I thought of their families preparing for Christmas without their little boys. Yet even in grief, our praise is still drawn heavenward. I praise God for His grace and mercy for the souls of these two little ones. My assured hope in Christ draws me to yearn for the one eternal day when all of us who follow Him will worship our Savior together in the pure holiness of heaven. I thank the Lord that the grace of Christ covers babies, in and out of the womb, and very young children like Campbell and Brandon too.

For we know that if the tent that is our earthly home is destroyed, we have a building from God, a house not made with hands, eternal in the heavens. . . . He who has prepared us for this very thing is God, who has given us the Spirit as a guarantee. . . . Therefore, we are ambassadors for Christ, God making his appeal through us. We implore you on behalf of Christ, be reconciled to God. For our sake he made him to be sin who knew no sin, so that in him we might become the righteousness of God.
—2 Corinthians 5:1, 5, 20-21

These verses remind me of David and Jill Dale. What strong ambassadors they have been for the kingdom of Christ! By submitting themselves to the Lord, the Holy Spirit has worked through them to bless so many people while enduring one of the most arduous circumstances one can imagine. They must have been tempted not to be so public with their private lives, struggles, and heartaches as Campbell fought for his life against a terrible enemy called cancer. Yet they were willing to share their deepest pains to give God glory through their suffering. One can only wonder about the short-term and eternal impact their repeated proclamation of their hope in Christ has had on the lives of others.

In 2015, I often referred to Campbell as my favorite superhero. In hindsight, I know I must regard the Dales as an entire family of conquering heroes because they consistently surrendered their fight into the hands of Almighty God. They have used their platform to glorify the Lord, raise funds for fighting children's cancer, and demonstrate joy and unshakable faith in Christ, even in the face of terrible sorrow. I admire them so much and pray the Lord will bless them just as He has used them to be a blessing to many.

Campbell Dale, 2015[34]

No, in all these things we are more than conquerors through him who loved us. For I am sure that neither death nor life, nor angels nor rulers, nor things present nor things to come, nor powers, nor height nor depth, nor anything else in all creation, will be able to separate us from the love of God in Christ Jesus our Lord.
—Romans 8:37-39

I hope this story has been meaningful to you. I hope it will cause you to consider the American judicial system's impact on our society and the vital role juries play in that system. Most people I know are inclined to avoid jury duty if possible because it is viewed as an inconvenient intrusion into our everyday lives. And to be fair, it is. But shouldn't we Christians have a different perspective on this civic responsibility? We want our judicial system to be as strong, fair, and healthy as possible. We have seen the harm done to our society when people with influential positions in the judicial system seem to abdicate their responsibilities. Don't we want a biblical view of justice and fairness involved in our legal and court processes? Most of us are limited in the amount of direct influence we can have in the judicial system. We can, however, pray, vote responsibly, and willingly serve on juries when the opportunity arises.

Chapter 29

MY HEROES

Precious in the sight of the LORD is the death of his saints.
—Psalm 116:15

They shall not die prematurely; they shall be immortal till their work is done; and when their time shall come to die, then their deaths shall be precious. The Lord watches over their dying beds, smooths their pillows, sustains their hearts, and receives their souls. Those who are redeemed with precious blood are so dear to God that even their deaths are precious to him. The death-beds of saints are very precious to the church, she often learns much from them; they are very precious to all believers, who delight to treasure up the last words of the departed; but they are most of all precious to the Lord Jehovah himself, who views the triumphant deaths of his gracious ones with sacred delight. If we have walked before him in the land of the living, we need not fear to die before him when the hour of our departure is at hand. (Charles Haddon Spurgeon)[28]

It is my honor to tell you a bit about the five people to whom this book is dedicated. Each has had an enormous influence on my life. Four of the five provided an unforgettable example of how a true believer in Christ is to handle a battle with cancer. The other did not have cancer but passed away suddenly and honorably. I pray that by the power of the Holy Spirit, God will continue to teach me, enlighten me, convict me, and mold me to be more like Jesus. I pray that by doing so, I might live in a Christ-honoring way as these did, and I may pass away in a Christ-honoring way as they did. I will forever remember and regard them as heroes.

> *Therefore, my beloved brothers, be steadfast, immovable, always abounding in the work of the Lord, knowing that in the Lord your labor is not in vain.*
> —1 Corinthians 15:58

DR. BOB GUINTER

After moving to Collierville in 1996, one of the first things Candy did was find a reputable pediatrician for our kids. It didn't take long to get many recommendations about Dr. Bob Guinter. We quickly came to appreciate his medical knowledge and wisdom. We also soon came to know Bob, a fellow member of our church, as a solid Christian, an outstanding church leader of youth, and an active participant in mission trips around the world. Bob was also an accomplished musician and authored a children's book. But for all of us who knew Dr. Bob, one of the first things we recall is his exceedingly dry sense of humor and quick wit that never failed to bring smiles and laughter.

Dr. Bob became a friend, mentor, and example to me as a head and neck cancer patient. He had survived oral cancer and several recurrences before I ever got cancer and offered helpful advice and encouragement after my diagnosis. As is the case with a high percentage of head and neck cancer patients, Bob continued to have recurrences. He never lost his focus on Christ and always saw things from a heavenly perspective. Dr. Bob suffered greatly toward the end of his life, and it hurt my soul to witness it. Yet even then, he continued to encourage me. I will always cherish our enjoyable and meaningful one-on-one visits, as well as the visits Candy and I had with him and his dear wife, Dee, during the final months of his life. He passed away in 2014, and I was one of the countless people in our community and around the world who grieved his passing. Yet we were thankful for the blessing and honor of knowing Dr. Bob, relieved that his suffering had ended and elated that he will forever be at home with the Savior he loved.

> *Let your speech always be gracious, seasoned with salt, so that you may know how you ought to answer each person.*
> —Colossians 4:6

I always thought I would follow a path like Bob's, with multiple oral cancer recurrences and suffering, and I prayed that I would handle it as courageously as he did. By God's grace, that has not happened as of the time of this writing. If and when I do have another recurrence, I pray I will remain a strong ambassador of Christ until the end, as my friend Dr. Bob did.

"Thank You, O Lord, for having blessed my life and the lives of Candy, Michael, Laura, and Joseph by sovereignly putting Dr. Bob Guinter in our path. Thank You for his positive influence on me, even as he suffered. I am a better man for having known Dr. Bob."

JIM SIEGFRIED

I am deeply blessed to have had Jim as a friend and mentor for many years. His grandson, Cade Peeper, was a friend and teammate of my son Joseph in multiple church league sports and competitive soccer. Jim rarely missed a game if he could help it, nor did I. Cheering and visiting with Jim during games was always a treat because I got to see both his competitive and compassionate traits working in tandem. He was a busy lay leader at our church and was deeply involved with Memphis FCA leadership. Our mutual love for the St. Louis Cardinals further bonded our friendship.

Jim was diagnosed with Stage 4 non-smokers lung cancer in 2003. He surprised everyone by living an additional fifteen years, even though he had multiple metastases to other parts of his torso. Jim was an absolute warrior and hero in the battle against cancer. He and his wife, Cyndi, founded a marvelous ministry that functioned as a faith-based support group for people with cancer and other long-term illnesses and their caregivers. It was one of the best groups Candy and I have ever been a part of, as it ministered to us with deep empathy, understanding, and concern about the challenges we faced. Jim labored tirelessly in visiting cancer patients at clinics and hospitals and by phone, even though he was a cancer patient himself.

I still miss Jim terribly, yet I cannot help but smile when I remember his infectious smile and unwaning upbeat attitude. No one has influenced me more than Jim in showing how a follower of Christ deals with cancer and ministers to fellow cancer patients and survivors in a compassionate, involved, and effective manner. I praise God for allowing this special friend and me to cross paths, for I am a better man for it.

"Thank You, O Lord, for Jim Siegfried, for he was one of Your most gracious, loving, and impactful gifts to me. Our cancer journey and the years after would have been far more difficult for Candy and me without the invaluable lessons we learned from You through the actions and words of Jim and Cyndi. I will be forever grateful to You for the warm friendship and Christ-honoring brotherhood I shared with him and will again someday."

Blessed be the God and Father of our Lord Jesus Christ, the Father of mercies and God of all comfort, who comforts us in all our affliction, so that we may be able to comfort those who are in any affliction, with the comfort with which we ourselves are comforted by God.
—2 Corinthians 1:3-4

But in your hearts honor Christ the Lord as holy, always being prepared to make a defense to anyone who asks you for a reason for the hope that is in you; yet do it with gentleness and respect.
—1 Peter 3:15

STEVE ALM

Candy and I met Steve and his wife, Nadia, at Germantown Baptist Church shortly after we moved back to the Memphis area in 1996. The four of us quickly became friends. Soon Steve and I became accountability partners, along with a few other men from our church, and that budded into one of the best and closest friendships I've ever had. By God's grace, my relationship with Steve deepened and grew throughout all the years that followed, even though we went to different churches for most of that time.

Steve, the ultimate "even Stephen," was one of the most even-keeled people I have ever known. His eyebrows might rise from time to time but rarely did his voice. Steve was a lifelong learner, always passionate about being a student of the word of God, a great man of prayer, and one who never stopped pursuing a life of righteousness. Like Bob and Jim, Steve was a man of integrity, dependability, and sound character, and he was an excellent example for me for many years. I greatly admired his devotion to excellence in all that he did, as well as his unshakable devotion to his wife, parents, children, grandson, siblings, and extended family.

In the many years of our friendship, Steve's excellent health contrasted my frequent battles with some sort of affliction or its aftermath. I always assumed my well-spoken friend would be one of the primary speakers at my funeral one day. I never, ever dreamed I would attend his funeral.

God providentially and graciously led me to start visiting Grace Evangelical Church with Steve in June 2020. I quickly discerned the Lord was leading Candy and me to make Grace Evan our new church home, although, at the time, I certainly did not understand all the reasons why. Five weeks after my first visit, one of the reasons became clearly evident when Steve received a diagnosis of bladder cancer. I rejoiced that the Lord put me in a position to walk closely with my dear friend in his cancer journey, for he had been exceptionally supportive of me during mine.

A few months into Steve's battle, he learned that his was a very rare and lethal type of bladder cancer. I will long remember the evening he gave me the news as we walked through my neighborhood. He remained true to his nature, being very calm and candid as he shared the statistical improbability of him living another year. Steve, mildly yet with great resolve, spoke of the things he wanted to take care of and accomplish for his family in the months ahead. We talked of our gratitude to God for our friendship, our families, our shared church homes, and our other friends. We prayed for healing and wisdom. Steve chose not to share the news broadly yet, and I was honored that he entrusted me to support him in prayer about these matters.

Steve battled cancer valiantly to the end. True to his nature of dependability, he did take care of and accomplish all the things we had discussed before he passed away on July 19, 2021. Like Bob and Jim, Steve suffered terribly yet bravely at the end and was quite ready to go home to the Lord.

I can still scarcely believe that I have outlived my beloved friend Steve. When I say "outlived," I mean my life on earth has been quantitatively longer. As far as making the most of one's short time here on earth, I am certain that Steve "outlived" me more days than not. And now that he is in the *one eternal day*, he continues to outlive me. Yet we are still prone to wonder why God chose to take Steve at the relatively early age of fifty-nine. I fully trust in the goodness of the sovereign and holy Almighty God, and I know all things have been for His glory and our good.

I miss Steve so very much but will be forever grateful to God for allowing me to walk closely with him, especially during the final thirteen months of his life on earth. I praise God that Steve and I will worship our Savior together again one day and do so for all eternity.

"Thank You, O Lord, for the delightful, meaningful, and impactful friendship You gave me with Steve Alm. You used him to make me a better man, husband, dad, and friend. May You continue to bless his dear wife, Nadia, and their precious family. Oh, what a gracious and loving Father You are to us!"

A friend loves at all times, and a brother is born for adversity.
—Proverbs 17:17

"Let not your hearts be troubled. Believe in God; believe also in me. In my Father's house are many rooms. If it were not so, would I have told you that I go to prepare a place for you? And if I go and prepare a place for you, I will come again and will take you to myself, that where I am you may be also. And you know the way to where I am going."
—The words of Jesus in John 14:1-4

JACK EDMANDS

I have fondly considered Jack a hero since he profoundly impacted my life in 1983, as described earlier in this book. He was not only a close and wonderful friend but my first and most enduring spiritual mentor. There is simply no way to overstate Jack's influence on my life. But that is a blessing I share with many other people. Jack was widely known, admired, and loved as a gifted speaker, an insightful and dynamic teacher of God's word, and a great friend. I have lost count of how many men have told me, "I am a better man because of Jack Edmands." It is certainly no shock that I consider my friend a hero; the shock is that he is included in this chapter, the one about heroes who have passed away. As I write this, it has been only a few months since Jack passed away suddenly from a massive heart attack. I still deeply grieve the loss. My grief is exacerbated by the fact that another exceptionally close friend, Steve Alm, passed away a mere fourteen months earlier. Losing two such close, long-time friends has left a substantial void in my life.

Jack appeared to be the picture of health. When? Always. From the first time I met him in the summer of 1983 until the last time I saw him, a week before he passed. He was ever diligent in taking good care of his health in every respect, starting with his spiritual well-being and extending to his physical and mental health. It seemed appropriate that Jack exited this world between two of his favorite activities: working out at the gym and going to a weekly Bible study. Pictures of Jack from 1983 and 2022 are unfairly similar. The man just didn't seem to age. I never even considered the possibility that Jack would precede me to glory, and I don't think anyone would have guessed that he would pass away from a heart attack. Yet that is the manner God took him home. His death was apparently almost instantaneous, with little or no suffering.

When I first heard the news of Jack's passing, my first thought was of Enoch.

> *Enoch walked with God, and he was not, for God took him.*
> —Genesis 5:24

The phrase *walked with God* is used in the Bible only for Enoch and his great-grandson, Noah. Am I wrong to associate this term with Jack Edmands? I turn to Matthew Henry, the prolific eighteenth-century commentator, for insight on the meaning of this term:

> To walk with God is to set God always before us, and to act as those that are always under his eye. It is to live a life of com-

munion with God both in ordinances and providences. It is to make God's word our rule and his glory our end in all our actions. It is to make it our constant care and endeavour in every thing to please God, and nothing to offend him. It is to comply with his will, to concur with his designs, and to be workers together with him. (Matthew Henry)[29]

Perhaps it is wrong to place Jack on such a pedestal, but I can confidently say he lived in genuine pursuit of living in the manner described by Pastor Henry: as one who walks with God.

The second half of Genesis 5:24 says that Enoch "was not, for God took him." This is clearly an intentional departure from the repeated pattern of the genealogies in Genesis, which state how long each man lived, followed by his age when "he died." Therefore it seems clear that Enoch, like Elijah, was taken alive to heaven without experiencing physical death. My friend Jack certainly did experience death, but his suffering was only momentary, if at all. I don't think anyone is surprised that Jack's death, like his life, was a bold testimony of God's mercy and grace.

Four days after Jack's passing, while still reeling from deep grief, I prayed, "Lord, why does it have to hurt so much?" The Lord immediately put this thought in my head: *Because it must.* I hastily scribbled out the thoughts that followed before I forgot them. A few days later, I was honored to have my words read by Jack's sister, Lindsey Burns, during his funeral:

Missing Jack

Our sense of loss is so enormous
  because God's gift of Jack was so gracious.
The grief in our hearts is so painful
  because his love was so genuine.
His passing leaves such a gaping void
  because his presence was so meaningful.
This deep sadness is so persistent
  because our joy with him was so consistent.
Our loss seems so exceedingly costly
  because Jack's friendship was so enriching.

There was not nor will there be another one like him;
  praise be to God for His gift of the one and only Jack.

JB
9/23/22

"Thank you, O Lord, for enriching my life in immeasurable and eternal ways through my dear friend Jack."

But the LORD takes pleasure in those who fear him, in those who hope in his steadfast love.
—Psalm 147:11

MILDRED WOFFORD

She was born Mildred Massey but was usually called "Sister" by her parents and four younger siblings. Before she reached the age of twenty, she became Mildred Barton after marrying a dashing young pilot. To me, she was my "Mama," later shortened to "Mom." That's what Candy called her too. Besides Candy, Mom was the most important and admired person in my life.

Mildred was raised during the Great Depression in Starkville, Mississippi, just across the road from the campus of Mississippi State College. She was the oldest child of W. C. and Louise Massey. W. C. worked at the college's agricultural extension service and often drafted young Mildred to help him print bulletins and brochures with helpful information for the many farmers in Mississippi.

It was on the campus of Mississippi State that she met a handsome college student, Thomas Wayne "Buck" Barton. An older cousin of mine who knew Buck described him as "somewhat mischievous, with a smile and grin that instantly disarmed and charmed anyone on the receiving end." (Candy says she knows that smile and grin well.) When he and Mildred met, he was already enlisted in the United States Army Air Forces (the precursor to the U.S. Air Force, established in 1947) through the ROTC program. College life during World War II was not like it has been for most of us. Buck split his time between Mississippi State and Army airfields in San Marcos, Texas; Lincoln, Nebraska; Biloxi, Mississippi; and Rantoul, Illinois, training as a pilot and navigator. Mildred was four years younger than Buck, but he was captivated not only by her striking beauty and charm but also by her sense of humor and ability to match wits with him.

Buck graduated from State in January of 1948 and was commissioned as a second lieutenant in the Air Force. He and Mildred were married in September of that same year. He was 23; she was 19. In the years that followed, the happy young Barton couple lived in an array of places across the nation and world as Buck's career as a pilot, officer, and instructor steadily progressed. After a tour of duty in Japan during and after the Korean War, Buck, then a captain, was assigned to teach ROTC at Hobart College in Geneva, New York, for a few years before an anticipated assignment in Germany.

In January 1958, Mildred gave birth to their firstborn, Bruce. She and Buck expected the transfer to Germany in mid to late 1959 and hoped to have their second child before the transfer. If it was another boy, they planned to name him Brad. In January 1959, four days before Bruce's birthday, and two and a half months before the birth of their second child, Buck was tragically killed in an automobile accident on the icy streets of Geneva. Mildred immediately moved back home to Mississippi to be near her parents, and she and Bruce lived in her in-laws' spacious house. She was so taken by the kindness of her father-in-law that when her new son was born on the first day of spring, she changed her mind and did not name him Brad. Mildred gave her second son the same name as his kind and patient grandfather: John Thomas Barton. That baby boy was me.

Many years later, I asked Mom how she was emotionally able to handle the trauma of suddenly becoming a widow at age twenty-nine with a one-year-old and being seven months pregnant. She said she relied on God's word for guidance and received loving support from family and friends. She also said remaining emotionally and physically strong for my last two months of development in her womb was a tremendous motivation. Mom remarried three and a half years later to George Wofford, a man who worked exceptionally hard to provide for us. He and Mom successfully instilled a strong work ethic in Bruce and me as we grew from boys to young men, but we also had lots of fun at the Wofford family farm outside of town.

Mom was a beautiful lady with a beautiful, friendly, outgoing personality. When I think of Mom, I immediately see her ever-present smile, which reflected well her joyful disposition and nature. She read her Bible and devotional book daily and prayed regularly for many, including Bruce and me. Mom loved children and taught preschool Sunday school for decades. She also loved her husband and lovingly cared for her parents in their elderly years. And, oh, how much she loved her sons! She was the ultimate "boy's mom," and all our friends loved coming to our house. She meticulously cared for herself physically, spiritually, mentally, and emotionally.

What stands out most in my memory about Mom are the little things she did for people to brighten up their day. By "little things," I mean things that were not extravagant or costly but very personal and meaningful, often with a touch of beauty, such as giving them a bouquet of freshly cut flowers with a kind and encouraging note attached. A prolific note-writer, she touched many hearts with expressions of cheer, congratulations, concern, or sympathy. Most things she did were known only by the recipient of the gift; she never made a show of her kindness.

Mama was the first to teach me about Jesus and His saving grace. She taught me how to pray and how to read my Bible. She took Bruce and me to church with her two or three times every week. She encouraged me to follow Christ diligently and didn't give up on me when I didn't. She never stopped praying for me.

When Candy and I got engaged, Mom told Candy, "You will never be my daughter-in-law; you are and will always be my daughter." And that is the relationship my two favorite people had, as they loved each other dearly. Mom always came to spend at least a week with us whenever one of our children was born, and I don't know what we would have done without her. Candy always cried when she left.

Mom took great care of herself, waking up early each morning to exercise and always being careful with what she ate. She was one of the healthiest people I knew, so it was a terrible shock when she was diagnosed with advanced ovarian cancer in 1994 at age sixty-five. By the time she was diagnosed, the cancer was too widespread to be treated. She prayed for the Lord to heal her miraculously or take her home to Him quickly. The Lord answered her prayer about six weeks later, and she passed away peacefully from a blood clot. Nothing in my life has been as devastating as her passing.

This may sound strange for a man to say, but for the past four decades, I have wanted to be like my Mom, at least in certain ways. The purpose of sanctification is to make us more like Christ, and I always figured being a lot like Mom was a good place to start. I want to be a caring and kind person who lives out my faith in a way that makes a difference in the lives of others. I want to do "little" personal things that are meaningful to people and reflect Christ in all I do. I want to be a man of prayer who loves God's word, but in humble, not showy ways. I want to bravely face illness and death as she did. I know I have a long way to go, but I pray that some people who knew Mom will be able to see that I'm her son based on how I live. I also pray that something in this book will be a "little thing" to brighten up your day, similar to how Mom brightened many people's lives.

"Thank You, Lord, for giving me such a wonderful person for my mom. Help me to be more like You by patterning much of my attitude and behavior after her."

And I am sure of this, that he who began a good work in you will bring it to completion at the day of Jesus Christ. . . . And it is my prayer that your love may abound more and more, with knowledge

and all discernment, so that you may approve what is excellent, and so be pure and blameless for the day of Christ, filled with the fruit of righteousness that comes through Jesus Christ, to the glory and praise of God.
—Philippians 1:6, 9-11

And I heard a voice from heaven saying, "Write this: Blessed are the dead who die in the Lord from now on." "Blessed indeed," says the Spirit, "that they may rest from their labors, for their deeds follow them!"
—Revelation 14:13

Chapter 30

MY PERSONAL BEST

*He who finds a wife finds a good thing
and obtains favor from the L<small>ORD</small>.*
—Proverbs 18:22

There are a few pictures of Candy and me in the back of this book. The most recent of these was taken during the post-game celebration of the National Champion Mississippi State baseball Bulldogs after the final game on June 30, 2021. As you can imagine, we were deliriously happy about witnessing State's first NCAA championship, having been longtime fans of MSU. (When people ask how long I've been a Mississippi State fan, I often say I've been a Bulldog since the summer of 1958 and was born in Starkville in the spring of 1959.) But the very best part about that moment in Omaha was being there with Candy. I can't imagine going through life without my true love, my very best friend, my charming and gracious wife, my faithful helpmate, sweet Candy. I thank the Lord for her and for our beautiful marriage every day.

Soon after Candy and I started dating, I never wanted to date anyone else. Why would I? I thought she was kind and warm-hearted, exceptionally smart, cute, fun to be with, laughed easily, and had the prettiest light-up-the-room smile I had ever seen. Even better, she had a passionate and strong faith in Christ and was well-grounded in Scripture. It seemed like a near-perfect fit from the start, and by Christmas that year, neither of us had any doubt of our love for each other or our desire to be married. Some unhealthy and disruptive relationships within Candy's family complicated our courtship and delayed our marriage for more than two years. Yet working through and around those difficulties cemented our devotion to each other and deepened our commitment to a Christ-honoring relationship. We were officially engaged on my twenty-seventh birthday, March 20, 1986, and were married on June 7 of that year. Memories of Candy walking down the church aisle in her wedding gown, reciting our vows, exchanging rings, and being pronounced man and wife have continued to sweeten as we grow older.

By God's amazing grace, it has been a truly remarkable marriage. The Lord has graciously used our triumphs, trials, celebrations, and shortcomings for our good and His glory. He has used our varied experiences to grow our mutual faith in Christ, deepen our love for one another, increase our appreciation of one another, strengthen our marriage, and bring increasingly more joy and trust to our friendship. Candy and I fall more in love with each other with each passing year.

We are also blessed to have three sensational adult children, Michael, Laura, and Joseph, and two terrific daughters-in-law, Gwen and Allison. We are thankful to have healthy relationships with all of them.

Honestly, it's hard to imagine going through cancer and living with my unusual disabilities without Candy. After the rough start with my voicelessness chronicled earlier in this book, we learned how to function well with my voice and speech problems that I've had since then. Candy worked tirelessly as my caregiver while I had cancer and has been very patient and understanding in living with its aftermath. She makes most phone calls for me because my speech impediment makes it difficult for most people to understand me. Candy handles introductions for us when we are in public together because of my inability to pronounce most names correctly, including hers and mine. She often acts as my interpreter, especially when I speak to people who haven't yet become accustomed to my unusual dialect. Because I cannot eat or drink by mouth, we hardly ever go to restaurants, a date night and vacation staple for most couples. Yet Candy never complains, makes the best of whatever situation we are in, and helps find other fun activities we can do together. Every day she tells me she loves me, but her actions say it even better.

Candy also works extremely hard as a tax CPA and is excellent at her job. What a blessing it is to have a wife who is so knowledgeable and wise about financial matters! After working for International Paper for ten years as a post-cancer disabled employee, I needed to retire early in 2019 to better care for my health. That decision was only a possibility because of Candy's encouragement to me and willingness to keep earning a paycheck for us.

I tremendously appreciated Candy's encouragement for the 5,000 Amazing Days of Grace celebration and praise event we hosted in March

2022. I am also grateful for her support of my desire to write this book. Both initially seemed like unrealistic ideas, but Candy was onboard and encouraging from the start. As my ideas for each project grew in scope and complexity, her support never waned. She recognized the enduring potential of sharing a part of our story in writing, and we both pray the Lord will use this book to bless many.

By God's grace, His word includes some apt descriptions of my lovely helpmate:

> *Love is patient and kind; love does not envy or boast; it is not arrogant or rude. It does not insist on its own way; it is not irritable or resentful; it does not rejoice at wrongdoing, but rejoices with the truth. Love bears all things, believes all things, hopes all things, endures all things. Love never ends.*
> —1 Corinthians 13:4-8a

> *An excellent wife who can find? She is far more precious than jewels. The heart of her husband trusts in her, and he will have no lack of gain. She does him good, and not harm,*
> *all the days of her life. . . . Charm is deceitful, and beauty is vain, but a woman who fears the LORD is to be praised. Give her of the fruit of her hands, and let her works praise her in the gates.*
> —Proverbs 31:10-12, 30-31

Candy and I often remind each other that we are each thankful to be married to our best friend. Yet we also acknowledge that our true Best Friend, the One for all eternity, is our Savior and Lord, Jesus Christ. Without Him, we would not have a story worth telling. Our marriage and our entire lives would be meaningless and without purpose. We pray you have gotten a glimpse of His grace in every story in this book.

> *"This is my commandment, that you love one another as I have loved you. Greater love has no one than this, that someone lay down his life for his friends. You are my friends if you do what I command you. No longer do I call you servants, for the servant does not know what his master is doing; but I have called you friends, for all that I have heard from my Father I have made known to you."*
> —The words of Jesus in John 15:12-15

Chapter 31

BENEDICTIONS

Return, O my soul, to your rest;
for the LORD has dealt bountifully with you.
—Psalm 116:7

I have chosen to close this book with two of my favorite hymns.

MY MAGNETIC NORTH

"When I Survey the Wondrous Cross" was written by thirty-three-year-old Isaac Watts, often referred to as the "Father of English Hymnody," in 1707. This was a favorite hymn of my mom's when I was growing up, and it became a favorite of mine. Candy and I chose for it to be sung at our wedding because it was profoundly meaningful to us then and has remained so for all these years. I refer to it as a compass hymn, for it never fails to point me in the right direction.

You know the purpose of a compass. It points to the north based on the magnetic field of the earth. If you know which direction is north, you can accurately determine any direction you need to go. "When I Survey the Wondrous Cross" never fails to point me to my spiritual Magnetic North, the cross of Jesus Christ. The hymn beckons me to be not just an observer of the cross but a surveyor. I must inspect it thoroughly to understand its attributes and purposes. The hymn reminds me that without the cross of Jesus, my life is void of meaning and direction. Only in Christ and in His perfectly righteous life and atoning death do I have life. All the worldly things that captivate my attention are, at best, crippling misdirections from my focus on Christ. At worst, they are idolatrous and deadly substitutes. As this beautiful hymn tunes my heart to this Magnetic North, the cross of Christ, I am drawn like a magnet to my Savior. I am compelled to obediently, gratefully, joyfully, and faithfully follow the righteous paths God has planned for me, wherever they may lead.

When I Survey the Wondrous Cross

When I survey the wondrous cross
On which the Prince of glory died,
My richest gain I count but loss,
And pour contempt on all my pride.

Forbid it, Lord, that I should boast,
Save in the death of Christ my God!
All the vain things that charm me most,
I sacrifice them to His blood.

See from His head, His hands, His feet,
Sorrow and love flow mingled down!
Did e'er such love and sorrow meet,
Or thorns compose so rich a crown?

Were the whole realm of nature mine,
That were a present far too small;
Love so amazing, so divine,
Demands my soul, my life, my all.[30]

The final twelve words of the hymn never fail to bring a tremble in my soul. They call me to soberly consider what is required of me as a follower of Christ: "Love so amazing, so divine, demands my soul, my life, my all." Only the Lord knows how woefully short I have come to giving Christ my all, even for a day, but I have a pretty good idea. Only by the grace of God and the power of the blood of Jesus on the cross have my sins been forgiven. Only by His mercy and might can I fear God with both trembling and rejoicing. Only in His strength and through the wisdom of His word can I prayerfully respond to His sacrificial love by striving to live in Christ, with Christ, and for Christ. The cross of Christ is how I was reconciled to Almighty God and have been granted prayerful access to His throne room. How can I not bow before Him in humility and gratitude?

This powerful and beautiful hymn reminds me of my wonderful mom, my wonderful marriage to dear, sweet Candy, and, most of all, my wonderful Savior and the life I have in Him by grace through faith. This compass hymn points me to whence I've come, where I stand, and my ultimate destination. It reminds me of my assured hope in Christ and my responsibilities as His servant. I pray that it will always serve as a reliable compass for my soul, ever pointing me to its Magnetic North.

AMAZING DAYS INDEED

I doubt many people in the United States, Christian or not, have never heard the hymn "Amazing Grace." It was penned in 1772 by John Newton of England, a former slave trader who was reborn in Christ and became an Anglican priest. Years later, Newton became an abolitionist and ally of William Wilberforce in fighting to end slavery. The hymn was first published in 1779 and, in 1847, linked to the tune we now know by American composer William Walker. Newton's hymn ended with the line, "But God, Who called me here below, will be forever mine." There is some disagreement on who wrote the beloved sixth and final verse we sing, but we know it was not Newton. Many saw that verse in print for the first time while reading Harriet Beecher Stowe's influential 1852 novel, *Uncle Tom's Cabin*, but it had been sung for many years before then.

The hymn records Newton's emotional testimony of salvation and surety of eternal life in Christ. I pray that it is not so familiar that you've quit pondering the lyrics you know so well, for it shall surely stir the soul of every Christ-follower who listens with freshness and intensity. While it was the testimony of John Newton's personal conversion, sanctification, and assured hope of eternal life in heaven, its words are broad enough to apply to every Christian's faith story.

"Amazing Grace" was a favorite of my grandparents, parents, and almost everyone else I knew while growing up. Candy's family heritage is Jewish, but after the conversion to Christ of Candy, her dad, and her sisters, the hymn also became a staple in their family. For me, it is another compass hymn, as it never fails to point me to my Savior and to His righteous life, sacrificial death, victorious resurrection, and eternal reign. It never fails to remind me how great is the grace that has chosen me, rescued me from the penalty of sin, is freeing me from the power of sin, and will one day deliver me from the presence of sin. It is the amazing grace of our holy, righteous, just, merciful, good, loving, all-powerful, all-knowing, ever-present God, the Fountain of all blessings, who never, ever lets go of me.

Amazing Grace

Amazing Grace how sweet the sound,
That saved a wretch like me!
I once was lost, but now am found;
Was blind, but now I see.

'Twas grace that taught my heart to fear,
And grace my fears relieved;
How precious did that grace appear
The hour I first believed!

Through many dangers, toils and snares,
I have already come;
'Tis grace hath brought me safe thus far,
And grace will lead me home.

The Lord has promised good to me,
His word my hope secures;
He will my shield and portion be,
As long as life endures.

Yea, when this flesh and heart shall fail,
And mortal life shall cease,
I shall possess, within the veil,
A life of joy and peace.

The earth shall soon dissolve like snow,
The sun forbear to shine;
But God, who called me here below,
Will be forever mine.

When we've been there ten thousand years,
Bright shining as the sun,
We've no less days to sing God's praise
Than when we'd first begun.[31]

I pray these two closing hymns have stirred your heart. I hope they are or will become compass hymns for you too. Both are saturated with sound theology and application for the realities of life. Both are filled with the power of God's love for us and our obedient response to Him. Both speak from hearts filled with the fear of, love for, and assured hope in Almighty God.

Thank you for reading these stories. They tell only a portion of the ways God has lovingly, faithfully, and abundantly blessed me through unique situations in my life. It has been my honor to share with you how God's amazing grace has shaped and molded me, about my delightful marriage to Candy, about my invaluable friendships, and, most of all, about my relationship with my Savior, Jesus Christ. Because of His grace, each day has indeed been an "amazing day of grace," a twenty-four-hour gift of life, blessings, joy, and peace.

The Lord only knows how many more days of grace remain for us in this world, for none of us is guaranteed a tomorrow in this life. Candy and I know not what lies ahead for us in this world, but we know with certainty that the most amazing day of all, the one eternal day of heaven, is indeed guaranteed for us because of Jesus. Until that day, we know we must gratefully, faithfully, and prayerfully keep our eyes on the wondrous cross of Christ, His perfect word of truth, and His amazing grace wherever life leads.

The LORD is my chosen portion and my cup; you hold my lot.
The lines have fallen for me in pleasant places; indeed, I have a
beautiful inheritance.
—Psalm 16:5-6

"Father God, it is in the name of Christ Jesus and in the power of the Holy Spirit that Candy and I pray. We praise You for who You are, for You are the only true God, the triune God, the Redeemer and Master of our souls, and the Lord of our lives. You alone are perfectly holy, righteous, just, and good. We thank You for how You have lovingly poured Your mercy and grace over us, for it is only in You that we have life. We thank You for leading us safely this far and for the assurance that You will indeed lead us home to our beautiful inheritance: face-to-face life with You for all eternity. We thank You for giving me the opportunity and guidance to write this book. Thank You for the countless blessings in our lives and the chance to use this book to share just a portion of them with others. May You bless each reader and use this book and our lives for Your glory. Amen."

APPENDIX A:
EXCERPTS FROM
JOHN BARTON'S
MD ANDERSON CAREPAGE

Between June 17, 2008 and December 25, 2008, Candy and I posted eighty-two entries in my MD Anderson CarePage blog. During that time we received nearly a thousand messages of encouragement, love, and prayer from family, friends, and even from people we did not know. Below is a sample of twenty-four of our posts.**

Note: Most Scripture references are from the NIV84.

CAREPAGE UPDATES

Posted Jun 17, 2008 7:06pm

We had our initial examination at MD Anderson with the primary oncologist (Dr. Diaz), physician's assistant, and scheduler this morning. We really like Dr. Diaz. He is very personable, frank, and comes highly recommended. I then had some lab work and x-rays, and attended an orientation class. Tomorrow morning at 6:30 I'll have a CT scan. Other tests are being scheduled; we should hear the schedule for them later today.

Dr. Diaz's initial observations are this: It's bad. He guesses that this is phase 4 cancer (on a scale of 1 to 4). It may involve most of the right side of the tongue. It has spread from the oral cavity part of the tongue (the part you can see) to the base part that is connected to the throat. That explains why I have had increasing amount of pain in swallowing. The cancer has also entered the nerves in the tongue, which explains why I have lots of pain and in the ear and most and the right side of my head. The treatment will almost certainly include surgery, radiation, and chemotherapy, although the order of those is yet to be determined. They may do surgery first, or it may make sense to try to try to shrink

---

** These CarePage entries have been copied verbatim. They were treated as historical text and have therefore not been edited.

the tumor with chemotherapy first. Dr. Diaz and the other doctors who will be involved will meet this Thursday night, and they will determine the best game plan. Dr. Diaz will present that game plan for my approval next Tuesday morning. He said it is good that I am young (I liked hearing that) and otherwise healthy, because to defeat this thing "we are going to beat the crap out of you." It won't be fun, but it can be beaten, and they have the weapons to do it. So while the diagnosis and prognosis are bad, the good news is that we are in the right place. For that we are most grateful.

That's about all we know at this point. They did give me some more potent pain medicine and gave me orders to try to put on some weight. Since I can't eat, that means lots of Ensure and milkshakes. We don't yet know if we will come home this weekend or stay down here; it depends on the scheduling of the other tests.

The bright spot of the day was visiting with dear friends Jim and Cyndi Siegfried for about an hour. They are in Houston while Jim is receiving radiation treatments. It is a great blessing and encouragement to know them and others who have gone down similar roads.

We know that the battle before us will be difficult, but we are in good hands. Psalm 46:1 tells us that *"God is our refuge and strength, an ever present help in trouble."*

Resting in Him,
John

Posted Jun 29, 2008 1:04pm

Happy Birthday, Candy!

"He who finds a wife finds what is good, and receives favor from the Lord."

Proverbs 18:22

I don't know what I would do without my lovely bride!

After a couple of days, Mr. PEG tube and I are slowly getting used to each other. I think we'll end up having a great relationship. Tomorrow is another big day, as I have my first appointment with Dr. Tauer at West Clinic, and we will find out the plan for my chemotherapy. Thanks for your prayers!

John

Posted Jul 3, 2008 6:54pm

Thursday, July 3, my first day of chemotherapy. The day I had hoped would never be necessary. The day I have fought not to be fearful of. The day was finally here. And this evening I can tell you it was a day that had "God" written all over it.

He filled the early morning with great encouragement and comfort from His word as I read in 2 Corinthians 12:9:

"But He said to me, 'My grace is sufficient for you, for My power is made perfect in weakness.'"

He arranged that my first day of chemo at West Clinic would be on friend Dana Carmen's last day of chemo treatments at West Clinic. Dana is one of three parents on our sons' soccer team that is battling cancer. A healthy Dana was a lively, bright, kind, friendly and funny lady. Dana with cancer has been all those things and more. She beams the joy of Christ and brightens the day for all in her path. Today in the West Clinic treatment room she and husband Don gave me a wonderful devotion book and a CD they burned with some great inspirational music. I could almost hear God telling me, "This is what a journey through difficulty looks like when you walk through it keeping your eyes and faith in Me. I can make your painful trial a time of great joy which you can share with others." Thanks, Dana and Don! Thank You, Lord!

The treatments themselves were pretty non-eventful. They took measures to minimize side effects, and so far I have not felt bad today, only tired. But other people in the treatment room probably didn't think I looked very tired as Candy and I cheered and high-fived at the softball news from Colorado. My friend Shawn Roberts sent numerous text messages, and in the end our Germantown Red Devils 16U team defeated two very good teams from Atlanta and Baton Rouge 4-2 and 4-3. The Red Devils are still undefeated in 6 games against some excellent competition from teams all over the country. Shaq (our Laura's softball name) continues having the greatest tournament of her life, going 4 for 6 at the plate today and making some great plays in right field. I commented the other day that when our kids' sports teams play well, other activities (meals, family relations) seem to go better too. Add chemotherapy to the list!

Twenty-five years ago, Candy was in a young singles class unofficially known as the Bellevue Bachelorettes. One of the other Bachelorettes was Anita Arnold, a good friend of a good friend of mine. Anita encouraged me to ask Candy for a date, and with her help, I finally got the courage to do so. Therefore, even though we have rarely seen Anita through our married life, she has remained one of my favorite people of all-time because of her role in me finding the girl of my dreams. So guess who comes to the treatment room at West Clinic today to hug us? You got it – Dr. Anita Arnold, an oncologist with West Clinic. When I saw Anita, my jaw dropped and I knew that it was just another sign from God, saying, "John, I am all over this situation. Just keep trusting Me, listening to Me, following Me, and sharing Me. Don't focus on the troubles that are to come, but on the blessings that will overflow."

Thanks to all of you. The Lord is using you to bless us greatly, and we are most thankful.

John

Posted Jul 7, 2008 11:51am

In the same way, the Spirit helps us in our weakness. We do not know what we ought to pray for, but the Spirit Himself intercedes for us with groans that words cannot express. And He who searches our hearts knows the mind of the Spirit, because the Spirit intercedes for the saints in accordance with God's will. And we know that in all things God works for the good of those who love Him, who have been called according to His purpose.

Romans 8:26-28

Folks, I'll be honest – these have been a very tough few days. This is the final day of Round 1 of chemotherapy, and we are glad to see it come to an end. We have had to simultaneously deal with a host of issues, ranging from bad side effects of chemo to bad direct effects from the cancer. We have prayed for strength, prayed for comfort, prayed for wisdom, prayed for healing, and sometimes we just don't know what to pray for. Yet God's word assures us that the Holy Spirit is always with us, interceding for us. None of the challenges we face can separate us from the love of God. By faith we know without a doubt that God is in this situation, and is working through it for the good of the body of Christ. For that, we choose this day to praise God for who He is, what He has done, and what He is doing. We thank Him for how He is working through so many people to pray for us and minister to us at this time.

I especially thank those of you who are praying for Candy. She is bearing a big load right now with great courage, faith, and diligence, and still has a long road ahead. I am so very thankful for her.

On a lighter family note, we will get daughter Laura back with us very late tonight. "Shaq" and her softball teammates are spending a final fun few hours in the mountains of Colorado today before heading home tonight (flying to Nashville, driving from there). The girls had an incredibly successful week of softball, winning 10 of 12 games, and finishing in second place in the prestigious Colorado Sparkler tournament. Way to go girls!

Thanks again to all of you,
John

Posted Jul 16, 2008 6:05pm

The Lord has been busy pouring blessings upon blessings over us in great and unexpected ways today!

Earlier this week some of my co-workers at International Paper organized a bake sale, with the intent of donating the proceeds to help us with our travel expenses. I was very grateful for their kindness. Regardless of the amount collected, the thoughtfulness would be a great blessing to us, and their kindness would be blessed by the Lord. But apparently God was in on this from the get-go. I don't know what they were selling at the bake sale, but my guess is that it was loaves and fishes. When my manager Dave Borchardt stopped by this afternoon to present the gift to us, our jaws dropped in total disbelief. We could only say thank you, even though that felt terribly inadequate. We are so very grateful for the generosity and friendship of these fine folks.

We continue to get cards, emails, and carepage messages that brighten our days, encourage us, assure us that we are loved and covered with prayer. We can never say thank you enough; we can only pray that the Lord will bless you as He has used you to bless us! The Lord has been so very good to us. He is so good and so gracious and so loving.

In His grip,
John

But as for me, it is good to be near God. I have made the Sovereign Lord my refuge; I will tell of all Your deeds.

Psalm 73:28

Posted Jul 21, 2008 11:01am

For we are God's workmanship, created in Christ Jesus to do good works, which God prepared in advance for us to do.

Ephesians 2:10

Yesterday was a very special day, as the elders of our church, Living Hope, came to our house to pray over me. It was a great honor and blessing for Candy and me. These men are not just elders in our church, but faithful friends who pray for me and my family on a regular basis. I pray that the Lord will greatly bless them, for they have been a great blessing to me. Each of these men has been through difficult days of testing and trials in the past. These aren't just men who talk the talk, but have walked the walk of difficult days. They have been great examples for me and countless others, as they display unwavering faith and dependence on God. In good and bad times, these men reflect the love, joy, and strength of Christ. I am so thankful for these men, and am so thankful for the time of worship we had with them Sunday afternoon.

Laura, aka Shaq, and her softball teammates will be getting home from Canada late tonight and be leaving tomorrow for a tournament in Oklahoma. Shaq has enjoyed playing in the various tournaments this summer, but she has been a bit homesick, and that feeling has been amplified by the fact that she has not had one of her parents with her at these far away tournaments, and by her concern for me. So we think it will be very good for Laura if Candy goes to Oklahoma with her, at least for a few days. It is an ideal time for Candy to be gone, since overall I am feeling pretty good, and am enjoying the last few days before the next round of chemotherapy, which starts Thursday.

Oh, by the way, the team did very well in the Canada Cup tournament. They won 8 of 11 games and finished in third place. Way to go, girls!

Michael is on his New York mission trip all week, so for at least a few days Joseph and I will be the only Barton in our house. But we will have many people from our expanded family of great friends and brothers and sisters in Christ helping us out. We continue to have many more offers to help than we have needs. It is such a wonderful blessing to have such a great family of friends, and to see God's workmanship in action.

Many thanks,
John

Posted Jul 24, 2008 7:21pm

And the peace of God, which transcends all understanding, will guard your hearts and your minds in Christ Jesus.

Philippians 4:7

Today was Day 1 of Round 2 of chemotherapy at West Clinic. I feel fine now. If things go as they did with Round 1, I will start feeling bad tomorrow and worse yet on Saturday and Sunday. But I think I am a little better prepared this time, so hopefully I will do better.

Before each doctor appointment at West Clinic, they have the patient fill out an inquiry on an electronic notebook. The answers are logged directly into a database that your doctor accesses before seeing you. It is a pretty neat tool, as the notebook also has several reports and articles on cancer and cancer recovery that you can read after the inquiry has been submitted and while you wait to see the doctor. The questions on the inquiry are about your current health status and what changes there have been since your last appointment. The format of the inquiry is that you answer each answer on a 0 to 10 scale, where 0 is "no problems" and 10 is "severe problems." The wise folk at West Clinic recognize the important link between physical health and emotional health, so the inquiry has several questions related to each.

After I answered all the questions, I reviewed my responses before submitting. My answers indicated that I have several physical health issues, yet virtually no emotional health problems. I asked myself if this is really an accurate picture. Am I being honest with myself? After all, it seems only natural that a person would have some degree of depression, sadness, isolation, or hopelessness when they have a very serious cancer and a very hard and long road ahead. I have indeed experienced some of those feelings, at least briefly, in the past several months. Yet today, I can honestly say that I have great joy despite the difficult circumstances we are in. I find it very easy to count many more blessings in my life than sorrows. I have an awesome family that loves me unconditionally. I have dozens of wonderful friends who minister to my family and me by being helping hands and feet, through visits, and through lots and lots of encouraging, loving, and inspiring messages. I have hundreds of people praying for me, some that I don't even know. And above it all, I have "the peace that transcends all understanding" through my relationship with Christ. It may be natural to have the blues when you have cancer, but they are overcome by the supernatural power of God!

The joy meter got another boost today when I heard that Shaq has been playing well this week in Oklahoma. After a super week in Colorado, her performance slipped some in Canada. I was not surprised, because I knew she was feeling homesick and missed not having her parents with her. Therefore I was not surprised to hear that she is playing much better now that Candy is with her. Of course the reason Candy is able to be with Shaq this week is because we have so many great friends helping me in Candy's absence. So whether you know it or not, you folks are a big help to the Germantown Red Devils summer team, because your help to me helps Candy and that helps Shaq and that helps her team. So on behalf of the Red Devils team coaches and players, thank you!

Gratefully yours,
John

Posted Jul 29, 2008 9:40am

For I am convinced that neither death nor life, neither angels nor demons, neither the present nor the future, nor any powers, neither height nor depth, nor anything else in all creation, will be able to separate us from the love of God that is in Christ Jesus our Lord.

Romans 8:38 -39

Sorry for not posting for a few days. This part of the journey has taken me through a dark tunnel of severe and unrelenting nausea for the past few days. Thankfully I have not had some of the other symptoms that we had to deal with in the first round of chemo. But the intensity of the nausea this time has made me so sick that I have not felt like doing anything. Yesterday (Monday) the pump was removed, thus ending this round of chemo, but the nausea has yet to fully subside. We hope that things will be much better by end of day today.

On days such as these have been, it is of great comfort to receive so many encouraging messages from people who are praying for us. I cannot begin to tell you how much your faithfulness is appreciated. For we know beyond a shadow of a doubt that God's hand is upon us, and He is listening to the prayers of His people. On good days and bad days, we are safe in His hands.

In family news, we have Michael back from his mission trip to New York, and Shaq has played her final softball tournament of the season. Joseph is spending this week with other students from Living Hope at a Service Over Self project in the Binghampton area.

John

Posted Jul 31, 2008 8:55am

Let the morning bring me word of Your unfailing love, for I have put my trust in You. Show me the way I should go, for to You I lift up my soul. Teach me to do Your will, for You are my God; may Your good Spirit lead me on level ground.

Psalm 143:8, 10

I awoke this morning just after dawn with the above verses on my mind. The last few days have continued to be very tough. I cannot seem to get over the nausea and vomiting from chemo and have been very sick. My weight continues to fall as I struggle to keep any nourishment down. Candy and I will be returning to West Clinic today; hopefully they will help get these turned around.

Yet each day has also brought blessings of encouragement. I have indeed felt quite discouraged at times, but a fresh word from the Lord or a note of gracious encouragement from a friend is never far behind. God's word never fails to assure of His great love for us, and that He is with us each step of the way. We also are constantly buoyed by the prayers, the love, the friendship, the encouragement, and the many helping hands and feet from people near and far.

Candy and I have been unable to individually thank each person that has helped us and encouraged us. I hope we can do a better job of that when things are better. Until then, please accept this as our expression of gratitude to you. I cannot imagine how dark this journey would be were it not for so many people standing with us and brightening our path.

John

May our Lord Jesus Christ Himself and God our Father, who loved us and by His grace gave us eternal encouragement and good hope, encourage your hearts and strengthen you in every good deed and word.

2 Thessalonians 2:16-17

Posted Aug 6, 2008 4:03pm

Candy and I got back home in Collierville Tuesday after flying to Jackson late Monday night and spending the night in Canton. We were both pretty tired yesterday, but feel rested today. Overall, things are pretty good now. The chemo was effective in shrinking the tumor to the point where I am no longer in any pain. The only issue now is the excessive secretions in my mouth, and we are expecting to get some better medicine for that today.

Our appointments at MD Anderson on Monday were interesting and provided some clarity to the issues we will be facing. We have a better understanding of what will be done during surgery and the challenges we will face afterwards. The basic plan is that Dr. Diaz will remove any cancerous cells he finds. We know that the tumor is large, and we expect that most and possibly all of the tongue will be removed. The plastic surgeon, Dr. Hanasono, will remove some flesh from my arm or leg to provide a "flap" to be attached in the mouth. The tongue is a very complex organ. The flap cannot provide any functions of the tongue, but would merely cover the space in the oral cavity. It is possible that the cancer has also spread to the throat and/or jaw bone. If so, Dr. Diaz will also have to remove those cancerous tissues. If some of the jaw bone has to be removed, Dr. Hanasono will use part of a bone from the lower leg to replace the lost jaw bone.

Obviously the more complex the surgery, the more difficult the recovery will be. We will also have to deal with six to seven weeks of radiation and probably more chemotherapy.

I have no idea of when it will be, but at some point we will finally be through all of the surgeries, treatments, and recovery, and be left with going through life in a different way than what we are used to. It is possible that I may not ever be able to eat solid food again. My speech will likely be very poor at best. I may look a good bit different than I do now. The severity of these things will depend a lot on how complex the surgery is.

Forgive me for posting such a lengthy update. From an emotional standpoint, it has not been easy thinking or writing about these things. I would have preferred not going into as much detail, but I dare not forsake the chance for you wonderful people to pray specifically about these matters. Please pray that the cancer is confined only to the tongue, and that some of the tongue can be salvaged. Please pray for wisdom for the surgeons and strength for Candy and me. Pray that the Lord's name will be glorified. Candy and I are thankful for your prayers and thankful that God hears them. As the word of God says in James 5:16, *"Therefore confess your sins to each other and pray for each other so that you may be healed. The prayer of a righteous man is powerful and effective."*

John

Posted Aug 8, 2008 9:13pm

A good Friday

The fruit of the Spirit is love, joy, peace, patience, kindness, goodness, faithfulness, gentleness and self-control.

Galatians 5:22-23

This verse came to mind today as I had a delightful visit with some of my International Paper work team members. I don't know how you could find a group of people as big-hearted and kind as my co-workers. In my July 16 update, I wrote that my work teammates decided to help Candy and me with our travel and medical expenses by raising funds with a bake sale. But this was no ordinary bake sale. We were completely blown away by how much money was raised. We thanked God for our work friends and thanked our friends for their generosity.

My manager is Dave Borchardt, a big guy from Wisconsin with a big heart. He is also a big Green Bay Packers fan and, up until this week, a big Brett Favre fan. Well, just like Brett doesn't know how to quit playing football, Dave and my other teammates apparently don't know how to quit bake-selling. They have continued to bake and bake and bake and sell and sell and sell over and over and over again. People from all over our building at Willow Lake have gotten involved and kept it going for 4 weeks now. As a result, they have raised a staggering amount of money for us. Candy and I have been simply overwhelmed by such loving generosity. Our thank you's seem far too inadequate. We pray that the Lord will greatly bless these kind-hearted people as He has greatly blessed us through them.

In family news, Candy and Joseph have arrived safely in Huntsville tonight for the first tournament of the new soccer season. Go Lobos! Michael is completing a very hot week of drum line camp at Mississippi State, and will start full band camp on Monday. Laura and I are holding down the fort this weekend. I am happy to report that I am feeling better now than I have in months. Many thanks for your faithful prayers!

John

Posted Aug 12, 2008 9:37pm

Reporting From Houston

Today (Tuesday) we had several appointments, starting with the most important, the appointment with Dr. Eduardo Diaz, the head and neck surgeon.

Dr. Diaz describes me as young, healthy (other than the cancer), tough, and motivated. Based on that assessment, I decided an apt description for Dr. Diaz would be highly intelligent, discerning, insightful, and quite observant! :-) Unfortunately, he said these things about me because he said all will be advantages during the very difficult recovery that he expects. As you may have guessed, he expects a difficult recovery because he anticipates a complex surgery. The latest scans and tests indicate a strong likelihood that the cancer has spread to places we had hoped that it would not. Of course, they will not know for sure until they start cutting Thursday morning. He asked us to not overlook the good news that surgery can be done, which is not always the case, and surgery is a must in defeating this cancer. For that we are grateful, yet Dr. Diaz could not help but notice the disappointment in our faces as he talked about the various procedures that are likely to be done. He said, "I'm sorry. I don't know if you were expecting miracles, but we're not in that business."

Fortunately, we do indeed know Someone in the miracle business. We continue to pray that the Lord will do something that only He can do. Perhaps that will be in providing a healing prior to the surgery. Perhaps He will leave the doctors wondering what went wrong with their scans. Perhaps He will strengthen me to recover faster and better than expected. Perhaps He will provide His wisdom and peace so that we may minister in His name more effectively than ever before, despite my physical condition. Or maybe He will do what He often does, bless us in ways that we never would have imagined. But this we do know with all certainty: There is no love greater than God's love for us. There is no place or circumstance that can separate us from the love of Christ. There is no greater hope than that which we place in Him.

Tomorrow I have but one appointment, an ultrasound tomorrow afternoon. We will also find out for sure the time of Thursday's surgery.

Thanks so much for all of your prayers, wonderfully encouraging messages, and for your friendship.

Blessings,
John

I remember my affliction and my wandering, the bitterness and the gall. I well remember them, and my soul is downcast within me. Yet this I call to mind and therefore I have hope: Because of the Lord's great love we are not consumed, for His compassions never fail. They are new every morning; great is Your faithfulness. I say to myself, "The Lord is my portion; therefore I will wait for Him." The

Lord is good to those whose hope is in Him, to the one who seeks Him; it is good to wait quietly for the salvation of the Lord.

Lamentations 3:19-26
(thanks, Steve)

Posted Aug 18, 2008 4:07pm

Recovery Day 4

We are doing very well! We got in to a private room from ICU late Saturday night and would have moved earlier, but the hospital didn't have any rooms available. (The nurse let us watch Michael Phelps' final race before we left ICU.) John is slowly getting various tubes and wires taken out (Yeah!) The foot-long incision on his thigh has been much more sore than the tongue, but it will heal much faster. John started walking a little on Sunday and will be increasing each day. The biggest risk in surgeries like these is pneumonia (in fact the doctors say that it is a given that he will get it), so he is doing tons of breathing treatments and exercises to try to keep his lungs opened up and not infected. Today we talked to a LOT of people, including a physical therapist and a speech therapist who told us John will need both therapies extensively in the months to come. We also had visits today from Dietary Dept., Social Services, Housekeeping, Volunteer Services, Accounting, Valet parking, and some guy named Kenny who just wanted to talk to someone. (Just kidding about Kenny!) As you can imagine, getting rest is quite a challenge. Last night, John sent me back to the hotel so that I could get some uninterrupted sleep and it helped tremendously! All in all, John is getting better every day. It is a good, strong start to a long road of recovery. We continue to see evidence of answered prayers with every step. Please pray that John will get some rest tonight and that he will not get pneumonia (a "given").

Ps. 103:8, 11, 13

The Lord is compassionate and gracious, slow to anger, abounding in love. . . . .For as high as the heavens are above the earth, so great is His love for those who fear Him. . . . As a father has compassion on his children, so the Lord has compassion on those who fear Him.

All for now,
Candy (with a lot of help from John)

Posted Aug 20, 2008 4:45pm

Travel Day

It was only a faint sound as we boarded the shuttle van, but I am pretty sure I heard a public announcement at the MD Anderson hospital that said, "John has left the building." After a very short drive – basically across the street – we were at our destination, the Rotary House (the hotel for the hospital).

Yep, I got discharged from the hospital today and am back in the hotel across the street, the Rotary House. The discharge is a day or two earlier than expected, and is based on the terrific progress I have made in recovery. One doctor told me this morning, "You have done as well as any person in your condition could possibly do." All I can say is thanks so much for your faithful prayers, and thank the Lord for answering them in this way.

Another view of the discharge is a bit of apprehension, for I still have need for many daily hours of health care, but that care will now be shifted from the MDA nursing staff to Candy and John Barton, with emphasis on Candy. We have gotten crash courses the last two days on taking care of a tracheostomy, the use of special devices used for breathing exercises, emptying drain bottles, using a feeding tube (we already knew that one), cleaning incisions, and other fun things, all of which will need to be done multiple times each day. In my spare time, I am supposed to walk as much as possible.

But please don't take that as a complaint. I am grateful to be in a position to go to the Rotary House today. It is by the grace of the Lord that I was the staff's primo patient for the week. Candy and I have a very long list of patient care to-do's each day, but guess who is in charge of the schedule for those things? It's not the therapist who has a breathing treatment for me at 2:15AM. We plan to see only one 2:15 each day from now on. It's not the nursing assistant who takes my vitals at 3:00AM. Candy has put me on notice that nothing will be vital between the hours of 10PM and whenever she wakes up AM.

We really appreciated our family members who came to see us. And we appreciated Bill, a friend of a friend of a friend of Candy's sister. Bill came to see Candy during the surgery, with doughnuts and assurance of his prayer support. He later came to see me in ICU. Bill is just a guy who doesn't know us but heard about us and decided to take action. I could not help but think of Matthew 25: 34-36:

"Then the King will say to those on his right, 'Come, you who are blessed by My Father; take your inheritance, the kingdom prepared for you since the creation of the world. 35For I was hungry and you gave me something to eat, I was thirsty and you gave me something to drink, I was a stranger and you invited me in, I needed clothes and you clothed me, I was sick and you looked after me, I was in prison and you came to visit me."

Hopefully, I will think of Bill and of these verses in a whole new light the next time I have a chance to be of service to someone. Hopefully I will respond like so many of you have helped my family and me in recent weeks and months.

Thanks so much,
John

Posted Aug 24, 2008 8:18pm

Visitors Day

"He who dwells in the shelter of the Most High will rest in the shadow of the Almighty. I will say of the Lord, He is my refuge and my fortress, my God, in whom I trust." Ps. 91:1-2

Greetings from Barton Refuge in Houston, TX! We have spent the last couple of days resting and decompressing from the surgery and hospital stay. John is doing very well and primarily caring for himself, so all I have to do is trach care. We are walking a couple of times of day, watching quite a bit of Olympics (so nice of them to schedule during John's surgery and recovery), reading, and generally chilling out. Today we had a special treat—visitors!

This morning we visited with John's college buddy Craig who drove to Houston from his home in Austin, Texas to see us. John hadn't seen Craig in 20 years, but they had exchanged e-mails over John's illness. I am so thankful that John and now I have such a fine, godly man for a friend.

This afternoon we visited with our good friends and mentors, Jim & Cyndi Siegfried. Jim has been a cancer patient in Houston on and off for six years. It is such a blessing to spend time with a Christian couple who have walked down the cancer road ahead of us, faced some of the same issues that we are facing, and have been strengthened in their faith through all of it.

We have a busy week ahead of us with doctors' appointments on Tuesday, Wednesday, and Friday. We will be getting the all important pathology report from Dr. Diaz on Tuesday and will hopefully get the trach out. Wednesday is the follow up appointment with the plastic surgeon who will take John's last drain out. Friday is the modified barium swallow which will show how John's swallow function is working (very important) and give us an indication of how much work John will need in speech therapy.

Life is different now. John looks a little different in some ways (but not as different as he thinks he looks) and will have to learn how to do some things like speaking and eating in different ways. However, he is still the same person—same smile, same corny jokes, same mischievous glint in his eye. He is the same John that I fell in love with 25 years ago and for that I am so thankful!

Resting in the Shadow,
Candy

Posted Aug 27, 2008 10:15pm

Wednesday Appointment

Today I had my surgical post-op appointment with the Plastic Surgery department. Those are the folks, headed by Dr. Matt Hanasono, who took part of my thigh to create a flap to replace the area in the mouth vacated by the cancerous tissue that Dr. Diaz removed. Dr. Hanasono was not in town today, so I was seen by a Physician's Assistant, Mindy. She said that the flap, and neck incision, and thigh incision all look good. Then Mindy made the Top Plays of the Day list when she removed the last remaining drain and stitches from my neck. Nice play, Mindy! My neck now has significantly less pain and I no longer have the annoyance of lugging around the drain tube and collection bottle. My next appointment with the Plastic Surgery department will be the same date as my next appointment with Dr. Diaz, which is scheduled for September 30 as of now.

For several weeks now I have had various things stuck in me that could not get wet, so I have had to take baths and sponge baths instead of showering. After the departure of the drain tube, the only medical accessory sticking in me is my feeding tube, which is OK to get wet. So as soon as we got back to the room, I had the long-awaited joy of a nice, warm, shower. Aaaaaahhh.

This afternoon Candy rode the hotel shuttle to do some shopping. Along the way, she met a couple from Chattanooga, who told Candy of a friend who has been battling cancer for seven years. She has had cancer in several different places, but it started in the tongue. Tonight Candy and I read more about the lady's story on her care page. It was very sobering.

Sobering. What a good word. So much more palatable than disturbing, frightening, or downright scary. So I will stick with sobering. It was sobering to read about how long she has been on the cancer road. It was sobering to read how painful and harmful some of her treatments have been. It was sobering to read about how many times cancer had appeared to be whipped, only to make an unwanted and unexpected comeback. It was sobering to consider how my cancer journey may be or may not be similar to hers.

At that point I decided that there was no profit in thinking any more about such things. None of us know what our future on earth holds. Each of us will have some joys and have some troubles. Rather than worrying about the unknown troubles, I choose to focus on some known joys for the upcoming journey:

Deuteronomy 31:6 - Be strong and courageous. Do not be afraid or terrified because of them, for the Lord your God goes with you; He will never leave you nor forsake you.

Psalm 119:105 - Your word is a lamp to my feet and a light for my path.

John 14: 1 and 6: Jesus told His disciples "Do not let your hearts be troubled. Trust in God, trust also in Me……. I am the way, and the truth, and the life. No one comes to the Father except through Me."

Philippians 4: 4-7 Rejoice in the Lord always. I will say it again: Rejoice! Let your gentleness be evident to all. The Lord is near. Do not be anxious about anything, but in everything, by prayer and petition, with thanksgiving, present your requests to God. And the peace of God, which transcends all understanding, will guard your hearts and your minds in Christ Jesus.

These are but a few joyous truths from God's word on which I can put my head and sleep well tonight. It is also wonderfully comforting to know that so many of you are praying for us. You fill our journey with love, encouragement, and friendship. You are greatly appreciated!

Many thanks,
John

Posted Aug 30, 2008 8:06am

Heading Home Saturday

Do you remember when you were a child and it seemed like it took Christmas Day FOREVER to finally arrive? Candy and I have been much like that about this date, August 30, the day we will finally fly home. Laura and Joseph, get ready for some really big hugs! We can't wait to see you!!! Please do not feel left out, Michael. We would love to see you, too, but I don't think the plane has a layover in Ruston. We hope the Famous Maroon Band and the MSU football team perform spectacularly tonight!

Of course we also look forward to seeing friends and neighbors who have been so wonderful in helping us, praying for us, encouraging us, and loving us. At this time we would like to express our most sincere appreciation to the Roberts family and the Tate family for taking care of Laura and Joseph while we have been away. Better friends were never had.

Oh yeah, this is supposed to be a medical update page, isn't it? Overall, I am continuing to progress, but as you would expect the rate of daily progress has slowed.

We decided to spend our last night in Houston (for a little while) having some fun. So last night we went to Minute Maid Field and watched the St. Louis Cardinals and Houston Astros play! It was the first major league game we have been to in a few years and we really enjoyed it. Candy had called the Astros ticket office and explained my situation that I can walk but cannot go up and down stairs yet. So they got us very good seats on the concourse level that required no step ups or down. We were not sure if I could handle such an adventure, but we made it through. I coughed quite a bit, but we were rather isolated, so it was OK. We have not been to that many major league games over the years, mostly because we would much rather see Shaq play softball and Joseph play soccer than Albert Pujols or Chipper Jones play baseball. But we have been fortunate enough to see some great major league games when we have gone. In fact, a majority of games we have seen have ended with a walk-off homer in the bottom of the ninth. I guess the lesson there is don't go see one of our favorite teams play on the road. Last night Lance Berkman of the Astros broke a 2-2 tie and ended the game with a homer in the bottom of the ninth. How exciting! What a good game! What a bummer that the Cardinals lost!

Thanks Candy, Jim, and Pete for talking me into making a go at attending the game last night. It was indeed fun, and there have not been many activities here the last three weeks that fall in the "fun" category. Yet there have been many, many very important and life-changing events in the last three weeks. Physically I will never be the same as before I got here. Emotionally there have been some highs and lows. Spiritually things have happened that I never dreamed would happen. We have been completely covered with the Lord's grace in ways we never have experienced before. We have been prayed for by hundreds of people and have definitely felt the support of those prayers. We have received so much love, encouragement, and support from hundreds of people that we are left grasping for new ways to say thank you in a deeper way. We simply pray that the Lord will abundantly bless you as He has worked through you to bless us. May His grace and peace fill your days.

If that sounded like a goodbye, it wasn't. This is just a rest station along a very long journey. We continue to ask for your faithful prayer support. We love you guys. We will now sign off from Houston with a favorite Scripture to which we cling today and will be doing so as we continue the journey:

Isaiah 40:28-31: Do you not know? Have you not heard? The LORD is the everlasting God, the Creator of the ends of the earth. He will not grow tired or weary, and His understanding no one can fathom. He gives strength to the weary and increases the power of the weak. Even youths grow tired and weary, and young men stumble and fall; but those who hope in the LORD will renew their strength. They will soar on wings like eagles; they will run and not grow weary, they will walk and not be faint.

Soaring John

Posted Oct 13, 2008 7:39pm

Paved Roads

The streets in our neighborhood were repaved during the last couple of weeks, and it has been a welcome improvement. The rough spots, dips, and bumps have all been covered and the driving is much smoother. I have been thinking about our streets as I ponder the figurative road my family and I have traveled during this journey through cancer, and of the road that lies ahead. We have certainly been through some bumps, dips, and very rough spots. Other times have been much smoother, especially during the past couple of weeks. The turn we are about to take, however, comes with lots of danger signs. Tomorrow (Tuesday) morning, I will get the first of six weekly doses of chemotherapy. Tomorrow night, I will receive the first of 30 radiation treatments, which will be received 5 days a week.

This is not a road I wish to travel, but one that I must. The radiation is designed to kill the residual cancer cells that linger. The chemo makes the cells more sensitive to the radiation. It is not a step that can be skipped in a cancer case like mine. The chemo will be in much lower doses than I received in July. We do not expect it to make me sick as it did then. The radiation treatments themselves are challenging but not painful, but the side effects are difficult. Some side effects are short-term, some are long-term, some are very long-term. I have read about head and neck radiation, heard what the doctors have to say about it, and have heard the stories of several people who have actually been through it. No one yet has said it will be easy. The unanimous opinion seems to be that this road will indeed be rough. For some, the road was merely difficult. For others it was a harrowing ride. How will it be for me? Since I am having so many different places radiated, it will probably be pretty tough, but only time will tell.

Yet I also know this is not a road I travel alone. God has promised to be with me, and He has indeed shown that He has been with my family and me every step of the journey thus far. I know beyond a shadow of a doubt that He will continue to be with us and bless us. I know that there will be pain on this road, but I pray that He will pave it over with His amazing love and grace. I know that this road will bring some discomfort, but I pray that He will pave it over with His comfort and His peace, the kind that is so great that it just doesn't make sense. I know that there will be difficult days, but I pray that the Lord will pave them with His joy, the kind that can only come from Him. I trust in the word of Lord, which says in Isaiah 26:7:

"The path of the righteous is level, O upright One, You make the way of the righteous smooth."

I also know that my family and I travel this road with the covering of prayer from hundreds of people, many of which read this carepage. I cannot begin to describe how comforting that is, and cannot begin to thank you enough for your faithfulness and friendship.

Gratefully yours,
John

Surely God is my salvation; I will trust and not be afraid. The Lord is my strength and my song; He has become my salvation.

Isaiah 12:2

Peace I leave with you; My peace I give you. I do not give to you as the world gives. Do not let your hearts be troubled and do not be afraid.

The words of Jesus in John 14:27

Posted Oct 21, 2008 6:14pm

Doubleheaders

Many of you know how much I enjoy baseball and softball. Oops, sorry Laura, I know that's supposed to be softball and baseball. When I was growing up in Starkville – my kids say such history is usually written on a stone tablet - I loved going to Mississippi State baseball games. For a number of years way back then, 3-game SEC series consisted of a doubleheader on Saturday and a single game on Sunday afternoon. I loved the Saturday games. What was better than watching a baseball game? Watching 2 baseball games! The Saturday doubleheaders eventually gave way to single games Friday through Sunday for SEC baseball, but the SEC softball girls still play Saturday doubleheaders. Laura is usually playing in tournaments of her own on weekends, but when possible, we try to catch a college softball doubleheader.

In the current phase of my journey through cancer, I have doubleheaders on Tuesdays. I have chemotherapy infusions on Tuesday morning, and radiation treatments Tuesday afternoons. These doubleheaders are not nearly as much fun as softball and baseball doubleheaders. [If we were having this discussion at the family dinner table, I would probably say the types of doubleheaders are not even in the same ball park, just to watch Laura roll her eyes and Joseph shake his head. That is Barton secret code for "We love your corny jokes, Dad!"] But I know the current doubleheaders are vitally necessary. The chemo makes the cancer cells look like big fat hanging curve balls so the radiation can knock them out of the park. [Come on, Laura, you know you liked that one.] The worst of the side effects from the treatments are expected to arrive in a week or two. Today I just feel more fatigued. One disappointment today was that my white blood cell count dropped 33% from last week to fall below the normal range. That reinforces the doctor's instructions to be careful about exposure to germs and viruses.

So I now have completed 2 of 6 chemo treatments and 5 of 30 radiation treatments. I must admit I went into this phase with some concern. Big concerns. I'll leave it at that since I am not supposed to be afraid. Yet when I confessed my fea …. I mean concerns... to God, He reassured me that He will be with me, and that as long as my trust in Him is greater than my ..uh. concerns, then I have nothing to worry about. And once again, He has provided tremendous peace as He assures me of His presence each and every time the radiation mask is clamped down on my head. In Psalm 139:5, the psalmist says, "You hem me in behind and before, and You lay Your hand upon me." In other words, I cannot get to the clinic early enough to beat God there. He is there with me the whole time, and lets me know that He is. He will be there for the remaining treatments, there for the next trip to Houston (now scheduled for December 14), and in those places the doctors don't know about but He does.

The next verse says that "Such knowledge is too wonderful for me, too lofty for me to attain." No I cannot figure out God, how He does what He does. But He only asked me to take Him at His word, and then proceeds to show me that He is faithful, perfectly faithful.

I got away from the softball metaphors, didn't I? Don't worry, Laura and Joseph. We'll be sitting down for dinner soon!

Many thanks for all your prayers,
John

Posted Oct 31, 2008 10:29am

Friday the 13th

This Halloween Friday morning I had my 13th radiation treatment. It is not really like a horror movie. In a horror movie, a mad scientist and his henchmen would take an innocent man, strip him of his shirt, and force him flat on his back on a cold, hard, table. A mask that is eerily in the exact shape of the victim's own head and shoulders would be bolted down over the man and into the cold table, a fit so tight that the victim cannot move. The henchmen would have forced a piece of wax into the man's mouth so large that he could not swallow the phlegm and secretions that would soon be building up in the back of his throat. Then the mad scientist would use his latest evil invention, a terrifying machine that zaps the poor man with rays of radiation beams, over and over and over again. The horrific radiation would cause the man to have neck sunburn from the inside out, and to have painful sores in his mouth and throat that continue to get worse and worse and worse. The mad scientist would not be satisfied with such gruesome fun and games for a day or even a week, but would keep bringing the same victim back week after week after torturous week.

No, my experience is not like that all. Dr. Gieschen is certainly not mad, but quite sane, intelligent, and helpful. The radiation center uses only highly qualified technicians, not henchmen. The doctors, technicians, and assistants are all very caring and friendly. There is no evil laughter or scary music in the background as they zap me with radiation over and and over and over and .....

Sorry about that. I couldn't help having a Halloween theme to today's update. The truth is that the 22-minute treatments themselves are still a challenge, and the cumulative effect of the treatments is beginning to take their toll. The sores in my mouth have become more plentiful and have gotten more painful each day this week. Although I still have a problem with phlegm in my throat when I lie flat, my throat generally feels very dry and sore. We knew all this was coming, but were not sure when. These side effects are expected to get worse over the remaining 17 treatments. There are some mouth rinses and drugs to lessen the pain, but only to an extent.

Fortunately, there is a help for these times that is far greater than any medicine.

When my spirit grows faint within me, it is You who know my way. .....O Lord, hear my prayer, listen to my cry for mercy; In Your faithfulness and righteousness come to my relief. .....I spread out my hands to You; my soul thirsts for you like a parched land.....Let the morning bring me word of Your unfailing love, for I have put my trust in You. Show me the way I should go, for to You I lift up my soul.

Psalm 142:3, 143:1,6,8

The LORD is my rock, my fortress and my deliverer; my God is my rock, in whom I take refuge. He is my shield and the horn of my salvation, my stronghold.

Psalm 18:2

Be joyful in hope, patient in affliction, faithful in prayer.

Romans 12:12

The sores are still there, but their discomfort is overmatched by the indescribable comfort provided by the presence of the Lord. I am comforted by the reassurance of so many people praying for me. I comforted by friends that help me and my family in many ways many times a week. This is certainly no horror movie, but a challenging time that allows us to see God and His people doing some of their best work.

Thanks to Him and thanks to you,
John

Posted Nov 7, 2008 11:11am

Bacon, Eggs, and Toast

Because of the Lord's great love we are not consumed, for His compassions never fail. They are new every morning; great is Your faithfulness.

Lamentations 3:22-23

The law of the LORD is perfect, reviving the soul

Psalm 19:7

My Mom was a big believer in the concept that breakfast is the most important meal of the day, and most of my days started with a great breakfast, which usually included bacon, eggs, and toast. She rarely had trouble with my brother and me sleeping late, for it was practically impossible to lie in bed with the smell of bacon and eggs in the air! We ate well and then washed it down with a glass of Tang, just like the astronauts did! I surely did not know what a good life we had.

My current breakfast is not quite as alluring: 2 cans of Nutren poured down my feeding tube. I am grateful for it and it serves me well, but it just doesn't enliven the senses the way Mom's breakfast did. Over the years, however, I have found another top of the morning jump starter that really gets my day off on the right track: the word of God. The day always goes better if I start it by spending time with God in His word and in prayer. It is good food for the soul, no matter what our circumstances. It always gives me something I really need for that day: a word of encouragement, a word of correction, an assignment, or perhaps a change in perspective. But it is always refreshing and satisfying, even more so than a plate of hot eggs and bacon and a cold glass of Tang!

This week has been a challenging one. As expected the radiation treatments and their aftermath continue to get worse. When you look at me, it looks like I have been in a fight and gotten the worst of it, as my mouth and lips are quite swollen. The inside of my mouth looks like a war zone, with sores throughout. There is also thick, gunky saliva hanging about like cobwebs in an old house. I cannot see down my throat, but the pain lets me know it has received some battle wounds as well. None of this is unexpected; it is simply the collateral damage from radiation in this battle with cancer.

Yet even on difficult weeks like this, the word of God is there to refresh me, to give me hope and a word of encouragement that I need. His word reminds me that I am not walking this path alone, that God's strength and peace are there for the asking. He tells me to not lose heart and to not lose my joy in Him. I am encouraged to keep on doing what I can with good nutrition and exercise every day, and to remain faithful in praying for others as so many are praying for me.

I am indeed grateful for God's word, and grateful for your prayers. After this afternoon's visit to the radiation clinic, I will have completed 18 treatments and have 12 more to go (the dirty dozen; sounds like one of my carepage titles, doesn't it?). I welcome the two days rest this weekend. I hope you all will get to enjoy some bacon, eggs, and toast!

Many thanks,
John

The Lord gives strength to His people; the Lord blesses His people with peace.

Psalm 29:11

Therefore we do not lose heart. Though outwardly we are wasting away, yet inwardly we are being renewed day by day. For our light and momentary troubles are achieving for us an eternal glory that far outweighs them all. So we fix our eyes not on what is seen, but on what is unseen. For what is seen is temporary, but what is unseen is eternal.

2 Corinthians 4:16-18

Posted Nov 14, 2008 8:09pm

Sounds of the Season

During my radiation treatments, I can hear the radio music that plays in the radiation room. It is not very loud and I usually do not pay much attention to it. On Thursday of this week however, I noticed that all of the songs were Christmas songs. Yes, this particular radio station has already started playing continuous Christmas music and will do so for the next six weeks. Of course the radiation technicians also noticed and made comments about it. One said, "Isn't it a little early for Christmas music? It isn't even Thanksgiving yet." Another said, "Yes, but Thanksgiving is almost here and Christmas will be here before you know it." We have all heard that sentiment expressed at one time or the other. The rapidity of the passage of time, however, usually depends on your perspective. My last radiation treatment is scheduled for November 25, two days before Thanksgiving. The calendar says that is a mere week and half away. Yet when I consider that I must endure 7 more radiation treatments and the side effects thereof, Thanksgiving seems a very, very long time away.

This is not an easy season. Each treatment is more difficult and the side effects get a little worse each day. My digestive system has made lots of music this week, but can't seem to decide between just Sitting on the Dock of the Bay or doing the Flight of the Bumblebee. In addition to the sores in my throat, mouth, and lips, some skin on my neck and face is chafed and painful. All my neck and lower face are red and hairless, as the hair follicles have been destroyed by the radiation. My face has taken on a definite starboard list, as the right side of my face and neck are quite swollen. The thick secretions continue to be difficult to manage. Speaking continues to get more difficult.

My intention is not to whine about my situation. I do want to be honest with you folks on the difficulties of going through radiation. But I also want to share the great message of hope, that even in times like this our days can be full of joy and joyous songs as we read and hear the Lord's melodious words of truth, and our hearts sing praises to Him. Even on a dark and rainy night like this, the love of God can shine brightly in our lives. God wants me to cry out to Him, to come to Him, to listen to Him, to talk to Him, and yes, even sing to Him.

In my distress I called to the LORD; I called out to my God. From his temple He heard my voice; my cry came to His ears.

2 Samuel 22:7

"Come to me, all you who are weary and burdened, and I will give you rest."

The words of Jesus in Matthew 11:28

"My sheep listen to my voice; I know them, and they follow me."

The words of Jesus in John 10:27

In the morning, O LORD, you hear my voice; in the morning I lay my requests before you and wait in expectation.

Psalm 5:3

I will sing to the LORD, for he has been good to me.

Psalm 13:6

I don't think that I'm quite ready to sing Christmas carols just yet, but the enduring song the Lord has put in my heart sure makes it a lot easier to endure times like this.

Thanks for your many prayers,
John

Posted Nov 25, 2008 5:35pm

Back in the Saddle Again

The stomach infection kept me from mounting up yesterday, but I am back on the trail today, and completed treatment #29. The final treatment is scheduled for tomorrow (Wednesday) at 12:30. Yea!

Candy and I have been completely overwhelmed by the response we got after sending out a request for prayer Sunday night. Less than 24 hours later we had heard from dozens of people. We heard from friends and family through care page messages, emails, phone calls, and text messages. We heard from family and friends who have known me my whole life, friends we have only recently met, and all sorts in between. We heard from friends from Texas to North Carolina. We heard from church friends, work friends, sports friends, Collierville friends. We had friends bring us food, books, monetary gifts, and cards. The outpouring of prayer, love, and support was simply amazing. We are indeed blessed.

In my devotional book, I read today that "thankfulness takes the sting out of adversity." The writer also adds that it is a mysterious transaction, certainly not a logical one, whereby we offer our thanks for God for everything, regardless of our feelings, and He clearly blesses us with joy, regardless of our circumstances. I can surely attest to those observations. This is certainly a time of adversity, with a terribly sore mouth and very painful burns on my neck. Both will take a long time to heal. Add to that a belly full of pain over the weekend, and you got a strong case of adversity. Yet the pain has definitely had its sting dulled by thankfulness. We are thankful for the Lord's clear hand on us as we have traveled this rocky road. We are thankful that He has put us in a position to see Him work as we never have before. We are thankful for an amazing outpouring of love, support, and prayers we have had from hundreds of people. We are thankful that the Lord has worked through so many people to bless us. We are thankful for our three fine children, and for the many friends who have helped them.

Romans 15:13 says:

"May the God of hope fill you with all joy and peace as you trust in Him, so that you may overflow with hope by the power of the Holy Spirit."

I can think of no better description of our experiences along this trail. God has blessed our lives, and blessed us again by allowing us to share the love of God as He overflows our lives with His joy and peace.

As we approach the Thanksgiving Day, I can honestly say I am aware of blessings this year more than any year before. Yes, I have some physical pain and challenges, and will have some for a while. Yet I think I could write up those quite thoroughly in five minutes time, while I would need at least 5 hours to get a good start on things for which I am thankful.

Thankfully yours,
John

You are my God, and I will give You thanks;
You are my God, and I will exalt You.
Give thanks to the LORD, for He is good; His love endures forever.
Psalm 118:28-29

Posted Nov 26, 2008 2:46pm

Thanksgiving Eve

"Come to me, all you who are weary and burdened, and I will give you rest."

The words of Jesus in Matthew 11:28

It is indeed a day of thanksgiving at the Barton home, as I had my last radiation treatment this afternoon. I am thankful that I was able to complete it before Thanksgiving Day. I am thankful that I can now focus on healing from these terrible burns and sores. I admit that it takes a little effort to be thankful for the radiation treatments themselves, for they have caused such great pain and discomfort. But I only have to think of the horror of another cancer recurrence to indeed be thankful that the radiation beams have hopefully burned up any remaining cancer cells. I am thankful for the kindness of those at the radiation clinic.

I am thankful for the Lord's comforting hand on me throughout this process. I am thankful that nothing can separate me from the love of Christ. I am thankful that He continues to overflow my life with hope, love, joy, and peace.

And if you are reading this, I am thankful for you. I am thankful for your prayers. I am thankful for your compassion, for your kindness, for your words, for your thoughts, for your love, and for your faith. I am thankful for your friendship and what your words and deeds have meant to my family and me.

I am thankful for my family. I am thankful for lovely bride Candy, and for her love, her faith, her stamina, her strength, and her care. I am thankful for my son Michael, and am thankful that he is with us for a few days this week. Michael has accepted a co-op job for the spring semester with United Space Alliance, a contractor for NASA in Cape Canaveral. We are thankful for this great opportunity for him. I am thankful for my beautiful daughter Laura, one of Collierville's most recent solo drivers. I am thankful for the example she sets for me and others to work hard to use the talents God gives you to their fullest. I am thankful for my youngest son Joseph. I am thankful that for the fine young man that he is becoming. He has had to shoulder more responsibilities since I have been ill, and he has done well. I am thankful for the joy brought to me each day from Joseph, Laura, Michael, and Candy.

It is my sincere hope that each of you has a wonderful and blessed Thanksgiving and holiday season.

Love,
John

Hear my cry, O God; listen to my prayer. From the ends of the earth I call to you, I call as my heart grows faint; lead me to the rock that is higher than I. For You have been my refuge, a strong tower against the foe. I long to dwell in Your tent forever and take refuge in the shelter of Your wings.

Psalm 61:1-4

APPENDIX B:
IMAGE GALLERY

Candy and John, June 7, 1986 (left) - Candy and John, Easter 2021 (right)[35]

Michael, Joseph, Laura, John, and Candy in Canyonlands National Park, 2016[36]

Dr. Bob Guinter[37]

Jim Siegfriend

Steve Alm

Jack Edmands

My Mom[39]

*John and Candy at the 2021
College World Series in Omaha*[38]

*These pictures and others in this book may be viewed in color by
scanning this QR code:

ENDNOTES

1   Charles H. Spurgeon, *Treasury of David*, Volume 2, Part 2 (Peabody, MA: Hendrickson Publishers, 2021), 145. Public domain.

2   Spurgeon, *Treasury of David*, Volume 3, Part 1, p. 240.

3   Spurgeon, *Treasury of David*, Volume 2, Part 2, p. 65.

4   Ibid, Volume 3, Part 1, p. 343.

5   Ibid, Volume 2, Part 2, p. 93.

6   Thomas Watson, *All Things for Good* (Shawnee, KS: Gideon House Books, 2015), 21. Originally published with the title *A Divine Cordial* (written in 1663): Public domain (https://librivox.org/a-divine-cordial-by-thomas-watson/).

7   Spurgeon, *Treasury of David*, Volume 1, Part 1, p. 355.

8   Spurgeon, *Treasury of David*, Volume 2, Part 2, p. 65.

9   Ibid, Volume 1, Part 2, p. 160.

10 Jeremiah Burroughs, *The Rare Jewel of Christian Contentment—Annotated*, Henry G. Bohn, New York Street, Covenant Garden, 1845, reprinted 2018), 13. Originally published in 1651. The annotated version was published in 1845. Public domain (page iii of the book).

11 Final stanza of "Charge of the Light Brigade" by Alfred, Lord Tennyson from poetryfoundation.org. Public domain (https://en.m.wikipedia.org/wiki/The_Charge_of_the_Light_Brigade_(poem)).

12 R. C. Sproul, "Cosmic Treason" article, ligonier.org. Used under fair use from Ligonier Ministries.

13 J. C. Ryle, *Holiness: Its Nature, Hindrances, Difficulties, and Roots* (Apollo, Pennsylvania: Ichthus Publications, 2017), 118. Originally published in 1877. Public domain (https://www.jcryle.info/p/home_21.html).

14 Spurgeon, *Treasury of David*, Volume 1, Part 2, p. 2.

15 Martyn Lloyd-Jones, Taken from *The Assurance of Our Salvation* by Martyn Lloyd-Jones, Copyright © 2013, pp. 432. Used by permission of Crossway, a publishing ministry of Good News Publishers, Wheaton, IL 60187, www.crossway.org.

16 Watson, "All Things for Good," page 23.

17 Spurgeon, *Treasury of David*, Volume 3, Part 1, p. 141.

18 John Flavel, *The Fountain of Life* (London: Forgotten Books, 2018), 359. Public domain.

19   Spurgeon, *Treasury of David*, Volume 3, Part 1, pp. 171–172.

20   Matthew Henry's Commentary on Psalm 57:8, included in biblegateway.com resources. Matthew Henry's Commentaries on the Bible were published between 1708 and 1710. Public domain (http://m.biblestudyguide.org/comment/matthew-henry/mh-complete/MHC00000.HTM).

21   Spurgeon, *Treasury of David*, Volume 3, Part 2, p. 375.

22   Spurgeon, *Treasury of David*, Volume 1, Part 1, p. 271.

23   W. Robert Godfrey, "General Revelation" article on Ligonier.org.

24   Matthew Henry's Commentary on Psalm 145:10, included in biblegateway.com resources.

25   Martyn Lloyd-Jones, *Commentary on Romans 9* (Edinburgh, UK; Carlisle, PA: Banner of Truth Trust) 9. Quote used with permission by Banner of Truth.

26   Dustin Benge Twitter account posting, 2022.

27   Personal names and stories of Cambell and Avery Dale used with permission from their parents, David and Jill Dale.

28   Spurgeon, *Treasury of David*, Volume 3, Part 1, p. 71.

29   Matthew Henry's Commentary on Genesis 5:24, included in biblegateway.com resources.

30   Isaac Watts, "When I Survey the Wondrous Cross," from *Hymns and Spiritual Songs* (Coppell, TX: Pantianos Classics, 2022) p. 119, Hymn 3.7. Originally written in 1707. Public domain (https://liftupyourheartshymnal.org/songs/when-i-survey-wondrous-cross).

31   John Newton, "Amazing Grace," *Trinity Hymnal* (Suwanee, GA: Great Commission Publications, Inc., 1990), hymn 460. Originally written in 1779. Public domain (https://library.timelesstruths.org/music/Amazing_Grace/).

32   Photo by Steve Austell, owned by John Barton.

33   Photo by Steve Austell, owned by John Barton.

34   Photo used with permission from Cambell's parents, David and Jill Dale.

35   Photos owned by John Barton.

36   Photo by Michael Barton.

37   Photos (and contained stories) of those on this page have been used with permission.

38   Photo owned by John Barton.

39   Photo owned by John Barton.